Beautiful Feet Books

Anthology of Medieval Literature

for use with
Medieval History Through Literature

edited by
Rebecca Berg Manor

HISTORY THROUGH LITERATURE

Beautiful Feet Books, Inc.
800.889.1978
www.bfbooks.com

Manufactured in the United States of America.

ISBN: 978-1-893103-50-4

Cover artwork is from the Devonshire Hunting Tapestries, specifically The Boar and Bear Hunt.
The tapestry is part of the permanent collection at the Victoria and Albert Museum, London.
The image is in the public domain.

CONTENTS

LITERATURE OF THE EARLY CHRISTIAN TRADITION

The Nicene Creed
(circ. 325)

We believe in one God, the Father, the Almighty, maker of heaven and earth, of all that is, seen and unseen. We believe in one Lord, Jesus Christ, the only Son of God, eternally begotten of the Father, God from God, light from light, true God from true God, begotten, not made, of one Being with the Father; through him all things were made. For us and for our salvation he came down from heaven, was incarnate of the Holy Spirit and the Virgin Mary and became truly human. For our sake he was crucified under Pontius Pilate; he suffered death and was buried. On the third day he rose again in accordance with the Scriptures; he ascended into heaven and is seated at the right hand of the Father. He will come again in glory to judge the living and the dead, and his kingdom will have no end.

We believe in the Holy Spirit, the Lord, the giver of life, who proceeds from the Father [and the Son], who with the Father and the Son is worshiped and glorified, who has spoken through the prophets. We believe in one holy catholic and apostolic Church. We acknowledge one baptism for the forgiveness of sins. We look for the resurrection of the dead, and the life of the world to come. Amen.

Te Deum
by Nicetas of Remesiana (AD 335-415?)

A hymn of joy and thanksgiving long associated with Saint Ambrose. Scholars now commonly accept that it was written by the fourth century cleric Nicetas of Remesiana. The hymn is still used today on Sundays outside Lent, daily during the Octaves of Christmas and Easter, and on Solemnities and Feast Days.

I. Praise to the Trinity

We praise thee, O God: we acknowledge Thee to be the Lord.
All the earth doth worship Thee, the Father everlasting.
To Thee all Angels cry aloud: the Heavens and all the powers therein.
To Thee Cherubim and Seraphim continually do cry,
Holy, Holy, Holy: Lord God of Sabaoth;
Heaven and earth are full of the Majesty of Thy Glory.
The glorious company of the Apostles praise Thee.
The godly fellowship of the Prophets praise Thee.
The noble army of Martyrs praise Thee.
The holy Church throughout all the world doth acknowledge Thee;
The Father of an infinite Majesty;
Thine honorable, true, and only Son;
Also the Holy Ghost: the Comforter.

II. Praise of Christ

Thou art the King of Glory, O Christ.
Thou art the everlasting Son of the Father.
When Thou tookest upon Thee to deliver man:
Thou didst not abhor the Virgin's womb.
When Thou hadst overcome the sharpness of death,
Thou didst open the Kingdom of Heaven to all believers.
Thou sittest at the right hand of God in the glory of the Father.
We believe that Thou shalt come to be our Judge.
We therefore pray Thee, help Thy servants whom
Thou hast redeemed with Thy precious blood.
Make them to be numbered with Thy Saints in glory everlasting.

III. Prayers

O Lord, save Thy people: and bless Thine heritage.

Govern them and lift them up for ever.

Day by day we magnify Thee;

And we worship Thy Name, ever world without end.

Vouchsafe, O Lord, to keep us this day without sin.

O Lord, have mercy upon us.

O Lord, let Thy mercy lighten upon us: as our trust is in Thee.

O Lord, in Thee have I trusted: let me never be confounded.

Hymn

by Ambrose of Milan (AD 340?-397)
translated by John Henry Newman

Aeterne rerum conditor,
Noctem diemque qui regis,
Et temporum das dempora,
Ut alleves fastidium;

Framer of the earth and sky,
Ruler of the day and night
With a glad variety
Tempering all, and making light.

Gleams upon our dark path flinging,
Cutting short each night begun.
Hark! for chanticleer is singing,
Hark! he chides the lingering sun.

And the morning star replies
And lets loose the imprisoned day;
And the godless bandit flies
From his haunt and from his prey.

Shrill it sounds; the storm relenting
Soothes the weary seaman's ears;
Once it wrought a great repenting
In that flood of Peter's tears.

Rouse we; the blithesome cry
Of that bird our hearts awaken,
Chide the slumberers as they lie,
And arrest the sin o'ertaken.

Hope and health are in his strain
To the fearful and the ailing;
Murder sheathes his blade profane;
Faith revives when faith was failing.

Jesu, Master! When we sin
Turn on us Thy healing face;
It will melt the offence within
Into penitential grace.

Beam on our bewildered mind
Till its dreamy shadows flee:
Stones cry out where Thou has shined,
Jesu! Musical with Thee.

To the Father and the Son
And the Spirit, who in heaven
Ever witness, Three in One,
Praise on earth be ever given.

Confessions
by Augustine of Hippo (354-430)
translated by Edward Bouverie Pusey

BOOK I:
*Commencing with the invocation of God, Augustine relates in
detail the beginning of his life, his infancy and boyhood up to his
fifteenth year; at which age he acknowledges that he was more
inclined to all youthful pleasures and vices than to the study of
letters.*

Great art Thou, O Lord, and greatly to be praised; great is Thy
power, and Thy wisdom infinite. And Thee would man praise;
man, but a particle of Thy creation; man, that bears about him his
mortality, the witness of his sin, the witness that Thou resistest the
proud: yet would man praise Thee; he, but a particle of Thy
creation. Thou awakest us to delight in Thy praise; for Thou
madest us for Thyself, and our heart is restless, until it finds its rest
in Thee. Grant me, Lord, to know and understand which is first, to
call on Thee or to praise Thee? And, again, to know Thee or to call
on Thee? For who can call on Thee, not knowing Thee? For he that
knoweth Thee not, may call on Thee as other than Thou art. Or, is
it rather, that we call on Thee that we may know Thee? But how
shall they call on Him in whom they have not believed? Or how
shall they believe without a preacher? And they that seek the Lord
shall praise Him: for they that seek shall find Him, and they that
find shall praise Him. I will seek Thee, Lord, by calling on Thee;
and will call on Thee, believing in Thee; for to us hast Thou been
preached. My faith, Lord, shall call on Thee, which Thou hast
given me, wherewith Thou hast inspired me, through the
Incarnation of Thy Son, through the ministry of the Preacher.

And how shall I call upon my God, my God and Lord, since,
when I call for Him, I shall be calling Him to myself? And what
room is there within me, whither my God can come into me?
Whither can God come into me, God who made heaven and earth?
Is there, indeed, O Lord my God, aught in me that can contain
Thee? So then heaven and earth, which Thou hast made, and
wherein Thou hast made me, contain Thee? Or, because nothing
which exists could exist without Thee, doth therefore whatever

exists contain Thee? Since, then, I too exist, why do I seek that Thou shouldest enter into me, who were not, wert Thou not in me? Why? Because I am not gone down in hell, and yet Thou art there also. For if I go down into hell, Thou art there. I could not be then, O my God, could not be at all, wert Thou not in me; or, rather, unless I were in Thee, of whom are all things, by whom are all things, in whom are all things? Even so, Lord, even so. Whither do I call Thee, since I am in Thee? Or whence canst Thou enter into me? For whither can I go beyond heaven and earth, that thence my God should come into me, who hath said, I fill the heaven and the earth.

Do the heaven and earth then contain Thee, since Thou fillest them? Or dost Thou fill them and yet overflow, since they do not contain Thee? And whither, when the heaven and the earth are filled, pourest Thou forth the remainder of Thyself? Or hast Thou no need that aught contain Thee, who containest all things, since what Thou fillest Thou fillest by containing it? For the vessels which Thou fillest uphold Thee not, since, though they were broken, Thou wert not poured out. And when Thou art poured out on us, Thou art not cast down, but Thou upliftest us; Thou art not dissipated, but Thou gatherest us. But Thou who fillest all things, fillest Thou them with Thy whole self? Or, since all things cannot contain Thee wholly, do they contain part of Thee? And all at once the same part? Or each its own part, the greater more, the smaller less? And is, then one part of Thee greater, another less? Or, art Thou wholly every where, while nothing contains Thee wholly?

What art Thou then, my God? What, but the Lord God? For who is Lord but the Lord? Or who is God save our God? Most highest, most good, most potent, most omnipotent; most merciful, yet most just; most hidden, yet most present; most beautiful, yet most strong, stable, yet incomprehensible; unchangeable, yet all-changing; never new, never old; all-renewing, and bringing age upon the proud, and they know it not; ever working, ever at rest; still gathering, yet nothing lacking; supporting, filling, and overspreading; creating, nourishing, and maturing; seeking, yet having all things. Thou lovest, without passion; art jealous, without anxiety; repentest, yet grievest not; art angry, yet serene; changest Thy works, Thy purpose unchanged; receivest again what Thou findest, yet didst never lose; never in need, yet rejoicing in gains;

never covetous, yet exacting usury. Thou receivest over and above, that Thou mayest owe; and who hath aught that is not Thine? Thou payest debts, owing nothing; remittest debts, losing nothing. And what had I now said, my God, my life, my holy joy? Or what saith any man when he speaks of Thee? Yet woe to him that speaketh not, since mute are even the most eloquent. Oh! that I might repose on Thee!

Oh! that Thou wouldest enter into my heart, and inebriate it, that I may forget my ills, and embrace Thee, my sole good! What art Thou to me? In Thy pity, teach me to utter it. Or what am I to Thee that Thou demandest my love, and, if I give it not, art wroth with me, and threatenest me with grievous woes? Is it then a slight woe to love Thee not? Oh! for Thy mercies' sake, tell me, O Lord my God, what Thou art unto me. Say unto my soul, I am thy salvation. So speak, that I may hear. Behold, Lord, my heart is before Thee; open Thou the ears thereof, and say unto my soul, I am thy salvation. After this voice let me haste, and take hold on Thee. Hide not Thy face from me. Let me die–lest I die–only let me see Thy face.

Narrow is the mansion of my soul; enlarge Thou it, that Thou mayest enter in. It is ruinous; repair Thou it. It has that within which must offend Thine eyes; I confess and know it. But who shall cleanse it? Or to whom should I cry, save Thee? Lord, cleanse me from my secret faults, and spare Thy servant from the power of the enemy. I believe, and therefore do I speak. Lord, Thou knowest. Have I not confessed against myself my transgressions unto Thee, and Thou, my God, hast forgiven the iniquity of my heart? I contend not in judgment with Thee, who art the truth; I fear to deceive myself; lest mine iniquity lie unto itself. Therefore I contend not in judgment with Thee; for if Thou, Lord, shouldest mark iniquities, O Lord, who shall abide it?

Yet suffer me to speak unto Thy mercy, me, dust and ashes. Yet suffer me to speak, since I speak to Thy mercy, and not to scornful man. Thou too, perhaps, despisest me, yet wilt Thou return and have compassion upon me. For what would I say, O Lord my God, but that I know not whence I came into this dying life (shall I call it?) or living death. Then immediately did the comforts of Thy compassion take me up, as I heard (for I remember it not) from the parents of my flesh, out of whose substance Thou didst sometime fashion me. Thus there received me the comforts of woman's milk. For neither my mother nor my nurses stored their own breasts for me; but Thou didst bestow the food of my infancy through them, according to Thine ordinance, whereby Thou distributest Thy riches through the hidden springs of all things. Thou also gavest me to desire no more than Thou gavest; and to my nurses willingly to give me what Thou gavest them. For they, with a heaven-taught affection, willingly gave me what they abounded with from Thee. For this my good from them, was good for them. Nor, indeed, from them was it, but through them; for from Thee, O God, are all good things, and from my God is all my health. This I since learned, Thou, through these Thy gifts, within me and without, proclaiming Thyself unto me. For then I knew but to suck; to repose in what pleased, and cry at what offended my flesh; nothing more.

Afterwards I began to smile; first in sleep, then waking: for so it was told me of myself, and I believed it; for we see the like in other infants, though of myself I remember it not. Thus, little by little, I became conscious where I was; and to have a wish to express my wishes to those who could content them, and I could not; for the wishes were within me, and they without; nor could they by any sense of theirs enter within my spirit. So I flung about at random limbs and voice, making the few signs I could, and such as I could, like, though in truth very little like, what I wished. And when I was not presently obeyed (my wishes being hurtful or unintelligible), then I was indignant with my elders for not submitting to me, with those owing me no service, for not serving me; and avenged myself on them by tears. Such have I learnt infants to be from observing them; and that I was myself such, they, all unconscious, have shown me better than my nurses who knew it.

And, lo! my infancy died long since, and I live. But Thou, Lord, who for ever livest, and in whom nothing dies: for before the foundation of the worlds, and before all that can be called "before," Thou art, and art God and Lord of all which Thou hast created: in Thee abide, fixed for ever, the first causes of all things unabiding; and of all things changeable, the springs abide in Thee unchangeable: and in Thee live the eternal reasons of all things unreasoning and temporal. Say, Lord, to me, Thy suppliant; say, all-pitying, to me, Thy pitiable one; say, did my infancy succeed another age of mine that died before it? Was it that which I spent within my mother's womb? For of that I have heard somewhat, and have myself seen women with child? And what before that life again, O God my joy, was I any where or any body? For this have I none to tell me, neither father nor mother, nor experience of others, nor mine own memory. Dost Thou mock me for asking this, and bid me praise Thee and acknowledge Thee, for that I do know?

I acknowledge Thee, Lord of heaven and earth, and praise Thee for my first rudiments of being, and my infancy, whereof I remember nothing; for Thou hast appointed that man should from others guess much as to himself; and believe much on the strength of weak females. Even then I had being and life, and (at my infancy's close) I could seek for signs whereby to make known to others my sensations. Whence could such a being be, save from Thee, Lord? Shall any be his own artificer? Or can there elsewhere be derived any vein, which may stream essence and life into us, save from thee, O Lord, in whom essence and life are one? For Thou Thyself art supremely Essence and Life. For Thou art most high, and art not changed, neither in Thee doth today come to a close; yet in Thee doth it come to a close; because all such things also are in Thee. For they had no way to pass away, unless Thou upheldest them. And since Thy years fail not, Thy years are one today. How many of ours and our fathers' years have flowed away through Thy "today," and from it received the measure and the mould of such being as they had; and still others shall flow away, and so receive the mould of their degree of being. But Thou art still the same, and all things of tomorrow, and all beyond, and all of yesterday, and all behind it, Thou hast done today. What is it to me, though any comprehend not this? Let him also rejoice and say, What thing is this? Let him rejoice even thus! and be content rather by not discovering to discover Thee, than by discovering not to discover Thee.

Hear, O God. Alas, for man's sin! So saith man, and Thou pitiest him; for Thou madest him, but sin in him Thou madest not. Who remindeth me of the sins of my infancy? For in Thy sight none is pure from sin, not even the infant whose life is but a day upon the earth. Who remindeth me? Doth not each little infant, in whom I see what of myself I remember not? What then was my sin? Was it that I hung upon the breast and cried? For should I now so do for food suitable to my age, justly should I be laughed at and reproved. What I then did was worthy reproof; but since I could not understand reproof, custom and reason forbade me to be reproved. For those habits, when grown, we root out and cast away. Now no man, though he prunes, wittingly casts away what is good. Or was it then good, even for a while, to cry for what, if given, would hurt? Bitterly to resent, that persons free, and its own elders, yea, the very authors of its birth, served it not? That many besides, wiser than it, obeyed not the nod of its good pleasure? To do its best to strike and hurt, because commands were not obeyed, which had been obeyed to its hurt? The weakness then of infant limbs, not its will, is its innocence. Myself have seen and known even a baby envious; it could not speak, yet it turned pale and looked bitterly on its foster-brother. Who knows not this? Mothers and nurses tell you that they allay these things by I know not what remedies. Is that too innocence, when the fountain of milk is flowing in rich abundance, not to endure one to share it, though in extremest need, and whose very life as yet depends thereon? We bear gently with all this, not as being no or slight evils, but because they will disappear as years increase; for, though tolerated now, the very same tempers are utterly intolerable when found in riper years.

Thou, then, O Lord my God, who gavest life to this my infancy, furnishing thus with senses (as we see) the frame Thou gavest, compacting its limbs, ornamenting its proportions, and, for its general good and safety, implanting in it all vital functions, Thou commandest me to praise Thee in these things, to confess unto Thee, and sing unto Thy name, Thou most Highest. For Thou art God, Almighty and Good, even hadst Thou done naught but only this, which none could do but Thou: whose Unity is the mould of all things; who out of Thy own fairness makest all things fair; and orderest all things by Thy law. This age then, Lord, whereof I have no remembrance, which I take on others' word, and guess from other infants that I have passed, true though the guess be, I am yet loth to count in this life of mine which I live in this world. For no less than that which I spent in my mother's womb, is it hid from me in the shadows of forgetfulness. But if I was shapen in iniquity, and in sin did my mother conceive me, where, I beseech Thee, O my God, where, Lord, or when, was I Thy servant guiltless? But, lo! that period I pass by; and what have I now to do with that, of which I can recall no vestige?

Passing hence from infancy, I came to boyhood, or rather it came to me, displacing infancy. Nor did that depart (for whither went it?) and yet it was no more. For I was no longer a speechless infant, but a speaking boy. This I remember; and have since observed how I learned to speak. It was not that my elders taught me words (as, soon after, other learning) in any set method; but I, longing by cries and broken accents and various motions of my limbs to express my thoughts, that so I might have my will, and yet unable to express all I willed, or to whom I willed, did myself, by the understanding which Thou, my God, gavest me, practise the sounds in my memory. When they named any thing, and as they spoke turned towards it, I saw and remembered that they called what they would point out by the name they uttered. And that they meant this thing and no other was plain from the motion of their body, the natural language, as it were, of all nations, expressed by the countenance, glances of the eye, gestures of the limbs, and tones of the voice, indicating the affections of the mind, as it pursues, possesses, rejects, or shuns. And thus by constantly hearing words, as they occurred in various sentences, I collected gradually for what they stood; and having broken in my mouth to these signs, I thereby gave utterance to my will. Thus I exchanged with those about me these current signs of our wills, and so launched deeper into the stormy intercourse of human life, yet depending on parental authority and the beck of elders.

O God my God, what miseries and mockeries did I now experience, when obedience to my teachers was proposed to me, as proper in a boy, in order that in this world I might prosper, and excel in tongue-science, which should serve to the "praise of men," and to deceitful riches. Next I was put to school to get learning, in which I (poor wretch) knew not what use there was; and yet, if idle in learning, I was beaten. For this was judged right by our forefathers; and many, passing the same course before us, framed for us weary paths, through which we were fain to pass; multiplying toil and grief upon the sons of Adam. But, Lord, we found that men called upon Thee, and we learnt from them to think of Thee (according to our powers) as of some great One, who, though hidden from our senses, couldest hear and help us. For so I began, as a boy, to pray to Thee, my aid and refuge; and broke the fetters of my tongue to call on Thee, praying Thee, though small, yet with no small earnestness, that I might not be beaten at school. And when Thou heardest me not (not thereby giving me over to folly), my elders, yea my very parents, who yet wished me no ill, mocked my stripes, my then great and grievous ill.

Is there, Lord, any of soul so great, and cleaving to Thee with so intense affection (for a sort of stupidity will in a way do it); but is there any one who, from cleaving devoutly to Thee, is endued with so great a spirit, that he can think as lightly of the racks and hooks and other torments (against which, throughout all lands, men call on Thee with extreme dread), mocking at those by whom they are feared most bitterly, as our parents mocked the torments which we suffered in boyhood from our masters? For we feared not our torments less; nor prayed we less to Thee to escape them. And yet we sinned, in writing or reading or studying less than was exacted of us. For we wanted not, O Lord, memory or capacity, whereof Thy will gave enough for our age; but our sole delight was play; and for this we were punished by those who yet themselves were doing the like. But elder folks' idleness is called "business"; that of boys, being really the same, is punished by those elders; and none commiserates either boys or men. For will any of sound discretion approve of my being beaten as a boy, because, by playing a ball, I made less progress in studies which I was to learn, only that, as a man, I might play more unbeseemingly? And what else did he who beat me? Who, if worsted in some trifling discussion with his fellow-tutor, was more embittered and jealous than I when beaten at ball by a play-fellow?

And yet, I sinned herein, O Lord God, the Creator and Disposer of all things in nature, of sin the Disposer only, O Lord my God, I sinned in transgressing the commands of my parents and those of my masters. For what they, with whatever motive, would have me learn, I might afterwards have put to good use. For I disobeyed, not from a better choice, but from love of play, loving the pride of victory in my contests, and to have my ears tickled with lying fables, that they might itch the more; the same curiosity flashing from my eyes more and more, for the shows and games of my elders. Yet those who give these shows are in such esteem, that almost all wish the same for their children, and yet are very willing that they should be beaten, if those very games detain them from the studies, whereby they would have them attain to be the givers of them. Look with pity, Lord, on these things, and deliver us who call upon Thee now; deliver those too who call not on Thee yet, that they may call on Thee, and Thou mayest deliver them.

As a boy, then, I had already heard of an eternal life, promised us through the humility of the Lord our God stooping to our pride; and even from the womb of my mother, who greatly hoped in Thee, I was sealed with the mark of His cross and salted with His salt. Thou sawest, Lord, how while yet a boy, being seized on a time with sudden oppression of the stomach, and like near to death- Thou sawest, my God (for Thou wert my keeper), with what eagerness and what faith I sought, from the pious care of my mother and Thy Church, the mother of us all, the baptism of Thy Christ, my God and Lord. Whereupon the mother my flesh, being much troubled (since, with a heart pure in Thy faith, she even more lovingly travailed in birth of my salvation), would in eager haste have provided for my consecration and cleansing by the health-giving sacraments, confessing Thee, Lord Jesus, for the remission of sins, unless I had suddenly recovered. And so, as if I must needs be again polluted should I live, my cleansing was deferred, because the defilements of sin would, after that washing, bring greater and more perilous guilt. I then already believed: and my mother, and the whole household, except my father: yet did not he prevail over the power of my mother's piety in me, that as he did not yet believe, so neither should I. For it was her earnest care that Thou my God, rather than he, shouldest be my father; and in this Thou didst aid her to prevail over her husband, whom she, the better, obeyed, therein also obeying Thee, who hast so commanded.

I beseech Thee, my God, I would fain know, if so Thou willest, for what purpose my baptism was then deferred? was it for my good that the rein was laid loose, as it were, upon me, for me to sin? or was it not laid loose? If not, why does it still echo in our ears on all sides, "Let him alone, let him do as he will, for he is not yet baptized?" but as to bodily health, no one says, "Let him be worse wounded, for he is not yet healed." How much better then, had I been at once healed; and then, by my friends' and my own, my soul's recovered health had been kept safe in Thy keeping who gavest it. Better truly. But how many and great waves of temptation seemed to hang over me after my boyhood! These my mother foresaw; and preferred to expose to them the clay whence I might afterwards be moulded, than the very cast, when made.

In boyhood itself, however (so much less dreaded for me than youth), I loved not study, and hated to be forced to it. Yet I was forced; and this was well done towards me, but I did not well; for, unless forced, I had not learnt. But no one doth well against his will, even though what he doth, be well. Yet neither did they well who forced me, but what was well came to me from Thee, my God. For they were regardless how I should employ what they forced me to learn, except to satiate the insatiate desires of a wealthy beggary, and a shameful glory. But Thou, by whom the very hairs of our head are numbered, didst use for my good the error of all who urged me to learn; and my own, who would not learn, Thou didst use for my punishment–a fit penalty for one, so small a boy and so great a sinner. So by those who did not well, Thou didst well for me; and by my own sin Thou didst justly punish me. For Thou hast commanded, and so it is, that every inordinate affection should be its own punishment.

But why did I so much hate the Greek, which I studied as a boy? I do not yet fully know. For the Latin I loved; not what my first masters, but what the so-called grammarians taught me. For those first lessons, reading, writing and arithmetic, I thought as great a burden and penalty as any Greek. And yet whence was this too, but from the sin and vanity of this life, because I was flesh, and a breath that passeth away and cometh not again? For those first lessons were better certainly, because more certain; by them I obtained, and still retain, the power of reading what I find written, and myself writing what I will; whereas in the others, I was forced to learn the wanderings of one Aeneas, forgetful of my own, and to weep for dead Dido, because she killed herself for love; the while, with dry eyes, I endured my miserable self dying among these things, far from Thee, O God my life.

For what more miserable than a miserable being who commiserates not himself; weeping the death of Dido for love to Aeneas, but weeping not his own death for want of love to Thee, O God. Thou light of my heart, Thou bread of my inmost soul, Thou Power who givest vigor to my mind, who quickenest my thoughts,

I loved Thee not. I committed fornication against Thee, and all around me thus fornicating there echoed "Well done! well done!" for the friendship of this world is fornication against Thee; and "Well done! well done!" echoes on till one is ashamed not to he thus a man. And for all this I wept not, I who wept for Dido slain, and "seeking by the sword a stroke and wound extreme," myself seeking the while a worse extreme, the extremest and lowest of Thy creatures, having forsaken Thee, earth passing into the earth. And if forbid to read all this, I was grieved that I might not read what grieved me. Madness like this is thought a higher and a richer learning, than that by which I learned to read and write.

But now, my God, cry Thou aloud in my soul; and let Thy truth tell me, "Not so, not so. Far better was that first study." For, lo, I would readily forget the wanderings of Aeneas and all the rest, rather than how to read and write. But over the entrance of the Grammar School is a vail drawn! true; yet is this not so much an emblem of aught recondite, as a cloak of error. Let not those, whom I no longer fear, cry out against me, while I confess to Thee, my God, whatever my soul will, and acquiesce in the condemnation of my evil ways, that I may love Thy good ways. Let not either buyers or sellers of grammar-learning cry out against me. For if I question them whether it be true that Aeneas came on a time to Carthage, as the poet tells, the less learned will reply that they know not, the more learned that he never did. But should I ask with what letters the name "Aeneas" is written, every one who has learnt this will answer me aright, as to the signs which men have conventionally settled. If, again, I should ask which might be forgotten with least detriment to the concerns of life, reading and writing or these poetic fictions? who does not foresee what all must answer who have not wholly forgotten themselves? I sinned, then, when as a boy I preferred those empty to those more profitable studies, or rather loved the one and hated the other. "One and one, two", "two and two, four"; this was to me a hateful singsong, "the wooden horse lined with armed men," and "the burning of Troy," and "Creusa's shade and sad similitude," were the choice spectacle of my vanity.

Why then did I hate the Greek classics, which have the like tales? For Homer also curiously wove the like fictions, and is most sweetly vain, yet was he bitter to my boyish taste. And so I suppose would Virgil be to Grecian children, when forced to learn him as I was Homer. Difficulty, in truth, the difficulty of a foreign tongue, dashed, as it were, with gall all the sweetness of Grecian fable. For not one word of it did I understand, and to make me understand I was urged vehemently with cruel threats and punishments. Time was also (as an infant) I knew no Latin; but this I learned without fear or suffering, by mere observation, amid the caresses of my nursery and jests of friends, smiling and sportively encouraging me. This I learned without any pressure of punishment to urge me on, for my heart urged me to give birth to its conceptions, which I could only do by learning words not of those who taught, but of those who talked with me; in whose ears also I gave birth to the thoughts, whatever I conceived. No doubt, then, that a free curiosity has more force in our learning these things, than a frightful enforcement. Only this enforcement restrains the rovings of that freedom, through Thy laws, O my God, Thy laws, from the master's cane to the martyr's trials, being able to temper for us a wholesome bitter, recalling us to Thyself from that deadly pleasure which lures us from Thee.

Hear, Lord, my prayer; let not my soul faint under Thy discipline, nor let me faint in confessing unto Thee all Thy mercies, whereby Thou hast drawn me out of all my most evil ways, that Thou mightest become a delight to me above all the allurements which I once pursued; that I may most entirely love Thee, and clasp Thy hand with all my affections, and Thou mayest yet rescue me from every temptation, even unto the end. For lo, O Lord, my King and my God, for Thy service be whatever useful thing my childhood learned; for Thy service, that I speak, write, read, reckon. For Thou didst grant me Thy discipline, while I was learning vanities; and my sin of delighting in those vanities Thou hast forgiven. In them, indeed, I learnt many a useful word, but these may as well be learned in things not vain; and that is the safe path for the steps of youth.

But woe is thee, thou torrent of human custom! Who shall stand against thee? How long shalt thou not be dried up? How long roll the sons of Eve into that huge and hideous ocean, which even they scarcely overpass who climb the cross? Did not I read in thee of Jove the thunderer and the adulterer? Both, doubtless, he could not be; but so the feigned thunder might countenance and pander to

17

real adultery. And now which of our gowned masters lends a sober ear to one who from their own school cries out, "These were Homer's fictions, transferring things human to the gods; would he had brought down things divine to us!" Yet more truly had he said, "These are indeed his fictions; but attributing a divine nature to wicked men, that crimes might be no longer crimes, and whoso commits them might seem to imitate not abandoned men, but the celestial gods."

And yet, thou hellish torrent, into thee are cast the sons of men with rich rewards, for compassing such learning; and a great solemnity is made of it, when this is going on in the forum, within sight of laws appointing a salary beside the scholar's payments; and thou lashest thy rocks and roarest, "Hence words are learnt; hence eloquence; most necessary to gain your ends, or maintain opinions." As if we should have never known such words as "golden shower," "lap," "beguile," "temples of the heavens," or others in that passage, unless Terence had brought a lewd youth upon the stage, setting up Jupiter as his example of seduction.

"Viewing a picture, where the tale was drawn,

Of Jove's descending in a golden shower

To Danae's lap a woman to beguile."

And then mark how he excites himself to lust as by celestial authority:

"And what God? Great Jove,

Who shakes heaven's highest temples with his thunder,

And I, poor mortal man, not do the same!

I did it, and with all my heart I did it."

Not one whit more easily are the words learnt for all this vileness; but by their means the vileness is committed with less shame. Not that I blame the words, being, as it were, choice and precious vessels; but that wine of error which is drunk to us in them by intoxicated teachers; and if we, too, drink not, we are beaten, and have no sober judge to whom we may appeal. Yet, O my God (in whose presence I now without hurt may remember this), all this unhappily I learnt willingly with great delight, and for this was pronounced a hopeful boy.

Bear with me, my God, while I say somewhat of my wit, Thy gift, and on what dotages I wasted it. For a task was set me, troublesome enough to my soul, upon terms of praise or shame, and fear of stripes, to speak the words of Juno, as she raged and mourned that she could not

"This Trojan prince from Latinum turn."

Which words I had heard that Juno never uttered; but we were forced to go astray in the footsteps of these poetic fictions, and to say in prose much what he expressed in verse. And his speaking was most applauded, in whom the passions of rage and grief were most preeminent, and clothed in the most fitting language, maintaining the dignity of the character. What is it to me, O my true life, my God, that my declamation was applauded above so many of my own age and class? Is not all this smoke and wind? And was there nothing else whereon to exercise my wit and tongue? Thy praises, Lord, Thy praises might have stayed the yet tender shoot of my heart by the prop of Thy Scriptures; so had it not trailed away amid these empty trifles, a defiled prey for the fowls of the air. For in more ways than one do men sacrifice to the rebellious angels.

But what marvel that I was thus carried away to vanities, and went out from Thy presence, O my God, when men were set before me as models, who, if in relating some action of theirs, in itself not ill, they committed some barbarism or solecism, being censured, were abashed; but when in rich and adorned and well-ordered discourse they related their own disordered life, being bepraised, they gloried? These things Thou seest, Lord, and holdest Thy peace; long-suffering, and plenteous in mercy and truth. Wilt Thou hold Thy peace for ever? And even now Thou drawest out of this horrible gulf the soul that seeketh Thee, that thirsteth for Thy pleasures, whose heart saith unto Thee, I have sought Thy face; Thy face, Lord, will I seek. For darkened affections is removal from Thee. For it is not by our feet, or change of place, that men leave Thee, or return unto Thee. Or did that Thy younger son look out for horses or chariots, or ships, fly with visible wings, or journey by the motion of his limbs, that he might in a far country waste in riotous living all Thou gavest at his departure? A loving Father, when Thou gavest, and more loving unto him, when he returned empty. So then in lustful, that is, in darkened affections, is the true distance from Thy face.

This was the world at whose gate unhappy I lay in my boyhood; this the stage where I had feared more to commit a barbarism, than having committed one, to envy those who had not. These things I speak and confess to Thee, my God; for which I had praise from them, whom I then thought it all virtue to please. For I saw not the abyss of vileness, wherein I was cast away from Thine eyes. Before them what more foul than I was already, displeasing even such as myself? With innumerable lies deceiving my tutor, my masters, my parents, from love of play, eagerness to see vain shows and restlessness to imitate them! Thefts also I committed, from my parents' cellar and table, enslaved by greediness, or that I might have to give to boys, who sold me their play, which all the while they liked no less than I. In this play, too, I often sought unfair conquests, conquered myself meanwhile by vain desire of preeminence. And what could I so ill endure, or, when I detected it, upbraided I so fiercely, as that I was doing to others? And for which if, detected, I was upbraided, I chose rather to quarrel than to yield. And is this the innocence of boyhood? Not so, Lord, not so; I cry Thy mercy, my God. For these very sins, as riper years succeed, these very sins are transferred from tutors and masters, from nuts and balls and sparrows, to magistrates and kings, to gold and manors and slaves, just as severer punishments displace the cane. It was the low stature then of childhood which Thou our King didst commend as an emblem of lowliness, when Thou saidst, Of such is the kingdom of heaven.

Yet, Lord, to Thee, the Creator and Governor of the universe, most excellent and most good, thanks were due to Thee our God, even hadst Thou destined for me boyhood only. For even then I was, I lived, and felt; and had an implanted providence over my well-being- a trace of that mysterious Unity whence I was derived; I guarded by the inward sense the entireness of my senses, and in these minute pursuits, and in my thoughts on things minute, I learnt to delight in truth, I hated to be deceived, had a vigorous memory, was gifted with speech, was soothed by friendship, avoided pain, baseness, ignorance. In so small a creature, what was not wonderful, not admirable? But all are gifts of my God: it was not I who gave them me; and good these are, and these together are myself. Good, then, is He that made me, and He is my good; and before Him will I exult for every good which of a boy I had. For it was my sin, that not in Him, but in His creatures–myself and others–I sought for pleasures, sublimities, truths, and so fell headlong into sorrows, confusions, errors. Thanks be to Thee, my joy and my glory and my confidence, my God, thanks be to Thee for Thy gifts; but do Thou preserve them to me. For so wilt Thou preserve me, and those things shall be enlarged and perfected which Thou hast given me, and I myself shall be with Thee, since even to be Thou hast given me.

BOOK II:
He advances to puberty, and indeed to the early part of the sixteenth year of his age, in which having abandoned his studies, he indulged in lustful pleasures, and with his companions, committed theft.

I will now call to mind my past foulness, and the carnal corruptions of my soul; not because I love them, but that I may love Thee, O my God. For love of Thy love I do it; reviewing my most wicked ways in the very bitterness of my remembrance, that Thou mayest grow sweet unto me (Thou sweetness never failing, Thou blissful and assured sweetness); and gathering me again out of that my dissipation, wherein I was torn piecemeal, while turned from Thee, the One Good, I lost myself among a multiplicity of things. For I even burnt in my youth heretofore, to be satiated in things below; and I dared to grow wild again, with these various and shadowy loves: my beauty consumed away, and I stank in Thine eyes; pleasing myself, and desirous to please in the eyes of men.

And what was it that I delighted in, but to love, and be loved? but I kept not the measure of love, of mind to mind, friendship's bright boundary: but out of the muddy concupiscence of the flesh, and the bubblings of youth, mists fumed up which beclouded and overcast my heart, that I could not discern the clear brightness of love from the fog of lustfulness. Both did confusedly boil in me, and hurried my unstayed youth over the precipice of unholy desires, and sunk me in a gulf of flagitiousnesses. Thy wrath had gathered over me, and I knew it not. I was grown deaf by the clanking of the chain of my mortality, the punishment of the pride of my soul, and I strayed further from Thee, and Thou lettest me alone, and I was tossed about, and wasted, and dissipated, and I boiled over in my fornications, and Thou heldest Thy peace, O

21

Thou my tardy joy! Thou then heldest Thy peace, and I wandered further and further from Thee, into more and more fruitless seed-plots of sorrows, with a proud dejectedness, and a restless weariness.

Oh! that some one had then attempered my disorder, and turned to account the fleeting beauties of these, the extreme points of Thy creation! Had put a bound to their pleasureableness, that so the tides of my youth might have cast themselves upon the marriage shore, if they could not be calmed, and kept within the object of a family, as Thy law prescribes, O Lord: who this way formest the offspring of this our death, being able with a gentle hand to blunt the thorns which were excluded from Thy paradise? For Thy omnipotency is not far from us, even when we be far from Thee. Else ought I more watchfully to have heeded the voice from the clouds: Nevertheless such shall have trouble in the flesh, but I spare you. And it is good for a man not to touch a woman. And, he that is unmarried thinketh of the things of the Lord, how he may please the Lord; but he that is married careth for the things of this world, how he may please his wife.

To these words I should have listened more attentively, and being severed for the kingdom of heaven's sake, had more happily awaited Thy embraces; but I, poor wretch, foamed like a troubled sea, following the rushing of my own tide, forsaking Thee, and exceeded all Thy limits; yet I escaped not Thy scourges. For what mortal can? For Thou wert ever with me mercifully rigorous, and besprinkling with most bitter alloy all my unlawful pleasures: that I might seek pleasures without alloy. But where to find such, I could not discover, save in Thee, O Lord, who teachest by sorrow, and woundest us, to heal; and killest us, lest we die from Thee. Where was I, and how far was I exiled from the delights of Thy house, in that sixteenth year of the age of my flesh, when the madness of lust (to which human shamelessness giveth free licence, though unlicensed by Thy laws) took the rule over me, and I resigned myself wholly to it? My friends meanwhile took no care by marriage to save my fall; their only care was that I should learn to speak excellently, and be a persuasive orator.

For that year were my studies intermitted: whilst after my return from Madaura (a neighbor city, whither I had journeyed to learn grammar and rhetoric), the expenses for a further journey to

Carthage were being provided for me; and that rather by the resolution than the means of my father, who was but a poor freeman of Thagaste. To whom tell I this? Not to Thee, my God; but before Thee to mine own kind, even to that small portion of mankind as may light upon these writings of mine. And to what purpose? That whosoever reads this, may think out of what depths we are to cry unto Thee. For what is nearer to Thine ears than a confessing heart, and a life of faith? Who did not extol my father, for that beyond the ability of his means, he would furnish his son with all necessaries for a far journey for his studies' sake? For many far abler citizens did no such thing for their children. But yet this same father had no concern how I grew towards Thee, or how chaste I were; so that I were but copious in speech, however barren I were to Thy culture, O God, who art the only true and good Lord of Thy field, my heart.

But while in that my sixteenth year I lived with my parents, leaving all school for a while (a season of idleness being interposed through the narrowness of my parents' fortunes), the briers of unclean desires grew rank over my head, and there was no hand to root them out. When that my father saw me at the baths, now growing towards manhood, and endued with a restless youthfulness, he, as already hence anticipating his descendants, gladly told it to my mother; rejoicing in that tumult of the senses wherein the world forgetteth Thee its Creator, and becometh enamoured of Thy creature, instead of Thyself, through the fumes of that invisible wine of its self-will, turning aside and bowing down to the very basest things. But in my mother's breast Thou hadst already begun Thy temple, and the foundation of Thy holy habitation, whereas my father was as yet but a Catechumen, and that but recently. She then was startled with a holy fear and trembling; and though I was not as yet baptized, feared for me those crooked ways in which they walk who turn their back to Thee, and not their face.

Woe is me! and dare I say that Thou heldest Thy peace, O my God, while I wandered further from Thee? Didst Thou then indeed hold Thy peace to me? And whose but Thine were these words which by my mother, Thy faithful one, Thou sangest in my ears? Nothing whereof sunk into my heart, so as to do it. For she wished, and I remember in private with great anxiety warned me, "not to commit fornication; but especially never to defile another man's wife." These seemed to me womanish advices, which I should blush to obey. But they were Thine, and I knew it not: and I thought Thou wert silent and that it was she who spake; by whom Thou wert not silent unto me; and in her wast despised by me, her son, the son of Thy handmaid, Thy servant. But I knew it not; and ran headlong with such blindness, that amongst my equals I was ashamed of a less shamelessness, when I heard them boast of their flagitiousness, yea, and the more boasting, the more they were degraded: and I took pleasure, not only in the pleasure of the deed, but in the praise. What is worthy of dispraise but vice? But I made myself worse than I was, that I might not be dispraised; and when in any thing I had not sinned as the abandoned ones, I would say that I had done what I had not done, that I might not seem contemptible in proportion as I was innocent; or of less account, the more chaste.

Behold with what companions I walked the streets of Babylon, and wallowed in the mire thereof, as if in a bed of spices and precious ointments. And that I might cleave the faster to its very center, the invisible enemy trod me down, and seduced me, for that I was easy to be seduced. Neither did the mother of my flesh (who had now fled out of the center of Babylon, yet went more slowly in the skirts thereof as she advised me to chastity, so heed what she had heard of me from her husband, as to restrain within the bounds of conjugal affection (if it could not be pared away to the quick) what she felt to be pestilent at present and for the future dangerous. She heeded not this, for she feared lest a wife should prove a clog and hindrance to my hopes. Not those hopes of the world to come, which my mother reposed in Thee; but the hope of learning, which both my parents were too desirous I should attain; my father, because he had next to no thought of Thee, and of me but vain conceits; my mother, because she accounted that those usual courses of learning would not only be no hindrance, but even some furtherance towards attaining Thee. For thus I conjecture, recalling, as well as I may, the disposition of my parents. The reins, meantime, were slackened to me, beyond all temper of due severity, to spend my time in sport, yea, even unto dissoluteness in whatsoever I affected. And in all was a mist, intercepting from me,

O my God, the brightness of Thy truth; and mine iniquity burst out as from very fatness.

Theft is punished by Thy law, O Lord, and the law written in the hearts of men, which iniquity itself effaces not. For what thief will abide a thief? Not even a rich thief, one stealing through want. Yet I lusted to thieve, and did it, compelled by no hunger, nor poverty, but through a cloyedness of well-doing, and a pamperedness of iniquity. For I stole that, of which I had enough, and much better. Nor cared I to enjoy what I stole, but joyed in the theft and sin itself. A pear tree there was near our vineyard, laden with fruit, tempting neither for color nor taste. To shake and rob this, some lewd young fellows of us went, late one night (having according to our pestilent custom prolonged our sports in the streets till then), and took huge loads, not for our eating, but to fling to the very hogs, having only tasted them. And this, but to do what we liked only, because it was misliked. Behold my heart, O God, behold my heart, which Thou hadst pity upon in the bottom of the bottomless pit. Now, behold, let my heart tell Thee what it sought there, that I should be gratuitously evil, having no temptation to ill, but the ill itself. It was foul, and I loved it; I loved to perish, I loved mine own fault, not that for which I was faulty, but my fault itself. Foul soul, falling from Thy firmament to utter destruction; not seeking aught through the shame, but the shame itself!

For there is an attractiveness in beautiful bodies, in gold and silver, and all things; and in bodily touch, sympathy hath much influence, and each other sense hath his proper object answerably tempered. Wordly honor hath also its grace, and the power of overcoming, and of mastery; whence springs also the thirst of revenge. But yet, to obtain all these, we may not depart from Thee, O Lord, nor decline from Thy law. The life also which here we live hath its own enchantment, through a certain proportion of its own, and a correspondence with all things beautiful here below. Human friendship also is endeared with a sweet tie, by reason of the unity formed of many souls. Upon occasion of all these, and the like, is sin committed, while through an immoderate inclination towards these goods of the lowest order, the better and higher are forsaken—Thou, our Lord God, Thy truth, and Thy law. For these lower things have their delights, but not like my God, who made all things; for in Him doth the righteous delight, and He is the joy of the upright in heart.

When, then, we ask why a crime was done, we believe it not, unless it appear that there might have been some desire of obtaining some of those which we called lower goods, or a fear of losing them. For they are beautiful and comely; although compared with those higher and beatific goods, they be abject and low. A man hath murdered another; why? He loved his wife or his estate; or would rob for his own livelihood; or feared to lose some such things by him; or, wronged, was on fire to be revenged. Would any commit murder upon no cause, delighted simply in murdering? who would believe it? For as for that furious and savage man, of whom it is said that he was gratuitously evil and cruel, yet is the cause assigned, "lest" (saith he) "through idleness hand or heart should grow inactive." And to what end? That, through that practice of guilt, he might, having taken the city, attain to honors, empire, riches, and be freed from fear of the laws, and his embarrassments from domestic needs, and consciousness of villainies. So then, not even Catiline himself loved his own villainies, but something else, for whose sake he did them.

What then did wretched I so love in thee, thou theft of mine, thou deed of darkness, in that sixteenth year of my age? Lovely thou wert not, because thou wert theft. But art thou any thing, that thus I speak to thee? Fair were the pears we stole, because they were Thy creation, Thou fairest of all, Creator of all, Thou good God; God, the sovereign good and my true good. Fair were those pears, but not them did my wretched soul desire; for I had store of better, and those I gathered, only that I might steal. For, when gathered, I flung them away, my only feast therein being my own sin, which I was pleased to enjoy. For if aught of those pears came within my mouth, what sweetened it was the sin. And now, O Lord my God, I enquire what in that theft delighted me; and behold it hath no loveliness; I mean not such loveliness as in justice and wisdom; nor such as is in the mind and memory, and senses, and animal life of man; nor yet as the stars are glorious and beautiful in their orbs; or the earth, or sea, full of embryo-life, replacing by its birth that which decayeth; nay, nor even that false and shadowy beauty which belongeth to deceiving vices.

For so doth pride imitate exaltedness; whereas Thou alone art God exalted over all. Ambition, what seeks it, but honors and glory? Whereas Thou alone art to be honored above all, and glorious for evermore. The cruelty of the great would fain be feared; but who is to be feared but God alone, out of whose power what can be wrested or withdrawn? When, or where, or whither, or by whom? The tendernesses of the wanton would fain be counted love: yet is nothing more tender than Thy charity; nor is aught loved more healthfully than that Thy truth, bright and beautiful above all. Curiosity makes semblance of a desire of knowledge; whereas Thou supremely knowest all. Yea, ignorance and foolishness itself is cloaked under the name of simplicity and uninjuriousness; because nothing is found more single than Thee: and what less injurious, since they are his own works which injure the sinner? Yea, sloth would fain be at rest; but what stable rest besides the Lord? Luxury affects to be called plenty and abundance; but Thou art the fulness and never-failing plenteousness of incorruptible pleasures.

Prodigality presents a shadow of liberality: but Thou art the most overflowing Giver of all good. Covetousness would possess many things; and Thou possessest all things. Envy disputes for excellency: what more excellent than Thou? Anger seeks revenge: who revenges more justly than Thou? Fear startles at things unwonted and sudden, which endangers things beloved, and takes forethought for their safety; but to Thee what unwonted or sudden, or who separateth from Thee what Thou lovest? Or where but with Thee is unshaken safety? Grief pines away for things lost, the delight of its desires; because it would have nothing taken from it, as nothing can from Thee.

Thus doth the soul commit fornication, when she turns from Thee, seeking without Thee, what she findeth not pure and untainted, till she returns to Thee. Thus all pervertedly imitate Thee, who remove far from Thee, and lift themselves up against Thee. But even by thus imitating Thee, they imply Thee to be the Creator of all nature; whence there is no place whither altogether to retire from Thee. What then did I love in that theft? And wherein did I even corruptly and pervertedly imitate my Lord? Did I wish even by stealth to do contrary to Thy law, because by power I could not, so that being a prisoner, I might mimic a maimed liberty by doing with impunity things unpermitted me, a darkened likeness of Thy Omnipotency? Behold, Thy servant, fleeing from his Lord, and obtaining a shadow. O rottenness, O monstrousness of life, and depth of death! could I like what I might not, only because I might not?

What shall I render unto the Lord, that, whilst my memory recalls these things, my soul is not affrighted at them? I will love Thee, O Lord, and thank Thee, and confess unto Thy name; because Thou hast forgiven me these so great and heinous deeds of mine. To Thy grace I ascribe it, and to Thy mercy, that Thou hast melted away my sins as it were ice. To Thy grace I ascribe also whatsoever I have not done of evil; for what might I not have done, who even loved a sin for its own sake? Yea, all I confess to have been forgiven me; both what evils I committed by my own wilfulness, and what by Thy guidance I committed not. What man is he, who, weighing his own infirmity, dares to ascribe his purity and innocency to his own strength; that so he should love Thee the less, as if he had less needed Thy mercy, whereby Thou remittest sins to those that turn to Thee? For whosoever, called by Thee, followed Thy voice, and avoided those things which he reads me recalling and confessing of myself, let him not scorn me, who being sick, was cured by that Physician, through whose aid it was that he was not, or rather was less, sick: and for this let him love Thee as much, yea and more; since by whom he sees me to have been recovered from such deep consumption of sin, by Him he sees himself to have been from the like consumption of sin preserved.

What fruit had I then (wretched man!) in those things, of the remembrance whereof I am now ashamed? Especially, in that theft which I loved for the theft's sake; and it too was nothing, and therefore the more miserable I, who loved it. Yet alone I had not done it: such was I then, I remember, alone I had never done it. I loved then in it also the company of the accomplices, with whom I did it? I did not then love nothing else but the theft, yea rather I did love nothing else; for that circumstance of the company was also nothing. What is, in truth? who can teach me, save He that enlighteneth my heart, and discovereth its dark corners? What is it which hath come into my mind to enquire, and discuss, and consider? For had I then loved the pears I stole, and wished to enjoy them, I might have done it alone, had the bare commission of the theft sufficed to attain my pleasure; nor needed I have inflamed the itching of my desires by the excitement of accomplices. But since my pleasure was not in those pears, it was in the offence itself, which the company of fellow-sinners occasioned.

What then was this feeling? For of a truth it was too foul: and woe was me, who had it. But yet what was it? Who can understand his errors? It was the sport, which as it were tickled our hearts, that we beguiled those who little thought what we were doing, and much disliked it. Why then was my delight of such sort that I did it not alone? Because none doth ordinarily laugh alone? ordinarily no one; yet laughter sometimes masters men alone and singly when on one whatever is with them, if anything very ludicrous presents itself to their senses or mind. Yet I had not done this alone; alone I had never done it. Behold my God, before Thee, the vivid remembrance of my soul; alone, I had never committed that theft wherein what I stole pleased me not, but that I stole; nor had it alone liked me to do it, nor had I done it. O friendship too unfriendly! Thou incomprehensible inveigler of the soul, thou greediness to do mischief out of mirth and wantonness, thou thirst of others' loss, without lust of my own gain or revenge: but when it is said, "Let's go, let's do it," we are ashamed not to be shameless.

Who can disentangle that twisted and intricate knottiness? Foul is it: I hate to think on it, to look on it. But Thee I long for, O Righteousness and Innocency, beautiful and comely to all pure eyes, and of a satisfaction unsating. With Thee is rest entire, and life imperturbable. Whoso enters into Thee, enters into the joy of his Lord: and shall not fear, and shall do excellently in the All-Excellent. I sank away from Thee, and I wandered, O my God, too much astray from Thee my stay, in these days of my youth, and I became to myself a barren land.

29

BOOK III:

Of the seventeenth, eighteenth, and nineteenth years of his age, passed at Carthage, when, having completed his course of studies, he is caught in the snares of a licentious passion and falls into the snares of an heresy.

To Carthage I came, where there sang all around me in my ears a cauldron of unholy loves. I loved not yet, yet I loved to love, and out of a deep-seated want, I hated myself for wanting not. I sought what I might love, in love with loving, and safety I hated, and a way without snares. For within me was a famine of that inward food, Thyself, my God; yet, through that famine I was not hungered; but was without all longing for incorruptible sustenance, not because filled therewith, but the more empty, the more I loathed it. For this cause my soul was sickly and full of sores, it miserably cast itself forth, desiring to be scraped by the touch of objects of sense. Yet if these had not a soul, they would not be objects of love. To love then, and to be beloved, was sweet to me; but more, when I obtained to enjoy the person I loved, I defiled, therefore, the spring of friendship with the filth of concupiscence, and I beclouded its brightness with the hell of lustfulness; and thus foul and unseemly, I would fain, through exceeding vanity, be fine and courtly. I fell headlong then into the love wherein I longed to be ensnared. My God, my Mercy, with how much gall didst Thou out of Thy great goodness besprinkle for me that sweetness? For I was both beloved, and secretly arrived at the bond of enjoying; and was with joy fettered with sorrow-bringing bonds, that I might be scourged with the iron burning rods of jealousy, and suspicions, and fears, and angers, and quarrels.

Stage-plays also carried me away, full of images of my miseries, and of fuel to my fire. Why is it, that man desires to be made sad, beholding doleful and tragical things, which yet himself would no means suffer? Yet he desires as a spectator to feel sorrow at them, this very sorrow is his pleasure. What is this but a miserable madness? For a man is the more affected with these actions, the less free he is from such affections. Howsoever, when he suffers in his own person, it uses to be styled misery: when he compassionates others, then it is mercy. But what sort of compassion is this for feigned and scenical passions? For the auditor is not called on to relieve, but only to grieve: and he applauds the actor of these fictions the more, the more he grieves. And if the calamities of those persons (whether of old times, or mere fiction) be so acted, that the spectator is not moved to tears, he goes away disgusted and criticising; but if he be moved to passion, he stays intent, and weeps for joy.

Are griefs then too loved? Verily all desire joy. Or whereas no man likes to be miserable, is he yet pleased to be merciful? Which because it cannot be without passion, for this reason alone are passions loved? This also springs from that vein of friendship. But whither goes that vein? Whither flows it? Wherefore runs it into that torrent of pitch bubbling forth those monstrous tides of foul lustfulness, into which it is willfully changed and transformed, being of its own will precipitated and corrupted from its heavenly clearness? Shall compassion then be put away? By no means. Be griefs then sometimes loved. But beware of uncleanness, O my soul, under the guardianship of my God, the God of our fathers, who is to be praised and exalted above all for ever, beware of uncleanness. For I have not now ceased to pity; but then in the theaters I rejoiced with lovers when they wickedly enjoyed one another, although this was imaginary only in the play. And when they lost one another, as if very compassionate, I sorrowed with them, yet had my delight in both. But now I much more pity him that rejoiceth in his wickedness, than him who is thought to suffer hardship, by missing some pernicious pleasure, and the loss of some miserable felicity. This certainly is the truer mercy, but in it grief delights not. For though he that grieves for the miserable, be commended for his office of charity; yet had he, who is genuinely compassionate, rather there were nothing for him to grieve for. For if good will be ill willed (which can never be), then may he, who truly and sincerely commiserates, wish there might be some miserable, that he might commiserate. Some sorrow may then be allowed, none loved. For thus dost Thou, O Lord God, who lovest souls far more purely than we, and hast more incorruptible pity on them, yet are wounded with no sorrowfulness. And who is sufficient for these things?

But I, miserable, then loved to grieve, and sought out what to grieve at, when in another's and that feigned and personated misery, that acting best pleased me, and attracted me the most vehemently, which drew tears from me. What marvel that an unhappy sheep, straying from Thy flock, and impatient of Thy keeping, I became infected with a foul disease? And hence the love of griefs; not such as should sink deep into me; for I loved not to suffer, what I loved to look on; but such as upon hearing their fictions should lightly scratch the surface; upon which, as on envenomed nails, followed inflamed swelling, impostumes, and a putrefied sore. My life being such, was it life, O my God?

And Thy faithful mercy hovered over me afar. Upon how grievous iniquities consumed I myself, pursuing a sacrilegious curiosity, that having forsaken Thee, it might bring me to the treacherous abyss, and the beguiling service of devils, to whom I sacrificed my evil actions, and in all these things Thou didst scourge me! I dared even, while Thy solemnities were celebrated within the walls of Thy Church, to desire, and to compass a business deserving death for its fruits, for which Thou scourgedst me with grievous punishments, though nothing to my fault, O Thou my exceeding mercy, my God, my refuge from those terrible destroyers, among whom I wandered with a stiff neck, withdrawing further from Thee, loving mine own ways, and not Thine; loving a vagrant liberty.

Those studies also, which were accounted commendable, had a view to excelling in the courts of litigation; the more bepraised, the craftier. Such is men's blindness, glorying even in their blindness. And now I was chief in the rhetoric school, whereat I joyed proudly, and I swelled with arrogancy, though (Lord, Thou knowest) far quieter and altogether removed from the subvertings of those "Subverters" (for this ill-omened and devilish name was the very badge of gallantry) among whom I lived, with a shameless shame that I was not even as they. With them I lived, and was sometimes delighted with their friendship, whose doings I ever did abhor -i.e., their "subvertings," wherewith they wantonly persecuted the modesty of strangers, which they disturbed by a gratuitous jeering, feeding thereon their malicious birth. Nothing can be liker the very actions of devils than these. What then could they be more truly called than "Subverters"? Themselves subverted and altogether perverted first, the deceiving spirits secretly deriding and seducing them, wherein themselves delight to jeer at and deceive others.

Among such as these, in that unsettled age of mine, learned I books of eloquence, wherein I desired to be eminent, out of a damnable and vainglorious end, a joy in human vanity. In the ordinary course of study, I fell upon a certain book of Cicero, whose speech almost all admire, not so his heart. This book of his contains an exhortation to philosophy, and is called "Hortensius." But this book altered my affections, and turned my prayers to Thyself O Lord; and made me have other purposes and desires. Every vain hope at once became worthless to me; and I longed with an incredibly burning desire for an immortality of wisdom, and began now to arise, that I might return to Thee. For not to sharpen my tongue (which thing I seemed to be purchasing with my mother's allowances, in that my nineteenth year, my father being dead two years before), not to sharpen my tongue did I employ that book; nor did it infuse into me its style, but its matter.

How did I burn then, my God, how did I burn to re-mount from earthly things to Thee, nor knew I what Thou wouldest do with me? For with Thee is wisdom. But the love of wisdom is in Greek called "philosophy," with which that book inflamed me. Some there be that seduce through philosophy, under a great, and smooth, and honorable name coloring and disguising their own errors: and almost all who in that and former ages were such, are in that book censured and set forth: there also is made plain that wholesome advice of Thy Spirit, by Thy good and devout servant: Beware lest any man spoil you through philosophy and vain deceit, after the tradition of men, after the rudiments of the world, and not after Christ. For in Him dwelleth all the fulness of the Godhead bodily. And since at that time (Thou, O light of my heart, knowest) Apostolic Scripture was not known to me, I was delighted with that exhortation, so far only, that I was thereby strongly roused, and kindled, and inflamed to love, and seek, and obtain, and hold, and embrace not this or that sect, but wisdom itself whatever it were; and this alone checked me thus unkindled, that the name of Christ was not in it. For this name, according to Thy mercy, O Lord, this name of my Savior Thy Son, had my tender heart, even with my mother's milk, devoutly drunk in and deeply treasured; and whatsoever was without that name, though never so learned, polished, or true, took not entire hold of me.

I resolved then to bend my mind to the holy Scriptures, that I might see what they were. But behold, I see a thing not understood by the proud, nor laid open to children, lowly in access, in its recesses lofty, and veiled with mysteries; and I was not such as could enter into it, or stoop my neck to follow its steps. For not as I now speak, did I feel when I turned to those Scriptures; but they seemed to me unworthy to be compared to the stateliness of Tully: for my swelling pride shrunk from their lowliness, nor could my sharp wit pierce the interior thereof. Yet were they such as would grow up in a little one. But I disdained to be a little one; and, swollen with pride, took myself to be a great one.

Therefore I fell among men proudly doting, exceeding carnal and prating, in whose mouths were the snares of the Devil, limed with the mixture of the syllables of Thy name, and of our Lord Jesus Christ, and of the Holy Ghost, the Paraclete, our Comforter. These names departed not out of their mouth, but so far forth as the sound only and the noise of the tongue, for the heart was void of truth. Yet they cried out "Truth, Truth," and spake much thereof to me, yet it was not in them: but they spake falsehood, not of Thee only (who truly art Truth), but even of those elements of this world, Thy creatures. And I indeed ought to have passed by even philosophers who spake truth concerning them, for love of Thee, my Father, supremely good, Beauty of all things beautiful. O Truth, Truth, how inwardly did even then the marrow of my soul pant after Thee, when they often and diversely, and in many and huge books, echoed of Thee to me, though it was but an echo? And these were the dishes wherein to me, hungering after Thee, they, instead of Thee, served up the Sun and Moon, beautiful works of Thine, but yet Thy works, not Thyself, no nor Thy first works. For Thy spiritual works are before these corporeal works, celestial though they be, and shining. But I hungered and thirsted not even after those first works of Thine, but after Thee Thyself, the Truth, in whom is no variableness, neither shadow of turning: yet they still set before me in those dishes, glittering fantasies, than which better were it to love this very sun (which is real to our sight at least), than those fantasies which by our eyes deceive our mind. Yet because I thought them to be Thee, I fed thereon; not eagerly, for Thou didst not in them taste to me as Thou art; for Thou wast not these emptinesses, nor was I nourished by them, but exhausted rather. Food in sleep shows very like our food awake; yet are not those asleep nourished by it, for they are asleep. But those were not even any way like to Thee, as Thou hast now spoken to me; for those were corporeal fantasies, false bodies, than which these true bodies, celestial or terrestrial, which with our fleshly sight we behold, are far more certain: these things the beasts and birds discern as well as we, and they are more certain than when we fancy them. And again, we do with more certainty fancy them, than by them conjecture other vaster and infinite bodies which have no being. Such empty husks was I then fed on; and was not fed. But Thou, my soul's Love, in looking for whom I fail, that I may become strong, art neither those bodies which we see, though in heaven; nor those which we see not there; for Thou hast created them, nor dost Thou account them among the chiefest of Thy works. How far then art Thou from those fantasies of mine, fantasies of bodies which altogether are not, than which the images of those bodies, which are, are far more certain, and more certain still the bodies themselves, which yet Thou art not; no, nor yet the soul, which is the life of the bodies. So then, better and more certain is the life of the bodies than the bodies. But Thou art the life of souls, the life of lives, having life in Thyself; and changest not, life of my soul.

Where then wert Thou then to me, and how far from me? Far verily was I straying from Thee, barred from the very husks of the swine, whom with husks I fed. For how much better are the fables of poets and grammarians than these snares? For verses, and poems, and "Medea flying," are more profitable truly than these men's five elements, variously disguised, answering to five dens of darkness, which have no being, yet slay the believer. For verses and poems I can turn to true food, and "Medea flying," though I did sing, I maintained not; though I heard it sung, I believed not: but those things I did believe. Woe, woe, by what steps was I brought down to the depths of hell! Toiling and turmoiling through want of Truth, since I sought after Thee, my God (to Thee I confess it, who hadst mercy on me, not as yet confessing), not according to the understanding of the mind, wherein Thou willedst that I should excel the beasts, but according to the sense of the flesh. But Thou wert more inward to me than my most inward part; and higher than my highest. I lighted upon that bold woman, simple and knoweth nothing, shadowed out in Solomon, sitting at the door, and saying, Eat ye bread of secrecies willingly, and drink ye stolen waters which are sweet: she seduced me, because she found my soul dwelling abroad in the eye of my flesh, and ruminating on such food as through it I had devoured.

BOOK VIII:

He finally describes the thirty-second year of his age, the most memorable of his whole life, in which, being instructed by Simplicianus concerning the conversion of others, and the manner of action, he is, after a severe struggle, renewed in his whole mind, and is converted unto God.

O my God, let me, with thanksgiving, remember, and confess unto Thee Thy mercies on me. Let my bones be bedewed with Thy love, and let them say unto Thee, Who is like unto Thee, O Lord? Thou hast broken my bonds in sunder, I will offer unto Thee the sacrifice of thanksgiving. And how Thou hast broken them, I will declare; and all who worship Thee, when they hear this, shall say, "Blessed be the Lord, in heaven and in earth, great and wonderful is his name. " Thy words had stuck fast in my heart, and I was hedged round about on all sides by Thee. Of Thy eternal life I was now certain, though I saw it in a figure and as through a glass. Yet I had ceased to doubt that there was an incorruptible substance, whence was all other substance; nor did I now desire to be more certain of Thee, but more steadfast in Thee. But for my temporal life, all was wavering, and my heart had to be purged from the old leaven. The Way, the Savior Himself, well pleased me, but as yet I shrunk from going through its straitness. And Thou didst put into my mind, and it seemed good in my eyes, to go to Simplicianus, who seemed to me a good servant of Thine; and Thy grace shone in him. I had heard also that from his very youth he had lived most devoted unto Thee. Now he was grown into years; and by reason of so great age spent in such zealous following of Thy ways, he seemed to me likely to have learned much experience; and so he had. Out of which store I wished that he would tell me (setting before him my anxieties) which were the fittest way for one in my case to walk in Thy paths.

For, I saw the church full; and one went this way, and another that way. But I was displeased that I led a secular life; yea now that my desires no longer inflamed me, as of old, with hopes of honor and profit, a very grievous burden it was to undergo so heavy a bondage. For, in comparison of Thy sweetness, and the beauty of Thy house which I loved, those things delighted me no longer. But still I was enthralled with the love of woman; nor did the Apostle forbid me to marry, although he advised me to something better, chiefly wishing that all men were as himself was. But I being weak, chose the more indulgent place; and because of this alone, was tossed up and down in all beside, faint and wasted with withering cares, because in other matters I was constrained against my will to conform myself to a married life, to which I was given up and enthralled. I had heard from the mouth of the Truth, that there were some eunuchs which had made themselves eunuchs for the kingdom of heaven's sake: but, saith He, let him who can receive it, receive it. Surely vain are all men who are ignorant of God, and could not out of the good things which are seen, find out Him who is good. But I was no longer in that vanity; I had surmounted it; and by the common witness of all Thy creatures had found Thee our Creator, and Thy Word, God with Thee, and together with Thee one God, by whom Thou createdst all things. There is yet another kind of ungodly, who knowing God, glorified Him not as God, neither were thankful. Into this also had I fallen, but Thy right hand upheld me, and took me thence, and Thou placedst me where I might recover. For Thou hast said unto man, Behold, the fear of the Lord is wisdom, and, Desire not to seem wise; because they who affirmed themselves to be wise, became fools. But I had now found the goodly pearl, which, selling all that I had, I ought to have bought, and I hesitated.

To Simplicianus then I went, the father of Ambrose (a Bishop now) in receiving Thy grace, and whom Ambrose truly loved as a father. To him I related the mazes of my wanderings. But when I mentioned that I had read certain books of the Platonists, which Victorinus, sometime Rhetoric Professor of Rome (who had died a Christian, as I had heard), had translated into Latin, he testified his joy that I had not fallen upon the writings of other philosophers, full of fallacies and deceits, after the rudiments of this world, whereas the Platonists many ways led to the belief in God and His

Word. Then to exhort me to the humility of Christ, hidden from the wise, and revealed to little ones, he spoke of Victorinus himself, whom while at Rome he had most intimately known: and of him he related what I will not conceal. For it contains great praise of Thy grace, to be confessed unto Thee, how that aged man, most learned and skilled in the liberal sciences, and who had read, and weighed so many works of the philosophers; the instructor of so many noble Senators, who also, as a monument of his excellent discharge of his office, had (which men of this world esteem a high honor) both deserved and obtained a statue in the Roman Forum; he, to that age a worshipper of idols, and a partaker of the sacrilegious rites, to which almost all the nobility of Rome were given up, and had inspired the people with the love of

Anubis, barking Deity, and all
The monster Gods of every kind, who fought
'Gainst Neptune, Venus, and Minerva:

whom Rome once conquered, now adored, all which the aged Victorinus had with thundering eloquence so many years defended; -he now blushed not to be the child of Thy Christ, and the new-born babe of Thy fountain; submitting his neck to the yoke of humility, and subduing his forehead to the reproach of the Cross.

O Lord, Lord, Which hast bowed the heavens and come down, touched the mountains and they did smoke, by what means didst Thou convey Thyself into that breast? He used to read (as Simplicianus said) the holy Scripture, most studiously sought and searched into all the Christian writings, and said to Simplicianus (not openly, but privately and as a friend), "Understand that I am already a Christian." Whereto he answered, "I will not believe it, nor will I rank you among Christians, unless I see you in the Church of Christ." The other, in banter, replied, "Do walls then make Christians?" And this he often said, that he was already a Christian; and Simplicianus as often made the same answer, and the conceit of the "walls" was by the other as often renewed. For he feared to offend his friends, proud daemon-worshippers, from the height of whose Babylonian dignity, as from cedars of Libanus, which the Lord had not yet broken down, he supposed the weight of enmity would fall upon him. But after that by reading and earnest thought he had gathered firmness, and feared to be denied by Christ before the holy angels, should he now be afraid to confess Him before men, and appeared to himself guilty of a heavy offence, in being ashamed of the Sacraments of the humility of Thy Word, and not being ashamed of the sacrilegious rites of those proud daemons, whose pride he had imitated and their rites adopted, he became bold-faced against vanity, and shame-faced towards the truth, and suddenly and unexpectedly said to Simplicianus (as himself told me), "Go we to the Church; I wish to be made a Christian." But he, not containing himself for joy, went with him. And having been admitted to the first Sacrament and become a Catechumen, not long after he further gave in his name, that he might be regenerated by baptism, Rome wondering, the Church rejoicing. The proud saw, and were wroth; they gnashed with their teeth, and melted away. But the Lord God was the hope of Thy servant, and he regarded not vanities and lying madness.

To conclude, when the hour was come for making profession of his faith (which at Rome they, who are about to approach to Thy grace, deliver, from an elevated place, in the sight of all the faithful, in a set form of words committed to memory), the presbyters, he said, offered Victorinus (as was done to such as seemed likely through bashfulness to be alarmed) to make his profession more privately: but he chose rather to profess his salvation in the presence of the holy multitude. "For it was not salvation that he taught in rhetoric, and yet that he had publicly professed: how much less then ought he, when pronouncing Thy word, to dread Thy meek flock, who, when delivering his own words, had not feared a mad multitude!" When, then, he went up to make his profession, all, as they knew him, whispered his name one to another with the voice of congratulation. And who there knew him not? and there ran a low murmur through all the mouths of the rejoicing multitude, Victorinus! Victorinus! Sudden was the burst of rapture, that they saw him; suddenly were they hushed that they might hear him. He pronounced the true faith with an excellent boldness, and all wished to draw him into their very heart; yea by their love and joy they drew him thither, such were the hands wherewith they drew him.

Good God! what takes place in man, that he should more rejoice at the salvation of a soul despaired of, and freed from greater peril, than if there had always been hope of him, or the danger had been less? For so Thou also, merciful Father, dost more rejoice over one penitent than over ninety-nine just persons that need no repentance. And with much joyfulness do we hear, so often as we hear with what joy the sheep which had strayed is brought back upon the shepherd's shoulder, and the groat is restored to Thy treasury, the neighbours rejoicing with the woman who found it; and the joy of the solemn service of Thy house forceth to tears, when in Thy house it is read of Thy younger son, that he was dead, and liveth again; had been lost, and is found. For Thou rejoicest in us, and in Thy holy angels, holy through holy charity. For Thou art ever the same; for all things which abide not the same nor for ever, Thou for ever knowest in the same way.

What then takes place in the soul, when it is more delighted at finding or recovering the things it loves, than if it had ever had them? yea, and other things witness hereunto; and all things are full of witnesses, crying out, "So is it." The conquering commander triumpheth; yet had he not conquered unless he had fought; and the more peril there was in the battle, so much the more joy is there in the triumph. The storm tosses the sailors, threatens shipwreck; all wax pale at approaching death; sky and sea are calmed, and they are exceeding joyed, as having been exceeding afraid. A friend is sick, and his pulse threatens danger; all who long for his recovery are sick in mind with him. He is restored, though as yet he walks not with his former strength; yet there is such joy, as was not, when before he walked sound and strong. Yea, the very pleasures of human life men acquire by difficulties, not those only which fall upon us unlooked for, and against our wills, but even by self-chosen, and pleasure-seeking trouble. Eating and drinking have no pleasure, unless there precede the pinching of hunger and thirst. Men, given to drink, eat certain salt meats, to procure a troublesome heat, which the drink allaying, causes pleasure. It is also ordered that the affianced bride should not at once be given, lest as a husband he should hold cheap whom, as betrothed, he sighed not after.

This law holds in foul and accursed joy; this in permitted and lawful joy; this in the very purest perfection of friendship; this, in him who was dead, and lived again; had been lost and was found. Every where the greater joy is ushered in by the greater pain. What means this, O Lord my God, whereas Thou art everlastingly joy to Thyself, and some things around Thee evermore rejoice in Thee?

What means this, that this portion of things thus ebbs and flows alternately displeased and reconciled? Is this their allotted measure? Is this all Thou hast assigned to them, whereas from the highest heavens to the lowest earth, from the beginning of the world to the end of ages, from the angel to the worm, from the first motion to the last, Thou settest each in its place, and realisest each in their season, every thing good after its kind? Woe is me! how high art Thou in the highest, and how deep in the deepest! and Thou never departest, and we scarcely return to Thee.

Up, Lord, and do; stir us up, and recall us; kindle and draw us; inflame, grow sweet unto us, let us now love, let us run. Do not many, out of a deeper hell of blindness than Victorinus, return to Thee, approach, and are enlightened, receiving that Light, which they who receive, receive power from Thee to become Thy sons? But if they be less known to the nations, even they that know them, joy less for them. For when many joy together, each also has more exuberant joy for that they are kindled and inflamed one by the other. Again, because those known to many, influence the more towards salvation, and lead the way with many to follow. And therefore do they also who preceded them much rejoice in them, because they rejoice not in them alone. For far be it, that in Thy tabernacle the persons of the rich should be accepted before the poor, or the noble before the ignoble; seeing rather Thou hast chosen the weak things of the world to confound the strong; and the base things of this world, and the things despised hast Thou chosen, and those things which are not, that Thou mightest bring to naught things that are. And yet even that least of Thy apostles, by whose tongue Thou soundedst forth these words, when through his warfare, Paulus the Proconsul, his pride conquered, was made to pass under the easy yoke of Thy Christ, and became a provincial of the great King; he also for his former name Saul, was pleased to be called Paul, in testimony of so great a victory. For the enemy is more overcome in one, of whom he hath more hold; by whom he hath hold of more. But the proud he hath more hold of, through their nobility; and by them, of more through their authority. By how much the more welcome then the heart of Victorinus was esteemed, which the devil had held as an impregnable possession, the tongue of Victorinus, with which mighty and keen weapon he had slain many; so much the more abundantly ought Thy sons to rejoice, for that our King hath bound the strong man, and they saw his vessels taken from him and cleansed, and made meet for Thy honor; and become serviceable for the Lord, unto every good work.

But when that man of Thine, Simplicianus, related to me this of Victorinus, I was on fire to imitate him; for for this very end had he related it. But when he had subjoined also, how in the days of the Emperor Julian a law was made, whereby Christians were forbidden to teach the liberal sciences or oratory; and how he, obeying this law, chose rather to give over the wordy school than Thy Word, by which Thou makest eloquent the tongues of the dumb; he seemed to me not more resolute than blessed, in having thus found opportunity to wait on Thee only. Which thing I was sighing for, bound as I was, not with another's irons, but by my own iron will. My will the enemy held, and thence had made a chain for me, and bound me. For of a forward will, was a lust made; and a lust served, became custom; and custom not resisted, became necessity. By which links, as it were, joined together (whence I called it a chain) a hard bondage held me enthralled. But that new will which had begun to be in me, freely to serve Thee, and to wish to enjoy Thee, O God, the only assured pleasantness, was not yet able to overcome my former wilfulness, strengthened by age. Thus did my two wills, one new, and the other old, one carnal, the other spiritual, struggle within me; and by their discord, undid my soul.

Thus, I understood, by my own experience, what I had read, how the flesh lusteth against the spirit and the spirit against the flesh. Myself verily either way; yet more myself, in that which I approved in myself, than in that which in myself I disapproved. For in this last, it was now for the more part not myself, because in much I rather endured against my will, than acted willingly. And yet it was through me that custom had obtained this power of warring against me, because I had come willingly, whither I willed not. And who has any right to speak against it, if just punishment follow the sinner? Nor had I now any longer my former plea, that I therefore as yet hesitated to be above the world and serve Thee, for that the truth was not altogether ascertained to me; for now it too was. But I still under service to the earth, refused to fight under Thy banner, and feared as much to be freed of all incumbrances, as we should fear to be encumbered with it. Thus with the baggage of this present world was I held down pleasantly, as in sleep: and the thoughts wherein I meditated on Thee were like the efforts of such as would awake, who yet overcome with a heavy drowsiness, are again drenched therein. And as no one would sleep for ever, and in all men's sober judgment waking is better, yet a man for the most part, feeling a heavy lethargy in all his limbs, defers to shake off sleep, and though half displeased, yet, even after it is time to rise, with pleasure yields to it, so was I assured that much better were it for me to give myself up to Thy charity, than to give myself over to mine own cupidity; but though the former course satisfied me and gained the mastery, the latter pleased me and held me mastered. Nor had I any thing to answer Thee calling to me, Awake, thou that sleepest, and arise from the dead, and Christ shall give thee light. And when Thou didst on all sides show me that what Thou saidst was true, I, convicted by the truth, had nothing at all to answer, but only those dull and drowsy words, "Anon, anon," "presently," "leave me but a little." But "presently, presently," had no present, and my "little while" went on for a long while; in vain I delighted in Thy law according to the inner man, when another law in my members rebelled against the law of my mind, and led me captive under the law of sin which was in my members. For the law of sin is the violence of custom, whereby the mind is drawn and holden, even against its will; but deservedly, for that it willingly fell into it. Who then should deliver me thus wretched from the body of this death, but Thy grace only, through Jesus Christ our Lord?

And how Thou didst deliver me out of the bonds of desire, wherewith I was bound most straitly to carnal concupiscence, and out of the drudgery of worldly things, I will now declare, and confess unto Thy name, O Lord, my helper and my redeemer. Amid increasing anxiety, I was doing my wonted business, and daily sighing unto Thee. I attended Thy Church, whenever free from the business under the burden of which I groaned. Alypius was with me, now after the third sitting released from his law business, and awaiting to whom to sell his counsel, as I sold the skill of speaking, if indeed teaching can impart it. Nebridius had now, in consideration of our friendship, consented to teach under Verecundus, a citizen and a grammarian of Milan, and a very intimate friend of us all; who urgently desired, and by the right of friendship challenged from our company, such faithful aid as he greatly needed. Nebridius then was not drawn to this by any desire of advantage (for he might have made much more of his learning had he so willed), but as a most kind and gentle friend, he would not be wanting to a good office, and slight our request. But he acted herein very discreetly, shunning to become known to personages great according to this world, avoiding the distraction of mind thence ensuing, and desiring to have it free and at leisure, as many hours as might be, to seek, or read, or hear something concerning wisdom.

Upon a day then, Nebridius being absent (I recollect not why), to, there came to see me and Alypius, one Pontitianus, our countryman so far as being an African, in high office in the Emperor's court. What he would with us, I know not, but we sat down to converse, and it happened that upon a table for some game, before us, he observed a book, took, opened it, and contrary to his expectation, found it the Apostle Paul; for he thought it some of those books which I was wearing myself in teaching. Whereat smiling, and looking at me, he expressed his joy and wonder that he had on a sudden found this book, and this only before my eyes. For he was a Christian, and baptized, and often bowed himself before Thee our God in the Church, in frequent and continued prayers. When then I had told him that I bestowed very great pains upon those Scriptures, a conversation arose (suggested by his account) on Antony the Egyptian monk: whose name was in high reputation among Thy servants, though to that hour unknown to us. Which when he discovered, he dwelt the more upon that subject, informing and wondering at our ignorance of one so eminent. But we stood amazed, hearing Thy wonderful works most fully attested, in times so recent, and almost in our own, wrought in the true Faith and Church Catholic. We all wondered; we, that they were so great, and he, that they had not reached us.

Thence his discourse turned to the flocks in the monasteries, and their holy ways, a sweet-smelling savor unto Thee, and the fruitful deserts of the wilderness, whereof we knew nothing. And there was a monastery at Milan, full of good brethren, without the city walls, under the fostering care of Ambrose, and we knew it not. He went on with his discourse, and we listened in intent silence. He told us then how one afternoon at Triers, when the

Emperor was taken up with the Circensian games, he and three others, his companions, went out to walk in gardens near the city walls, and there as they happened to walk in pairs, one went apart with him, and the other two wandered by themselves; and these, in their wanderings, lighted upon a certain cottage, inhabited by certain of Thy servants, poor in spirit, of whom is the kingdom of heaven, and there they found a little book containing the life of Antony. This one of them began to read, admire, and kindle at it; and as he read, to meditate on taking up such a life, and giving over his secular service to serve Thee. And these two were of those whom they style agents for the public affairs. Then suddenly, filled with a holy love, and a sober shame, in anger with himself cast his eyes upon his friend, saying, "Tell me, I pray thee, what would we attain by all these labors of ours? what aim we at? what serve we for? Can our hopes in court rise higher than to be the Emperor's favorites? and in this, what is there not brittle, and full of perils? and by how many perils arrive we at a greater peril? and when arrive we thither? But a friend of God, if I wish it, I become now at once." So spake he. And in pain with the travail of a new life, he turned his eyes again upon the book, and read on, and was changed inwardly, where Thou sawest, and his mind was stripped of the world, as soon appeared. For as he read, and rolled up and down the waves of his heart, he stormed at himself a while, then discerned, and determined on a better course; and now being Thine, said to his friend, "Now have I broken loose from those our hopes, and am resolved to serve God; and this, from this hour, in this place, I begin upon. If thou likest not to imitate me, oppose not." The other answered, he would cleave to him, to partake so glorious a reward, so glorious a service. Thus both being now Thine, were building the tower at the necessary cost, the forsaking all that they had, and following Thee. Then Pontitianus and the other with him, that had walked in other parts of the garden, came in search of them to the same place; and finding them, reminded them to return, for the day was now far spent. But they relating their resolution and purpose, and how that will was begun and settled in them, begged them, if they would not join, not to molest them. But the others, though nothing altered from their former selves, did yet bewail themselves (as he affirmed), and piously congratulated them, recommending themselves to their prayers;

45

and so, with hearts lingering on the earth, went away to the palace. But the other two, fixing their heart on heaven, remained in the cottage. And both had affianced brides, who when they heard hereof, also dedicated their virginity unto God.

Such was the story of Pontitianus; but Thou, O Lord, while he was speaking, didst turn me round towards myself, taking me from behind my back where I had placed me, unwilling to observe myself; and setting me before my face, that I might see how foul I was, how crooked and defiled, bespotted and ulcerous. And I beheld and stood aghast; and whither to flee from myself I found not. And if I sought to turn mine eye from off myself, he went on with his relation, and Thou again didst set me over against myself, and thrustedst me before my eyes, that I might find out mine iniquity, and hate it. I had known it, but made as though I saw it not, winked at it, and forgot it.

But now, the more ardently I loved those whose healthful affections I heard of, that they had resigned themselves wholly to Thee to be cured, the more did I abhor myself, when compared with them. For many of my years (some twelve) had now run out with me since my nineteenth, when, upon the reading of Cicero's Hortensius, I was stirred to an earnest love of wisdom; and still I was deferring to reject mere earthly felicity, and give myself to search out that, whereof not the finding only, but the very search, was to be preferred to the treasures and kingdoms of the world, though already found, and to the pleasures of the body, though spread around me at my will. But I wretched, most wretched, in the very commencement of my early youth, had begged chastity of Thee, and said, "Give me chastity and continency, only not yet." For I feared lest Thou shouldest hear me soon, and soon cure me of the disease of concupiscence, which I wished to have satisfied, rather than extinguished. And I had wandered through crooked ways in a sacrilegious superstition, not indeed assured thereof, but as preferring it to the others which I did not seek religiously, but opposed maliciously.

And I had thought that I therefore deferred from day to day to reject the hopes of this world, and follow Thee only, because there did not appear aught certain, whither to direct my course. And now was the day come wherein I was to be laid bare to myself, and my conscience was to upbraid me. "Where art thou now, my tongue?

Thou saidst that for an uncertain truth thou likedst not to cast off the baggage of vanity; now, it is certain, and yet that burden still oppresseth thee, while they who neither have so worn themselves out with seeking it, nor for often years and more have been thinking thereon, have had their shoulders lightened, and received wings to fly away." Thus was I gnawed within, and exceedingly confounded with a horrible shame, while Pontitianus was so speaking. And he having brought to a close his tale and the business he came for, went his way; and I into myself. What said I not against myself? with what scourges of condemnation lashed I not my soul, that it might follow me, striving to go after Thee! Yet it drew back; refused, but excused not itself. All arguments were spent and confuted; there remained a mute shrinking; and she feared, as she would death, to be restrained from the flux of that custom, whereby she was wasting to death.

Then in this great contention of my inward dwelling, which I had strongly raised against my soul, in the chamber of my heart, troubled in mind and countenance, I turned upon Alypius. "What ails us?" I exclaim: "what is it? what heardest thou? The unlearned start up and take heaven by force, and we with our learning, and without heart, to, where we wallow in flesh and blood! Are we ashamed to follow, because others are gone before, and not ashamed not even to follow?" Some such words I uttered, and my fever of mind tore me away from him, while he, gazing on me in astonishment, kept silence. For it was not my wonted tone; and my forehead, cheeks, eyes, color, tone of voice, spake my mind more than the words I uttered. A little garden there was to our lodging, which we had the use of, as of the whole house; for the master of the house, our host, was not living there. Thither had the tumult of my breast hurried me, where no man might hinder the hot contention wherein I had engaged with myself, until it should end as Thou knewest, I knew not. Only I was healthfully distracted and dying, to live; knowing what evil thing I was, and not knowing what good thing I was shortly to become. I retired then into the garden, and Alypius, on my steps. For his presence did not lessen my privacy; or how could he forsake me so disturbed? We sate down as far removed as might be from the house. I was troubled in spirit, most vehemently indignant that I entered not into Thy will and covenant, O my God, which all my bones cried out unto me to enter, and praised it to the skies. And therein we enter not by ships, or chariots, or feet, no, move not so far as I had come from the house to that place where we were sitting. For, not to go only, but to go in thither was nothing else but to will to go, but to will resolutely and thoroughly; not to turn and toss, this way and that, a maimed and half-divided will, struggling, with one part sinking as another rose.

Lastly, in the very fever of my irresoluteness, I made with my body many such motions as men sometimes would, but cannot, if either they have not the limbs, or these be bound with bands, weakened with infirmity, or any other way hindered. Thus, if I tore my hair, beat my forehead, if locking my fingers I clasped my knee; I willed, I did it. But I might have willed, and not done it; if the power of motion in my limbs had not obeyed. So many things then I did, when "to will" was not in itself "to be able"; and I did not what both I longed incomparably more to do, and which soon after, when I should will, I should be able to do; because soon after, when I should will, I should will thoroughly. For in these things the ability was one with the will, and to will was to do; and yet was it not done: and more easily did my body obey the weakest willing of my soul, in moving its limbs at its nod, than the soul obeyed itself to accomplish in the will alone this its momentous will.

Whence is this monstrousness? and to what end? Let Thy mercy gleam that I may ask, if so be the secret penalties of men, and those darkest pangs of the sons of Adam, may perhaps answer me. Whence is this monstrousness? and to what end? The mind commands the body, and it obeys instantly; the mind commands itself, and is resisted. The mind commands the hand to be moved; and such readiness is there, that command is scarce distinct from obedience. Yet the mind is mind, the hand is body. The mind commands the mind, its own self, to will, and yet it doth not. Whence this monstrousness? and to what end? It commands itself, I say, to will, and would not command, unless it willed, and what it commands is not done. But it willeth not entirely: therefore doth it not command entirely. For so far forth it commandeth, as it willeth: and, so far forth is the thing commanded, not done, as it willeth not. For the will commandeth that there be a will; not another, but itself. But it doth not command entirely, therefore what it

48

commandeth, is not. For were the will entire, it would not even command it to be, because it would already be. It is therefore no monstrousness partly to will, partly to nill, but a disease of the mind, that it doth not wholly rise, by truth upborne, borne down by custom. And therefore are there two wills, for that one of them is not entire: and what the one lacketh, the other hath.

Let them perish from Thy presence, O God, as perish vain talkers and seducers of the soul: who observing that in deliberating there were two wills, affirm that there are two minds in us of two kinds, one good, the other evil. Themselves are truly evil, when they hold these evil things; and themselves shall become good when they hold the truth and assent unto the truth, that Thy Apostle may say to them, Ye were sometimes darkness, but now light in the Lord. But they, wishing to be light, not in the Lord, but in themselves, imagining the nature of the soul to be that which God is, are made more gross darkness through a dreadful arrogancy; for that they went back farther from Thee, the true Light that enlightened every man that cometh into the world. Take heed what you say, and blush for shame: draw near unto Him and be enlightened, and your faces shall not be ashamed. Myself when I was deliberating upon serving the Lord my God now, as I had long purposed, it was I who willed, I who nilled, I, I myself. I neither willed entirely, nor nilled entirely. Therefore was I at strife with myself, and rent asunder by myself. And this rent befell me against my will, and yet indicated, not the presence of another mind, but the punishment of my own. Therefore it was no more I that wrought it, but sin that dwelt in me; the punishment of a sin more freely committed, in that I was a son of Adam.

For if there be so many contrary natures as there be conflicting wills, there shall now be not two only, but many. If a man deliberate whether he should go to their conventicle or to the theater, these Manichees cry out, Behold, here are two natures: one good, draws this way; another bad, draws back that way. For whence else is this hesitation between conflicting wills? But I say that both be bad: that which draws to them, as that which draws back to the theater. But they believe not that will to be other than good, which draws to them. What then if one of us should deliberate, and amid the strife of his two wills be in a strait, whether he should go to the theater or to our church? would not these Manichees also be in a strait what to answer? For either they must confess (which they fain would not) that the will which leads to our church is good, as well as theirs, who have received and are held by the mysteries of theirs: or they must suppose two evil natures, and two evil souls conflicting in one man, and it will not be true, which they say, that there is one good and another bad; or they must be converted to the truth, and no more deny that where one deliberates, one soul fluctuates between contrary wills.

Let them no more say then, when they perceive two conflicting wills in one man, that the conflict is between two contrary souls, of two contrary substances, from two contrary principles, one good, and the other bad. For Thou, O true God, dost disprove, check, and convict them; as when, both wills being bad, one deliberates whether he should kill a man by poison or by the sword; whether he should seize this or that estate of another's, when he cannot both; whether he should purchase pleasure by luxury, or keep his money by covetousness; whether he go to the circus or the theater, if both be open on one day; or thirdly, to rob another's house, if he have the opportunity; or, fourthly, to commit adultery, if at the same time he have the means thereof also; all these meeting together in the same juncture of time, and all being equally desired, which cannot at one time be acted: for they rend the mind amid four, or even (amid the vast variety of things desired) more, conflicting wills, nor do they yet allege that there are so many divers substances. So also in wills which are good. For I ask them, is it good to take pleasure in reading the Apostle? or good to take pleasure in a sober Psalm? or good to discourse on the Gospel? They will answer to each, "it is good." What then if all give equal pleasure, and all at once? Do not divers wills distract the mind, while he deliberates which he should rather choose? yet are they all good, and are at variance till one be chosen, whither the one entire will may be borne, which before was divided into many. Thus also, when, above, eternity delights us, and the pleasure of temporal good holds us down below, it is the same soul which willeth not this or that with an entire will; and therefore is rent asunder with grievous perplexities, while out of truth it sets this first, but out of habit sets not that aside.

Thus soul-sick was I, and tormented, accusing myself much more severely than my wont, rolling and turning me in my chain, till that were wholly broken, whereby I now was but just, but still was, held. And Thou, O Lord, pressedst upon me in my inward parts by a severe mercy, redoubling the lashes of fear and shame, lest I should again give way, and not bursting that same slight remaining tie, it should recover strength, and bind me the faster. For I said with myself, "Be it done now, be it done now." And as I spake, I all but enacted it: I all but did it, and did it not: yet sunk not back to my former state, but kept my stand hard by, and took breath. And I essayed again, and wanted somewhat less of it, and somewhat less, and all but touched, and laid hold of it; and yet came not at it, nor touched nor laid hold of it; hesitating to die to death and to live to life: and the worse whereto I was inured, prevailed more with me than the better whereto I was unused: and the very moment wherein I was to become other than I was, the nearer it approached me, the greater horror did it strike into me; yet did it not strike me back, nor turned me away, but held me in suspense.

The very toys of toys, and vanities of vanities, my ancient mistresses, still held me; they plucked my fleshy garment, and whispered softly, "Dost thou cast us off? and from that moment shall we no more be with thee for ever? and from that moment shall not this or that be lawful for thee for ever?" And what was it which they suggested in that I said, "this or that," what did they suggest, O my God? Let Thy mercy turn it away from the soul of Thy servant. What defilements did they suggest! what shame! And now I much less than half heard them, and not openly showing themselves and contradicting me, but muttering as it were behind my back, and privily plucking me, as I was departing, but to look back on them. Yet they did retard me, so that I hesitated to burst and shake myself free from them, and to spring over whither I was called; a violent habit saying to me, "Thinkest thou, thou canst live without them?"

But now it spake very faintly. For on that side whither I had set my face, and whither I trembled to go, there appeared unto me the chaste dignity of Continency, serene, yet not relaxedly, gay, honestly alluring me to come and doubt not; and stretching forth to receive and embrace me, her holy hands full of multitudes of good examples: there were so many young men and maidens here, a multitude of youth and every age, grave widows and aged virgins;

and Continence herself in all, not barren, but a fruitful mother of children of joys, by Thee her Husband, O Lord. And she smiled on me with a persuasive mockery, as would she say, "Canst not thou what these youths, what these maidens can? or can they either in themselves, and not rather in the Lord their God? The Lord their God gave me unto them. Why standest thou in thyself, and so standest not? cast thyself upon Him, fear not He will not withdraw Himself that thou shouldest fall; cast thyself fearlessly upon Him, He will receive, and will heal thee." And I blushed exceedingly, for that I yet heard the muttering of those toys, and hung in suspense. And she again seemed to say, "Stop thine ears against those thy unclean members on the earth, that they may be mortified. They tell thee of delights, but not as doth the law of the Lord thy God." This controversy in my heart was self against self only. But Alypius sitting close by my side, in silence waited the issue of my unwonted emotion.

But when a deep consideration had from the secret bottom of my soul drawn together and heaped up all my misery in the sight of my heart; there arose a mighty storm, bringing a mighty shower of tears. Which that I might pour forth wholly, in its natural expressions, I rose from Alypius: solitude was suggested to me as fitter for the business of weeping; so I retired so far that even his presence could not be a burden to me. Thus was it then with me, and he perceived something of it; for something I suppose I had spoken, wherein the tones of my voice appeared choked with weeping, and so had risen up. He then remained where we were sitting, most extremely astonished. I cast myself down I know not how, under a certain fig-tree, giving full vent to my tears; and the floods of mine eyes gushed out an acceptable sacrifice to Thee. And, not indeed in these words, yet to this purpose, spake I much unto Thee: and Thou, O Lord, how long? how long, Lord, wilt Thou be angry for ever? Remember not our former iniquities, for I felt that I was held by them. I sent up these sorrowful words: How long, how long, "to-morrow, and tomorrow?" Why not now? why not is there this hour an end to my uncleanness?

So was I speaking and weeping in the most bitter contrition of my heart, when, lo! I heard from a neighbouring house a voice, as of boy or girl, I know not, chanting, and oft repeating, "Take up and read; Take up and read. " Instantly, my countenance altered, I began to think most intently whether children were wont in any kind of play to sing such words: nor could I remember ever to have heard the like. So checking the torrent of my tears, I arose; interpreting it to be no other than a command from God to open the book, and read the first chapter I should find. For I had heard of Antony, that coming in during the reading of the Gospel, he received the admonition, as if what was being read was spoken to him: Go, sell all that thou hast, and give to the poor, and thou shalt have treasure in heaven, and come and follow me: and by such oracle he was forthwith converted unto Thee. Eagerly then I returned to the place where Alypius was sitting; for there had I laid the volume of the Apostle when I arose thence. I seized, opened, and in silence read that section on which my eyes first fell: Not in rioting and drunkenness, not in chambering and wantonness, not in strife and envying; but put ye on the Lord Jesus Christ, and make not provision for the flesh, in concupiscence. No further would I read; nor needed I: for instantly at the end of this sentence, by a light as it were of serenity infused into my heart, all the darkness of doubt vanished away.

Then putting my finger between, or some other mark, I shut the volume, and with a calmed countenance made it known to Alypius. And what was wrought in him, which I knew not, he thus showed me. He asked to see what I had read: I showed him; and he looked even further than I had read, and I knew not what followed. This followed, him that is weak in the faith, receive; which he applied to himself, and disclosed to me. And by this admonition was he strengthened; and by a good resolution and purpose, and most corresponding to his character, wherein he did always very far differ from me, for the better, without any turbulent delay he joined me. Thence we go in to my mother; we tell her; she rejoiceth: we relate in order how it took place; she leaps for joy, and triumpheth, and blesseth Thee, Who are able to do above that which we ask or think; for she perceived that Thou hadst given her more for me, than she was wont to beg by her pitiful and most sorrowful groanings. For thou convertedst me unto Thyself, so that I sought neither wife, nor any hope of this world, standing in that rule of faith, where Thou hadst showed me unto her in a vision, so many years before. And Thou didst convert her mourning into joy, much more plentiful than she had desired, and in a much more precious and purer way than she erst required, by having grandchildren of my body.

ROMANESQUE LITERATURE

The Carolingian monarchs emerged in the late seventh century and throughout the next two centuries expanded their empire to include most of Europe. Charles Martel, the first ruler in the dynasty, was followed by his son Pippin the Short. He was succeeded by his two sons, Charles and Carloman, who reigned together for three years. Carloman died in 771 leaving Charles as the sole ruler. Until his death in 814 Charles worked tirelessly, and ferociously, to expand his power. He also instituted reforms and promoted education. Many of his works are recorded in *The Deeds of Charlemagne*, a work by a monk known as Notker Balbulus who wrote in 883. While this work does concern itself with being a historical record of Charlemagne's impressive reign, it is also inflated and fantastical. The author seems to want to entertain his audience as well as educate them! Selections from this work are presented here.

The Deeds of Charlemagne
by Notker of St. Gall (840-912)
From *The Early Lives of Charlemagne,* translated by A. J. Grant,
1922

BOOK I:
Concerning the piety of Charles and his care of the Church

After the omnipotent ruler of the world, who orders alike the fate of kingdoms and the course of time, had broken the feet of iron and clay in one noble statue, to wit the Romans, he raised by the hands of the illustrious Charles the golden head of another, not less admirable, among the Franks. Now it happened, when he had begun to reign alone in the western parts of the world, and the pursuit of learning had been almost forgotten throughout all his realm, and the worship of the true Godhead was faint and weak, that two Scots came from Ireland to the coast of Gaul along with certain traders of Britain. These Scotchmen were unrivalled for their skill in sacred and secular learning: and day by day, when the crowd gathered round them for traffic, they exhibited no wares for sale, but cried out and said, "Ho, everyone that desires wisdom, let him draw near and take it at our hands, for it is wisdom that we have for sale."

Now they declared that they had wisdom for sale because they said that the people cared not for what was given freely but only for what was sold, hoping that thus they might be incited to purchase wisdom along with other wares; and also perhaps hoping that by this announcement they themselves might become a wonder and a marvel to men: which indeed turned out to be the case. For so long did they make their proclamation that in the end those who wondered at these men, or perhaps thought them insane, brought the matter to the ears of King Charles, who always loved and sought after wisdom. Wherefore he ordered them to come with all speed into his presence and asked them whether it were true, as fame reported of them, that they had brought wisdom with them. They answered, "We both possess it and are ready to give it, in the name of God, to those who seek it worthily." Again he asked them what price they asked for it and they answered, "We ask no price, O king. We ask only for a fit place for teaching and quick minds to teach and food to eat and raiment to put on, for without these we cannot accomplish our pilgrimage."

This answer filled the king with a great joy and first he kept both of them with him for a short time. But soon, when he must needs go to war, he made one of them named Clement reside in Gaul, and to him he sent many boys both of noble, middle, and humble birth, and he ordered as much food to be given them as they required, and he set aside for them buildings suitable for study. But he sent the second scholar into Italy and gave him the monastery of Saint Augustine near Pavia, that all who wished might gather there to learn from him.

But when Albinus, also called Alcuin, an Englishman, heard that the most religious Emperor Charles gladly entertained wise men, he entered into a ship and came to him. Now Albinus was skilled in all learning beyond all others of our times, for he was the disciple of that most learned priest Bede,[1] who next to Saint

---

[1] Bede was an English best known for his work *The Ecclesiastical History of the English People* and is known as the father of English history.

Gregory was the most skillful interpreter of the scriptures. And Charles received Albinus kindly and kept him at his side to the end of his life, except when he marched with his armies to his vast wars: nay, Charles would even call himself Albinus's disciple, and Albinus he would call his master. He appointed him to rule over the abbey of Saint Martin, near to the city of Tours, so that, when he himself was absent, Albinus might rest there and teach those who had recourse to him. And his teaching bore such fruit among his pupils that the modern Gauls or Franks came to equal the ancient Romans or Athenians.

Then when Charles came back, after a long absence, crowned with victory, into Gaul, he ordered the boys whom he had entrusted to Clement to come before him and present to him letters and verses of their own composition. Now the boys of middle or low birth presented him with writings garnished with the sweet savors of wisdom beyond all that he could have hoped, while those of the children of noble parents were silly and tasteless. Then the most wise Charles, imitating the judgment of the eternal Judge, gathered together those who had done well upon his right hand and addressed them in these words, "My children, you have found much favor with me because you have tried with all your strength to carry out my orders and win advantage for yourselves. Wherefore now study to attain to perfection; and I will give you bishoprics[2] and splendid monasteries, and you shall be always honorable in my eyes." Then he turned severely to those who were gathered on his left, and, smiting their consciences with the fire of his eyes, he flung at them in scorn these terrible words, which seemed thunder rather than human speech, "You nobles, you sons of my chiefs, you superfine dandies, you have trusted to your birth and your possessions and have set at naught my orders to your own advancement: you have neglected the pursuit of learning and you have given yourselves over to luxury and sport, to idleness and profitless pastimes." Then solemnly he raised his august head and his unconquered right hand to the heavens and thus thundered against them, "By the King of Heaven, I take no account of your noble birth and your fine looks, though others may admire you for

---

[2] Bishoprics an ecclesiastical region run by a bishop in the Roman Catholic. Men appointed to these positions had political power as well as religious authority.

them. Know this for certain, that unless you make up for your former sloth by vigorous study, you will never get any favor from Charles."

Charles used to pick out all the best writers and readers from among the poor boys that I have spoken of and transferred them to his chapel; for that was the name that the kings of the Franks gave to their private oratory, taking the word from the cope of St. Martin, which they always took with them in war for a defense against their enemies. Now one day it was announced to this most wary King Charles that a certain bishop was dead and, when the king asked whether the dead bishop had made any bequests for the good of his soul, the messenger replied, "Sire, he has bequeathed no more than two pounds of silver." Thereupon one of his chaplains, sighing, and no longer able to keep the thoughts of his mind within his breast, spake in the hearing of the king these words, "That is small provision for a long, a never-ending journey."

Then Charles, the mildest of men, deliberated a space, and said to the young man, "Do you think then, if you were to get the bishopric, you would care to make more provision for that same long journey?" These cautious words fell upon the chaplain as ripe grapes into the mouth of one who stands agape for them and he threw himself at the feet of Charles and said, "Sire, the matter rests upon the will of God and your own power." Said the king, "Stand behind the curtain, that hangs behind me, and mark what kind of help you would receive if you were raised to that honor."

Now, when the officers of the palace, who were always on the watch for deaths or accidents, heard that the bishop was dead, one and all of them, impatient of delay and jealous of each other, began to make suit for the bishopric through the friends of the emperor. But Charles still persisted unmoved in his design; he refused everyone and said that he would not disappoint his young friend. At last Queen Hildigard sent some of the nobles of the realm, and at last came in person, to beg the bishopric for a certain clerk of her own. The emperor received her petition very graciously and said that he would not and could not deny her anything; but that he thought it shame to deceive his little chaplain. But still the queen, woman-like, thought that a woman's opinion and wish ought to outweigh the decrees of men, and so she concealed the passion that was rising in her heart. She sank her strong voice almost to a whisper and with caressing gestures tried to soften the emperor's unspoken mind. "My sire and king," she said, "what does it matter if that boy does lose the bishopric? Nay, I beseech you, sweet sire, my glory and my refuge, give it to your faithful servant, my clerk." Then that young man, who had heard the petitions from behind the curtain close to the king's chair where he had been placed, embraced the king through the curtain and cried, "Sir king, stand fast and do not let anyone take from you the power that has been given you by God."

Then that strict lover of truth bade him come out and said, "I intend you to have the bishopric; but you must be very careful to spend more and make fuller provision for that same long and unreturning journey both for yourself and for me."

But I must not seem to forget or to neglect Alcuin and will therefore make this true statement about his energy and his deserts: all his pupils without exception distinguished themselves by becoming either holy abbots or bishops. My master Grimald studied the liberal arts under him, first in Gaul and then in Italy. But those who are learned in these matters may charge me with falsehood for saying "all his pupils without exception" when the fact is that there were in his schools two young men, sons of a miller in the service of the monastery of Saint Columban, who did not seem fit and proper persons for promotion to the command of bishoprics or monasteries; but even these men were, by the influence probably of their teacher, advanced one after the other to the office of minister in the monastery of Bobbio, in which they displayed the greatest energy.

So the most glorious Charles saw the study of letters flourishing throughout this whole realm, but still he was grieved to find that it did not reach the ripeness of the earlier fathers and so, after super-human labors, he broke out one day with this expression of his sorrow, "Would that I had twelve clerks so learned in all wisdom and so perfectly trained as were Jerome and Augustine." Then the learned Alcuin, feeling himself ignorant indeed in comparison with these great names, rose to a height of daring, that no man else attained to in the presence of the terrible Charles, and said, with deep indignation in his mind but none in his countenance, "The Maker of heaven and earth has not many like those men and do you expect to have twelve?"

ॐ•ॐ

Here I must report something which the men of our time will find it difficult to believe, for I myself who write it could hardly believe it. So great is the difference between our method of chanting and the Roman,[3] were it not that we must trust rather the accuracy of our fathers than the false suggestions of modern sloth. Well then, Charles, that never-wearied lover of the service of God, when he could congratulate himself that all possible progress had been made in the knowledge of letters, was grieved to observe how widely the different provinces–nay, not the provinces only but districts and cities–differed in the praise of God, that is to say in their method of chanting. He therefore asked of Pope Stephen of blessed memory–the same who, after Hilderich King of the Franks had been deposed and tonsured, had anointed Charles to be ruler of the kingdom after the ancestral custom of the people–he asked of Pope Stephen, I say, that he should provide him with twelve clerks deeply learned in divine song. The Pope yielded assent to his virtuous wish and his divinely inspired design and sent to him in Frankland from the apostolic see clerks skilled in divine song, and twelve in number, according to the number of the twelve apostles.

Now, when I said Frankland just above, I meant all the provinces north of the Alps; for as it is written, "In those days ten men shall take hold out of all the languages of the nations, shall even take hold of the skirt of him that is a Jew," so at that time, by reason of the glory of Charles, Gauls, Aquitanians, Æduans, Spaniards, Germans, and Bavarians thought that no small honor was paid to them, if they were thought worthy to be called the servants of the Franks.

Now when the aforementioned clerks were departing from Rome, being, like all Greeks and Romans, torn with envy of the glory of the Franks, they took counsel among themselves, and determined so to vary their method of singing that his kingdom and dominion should never have cause to rejoice in unity and agreement. So when they came to Charles they were received most

---

[3] Throughout the vast area held by Charles, he discovered stylistic differences in the songs sung in churches. He felt that this would undermine the unity of the church and set about to create a uniform style of worship.

honorably and despatched to the chief places. And thereupon each in his allotted place began to chant as differently as possible and to teach others to sing in like fashion and in as false a manner as they could invent. But as the most cunning Charles celebrated one year the feast of the Birth and Coming of Christ at Trèves or Metz, and most carefully and cleverly grasped and understood the style of the singing; and then the next year passed the same solemn season at Paris or Tours, but found that the singing was wholly different from what he had heard in the preceding year; as moreover he found that those whom he had sent into different places were also at variance with one another, he reported the whole matter to Pope Leo, of holy memory, who had succeeded Stephen. The Pope summoned the clerks back to Rome and condemned them to exile or perpetual imprisonment and then said to Charles, "If I send you others they will be blinded with the same malice as their predecessors and will not fail to cheat you. But I think I can satisfy your wishes in this way. Send me two of the cleverest clerks that you have by you, in such a way that those who are with me may not know that they belong to you, and, with God's help, they shall attain to as perfect a knowledge of those things as you desire." So said, so done. Soon the Pope sent them back excellently trained to Charles. One of them he kept at his own court, the other upon the petition of his son Drogo, Bishop of Metz, he sent to that cathedral. And not only did his energy show itself powerful in that city, but it soon spread so widely throughout all Frankland, that now all in these regions who use the Latin tongue called the ecclesiastical chant Metensian; or, if they use the Teutonic or Teuthiscan tongue, they call it Mette; or if the Greek form is used it is called Mette. The most pious emperor also ordered Peter, the singer who had come to reside with him, to reside for a while in the monastery of St. Gall. There too Charles established the chanting as it is today, with an authentic songbook, and gave most careful instructions, being always a warm champion of Saint Gall, that the Roman method of singing should be both taught and learnt. He gave to the monastery also much money and many lands: he gave too relics, contained in a reliquary made of solid gold and gems, which is called the Shrine of Charles.

᭞᭞

There was a certain bishopric which lay full in Charles's path when he journeyed, and which indeed he could hardly avoid and the bishop of this place, always anxious to give satisfaction, put everything that he had at Charles's disposal. But once the emperor came quite unexpectedly and the bishop in great anxiety had to fly hither and thither like a swallow, and had not only the palaces and houses but also the courts and squares swept and cleaned, and then, tired and irritated, came to meet him. The most pious Charles noticed this, and after examining all the various details, he said to the bishop, "My kind host, you always have everything splendidly cleaned for my arrival." Then the bishop, as if divinely inspired, bowed his head and grasped the king's never-conquered right hand, and hiding his irritation, kissed it and said, "It is but right, my lord, that, wherever you come, all things should be thoroughly cleansed." Then Charles, of all kings the wisest, understanding the state of affairs said to him, "If I empty I can also fill." And he added, "You may have that estate which lies close to your bishopric, and all your successors may have it until the end of time."

As we have shown how the most wise Charles exalted the humble, let us now show how he brought low the proud. There was a bishop who sought above measure vanities and the fame of men. The most cunning Charles heard of this and told a certain Jewish merchant, whose custom it was to go to the land of promise and bring from thence rare and wonderful things to the countries beyond the sea, to deceive or cheat this bishop in whatever way he could. So the Jew caught an ordinary household mouse and stuffed it with various spices and then offered it for sale to the bishop, saying that he had brought this most precious never-before-seen animal from Judea. The bishop was delighted with what he thought a stroke of luck and offered the Jew three pounds of silver for the precious ware. Then said the Jew, "A fine price indeed for so precious an article! I had rather throw it into the sea than let any man have it at so cheap and shameful a price." So the bishop, who had much wealth and never gave anything to the poor, offered him ten pounds of silver for the incomparable treasure. But the cunning rascal, with pretended indignation, replied, "The God of Abraham forbid that I should thus lose the fruit of my labor and journeyings." Then our avaricious bishop, all eager for the prize, offered twenty pounds. But the Jew in high dudgeon wrapped up the mouse in the most costly silk and made as if he would depart. Then the bishop, as thoroughly taken in as he deserved to be, offered a full measure of silver for the priceless object. And so at last our trader yielded to his entreaties with much show of reluctance and, taking the money, went to the emperor and told him everything. A few days later the king called together all the bishops and chief men of the province to hold discourse with him and, after many other matters had been considered, he ordered all that measure of silver to be brought and placed in the middle of the palace. Then thus he spoke and said, "Fathers and guardians, bishops of our Church, you ought to minister to the poor, or rather to Christ in them, and not to seek after vanities. But now you act quite contrary to this and are vainglorious and avaricious beyond all other men." Then he added, "One of you has given a Jew all this silver for a painted mouse." Then the bishop, who had been so wickedly deceived, threw himself at Charles's feet and begged pardon for his sin. Charles upbraided him in suitable words and then allowed him to depart in confusion.

≈∽≈

Now since envy always rages among the envious, so it is customary and regular with the Romans to oppose or rather to fight against all strong Popes who are from time to time raised to the apostolic see. Whence it came to pass that certain of the Romans, themselves blinded with envy, charged the above-mentioned Pope Leo of holy memory with a deadly crime and tried to blind him. But they were frightened and held back by some divine impulse, and after trying in vain to gouge out his eyes, they slashed them across the middle with knives. The Pope had news of this carried secretly by his servants to Michael, Emperor of Constantinople but he refused all assistance saying, "The Pope has an independent kingdom and one higher than mine so he must act his own revenge upon his enemies." Thereupon the holy Leo invited the unconquered Charles to come to Rome; following in this the ordinance of God, that, as Charles was already in very deed ruler and emperor over many nations, so also by the authority of the apostolic see he might have now the name of Emperor, Cæsar and Augustus.

Now Charles, being always ready to march and in warlike array, though he knew nothing at all of the cause of the summons, came at once with his attendants and his vassals; himself the head of the world he came to the city that had once been the head of the world. And when the abandoned people heard of his sudden coming, at once, as sparrows hide themselves when they hear the voice of their master, so they fled and hid in various hiding-places, cellars, and dens. Nowhere howsoever under heaven could they escape from his energy and penetration and soon they were captured and brought in chains to the Cathedral of St. Peter. Then the undaunted Father Leo took the gospel of our Lord Jesus Christ and held it over his head, and then in the presence of Charles and his knights, in presence also of his persecutors, he swore in the following words, "So on the day of the great judgment may I partake in the promises, as I am innocent of the charge that is falsely laid against me." Then many of the prisoners asked to be allowed to swear upon the tomb of St. Peter that they also were innocent of the charge laid against them. But the Pope knew their falseness and said to Charles, "Do not, I pray you, unconquered servant of God, give assent to their cunning for well they know that Saint Peter is always ready to forgive. But seek among the tombs of the martyrs the stone upon which is written the name of St. Pancras, that boy of thirteen years, and if they will swear to you in his name you may know that you have them fast." It was done as the Pope ordered. And when many people drew near to take the oath upon this tomb straightway some fell back dead and some were seized by the devil and went mad. Then the terrible Charles said to his servants, "Take care that none of them escapes." Then he condemned all who had been taken prisoner either to some kind of death or to perpetual imprisonment.

As Charles stayed in Rome for a few days, the Pope called together all who would come from the neighboring districts and then, in their presence and in the presence of all the knights of the unconquered Charles, he declared him to be Emperor and Defender of the Roman Church. Now Charles had no guess of what was coming and, though he could not refuse what seemed to have been divinely preordained for him, nevertheless he received his new title with no show of thankfulness. For first he thought that the Greeks would be fired by greater envy than ever and would plan some harm against the kingdom of the Franks, or at least would take greater precautions against a possible sudden attack of Charles to subdue their kingdom, and add it to his own empire. And further the magnanimous Charles recalled how ambassadors from the King of Constantinople had come to him and had told him that their master wished to be his loyal friend and that, if they became nearer neighbors, he had determined to treat him as his son and relieve the poverty of Charles from his resources and how, upon hearing this, Charles was unable to contain any longer the fiery ardor of his heart and had exclaimed, "Oh, would that pool[4] were not between us for then we would either divide between us the wealth of the east, or we would hold it in common."

But the Lord, who is both the giver and the restorer of health, so showed his favor to the innocency of the blessed Leo that he restored his eyes to be brighter than they were before that wicked and cruel cutting except only that, in token of his virtue, a bright scar (like a very fine thread) marked his eyelids.

☙◦❧

When the most energetic Emperor Charles could rest awhile he sought not sluggish ease, but labored in the service of God. He desired therefore to build upon his native soil a cathedral finer even than the works of the Romans, and soon his purpose was realised. For the building thereof he summoned architects and skilled workmen from all lands beyond the seas and above all he placed a certain knavish abbot whose competence for the execution of such tasks he knew, though he knew not his character. When the August emperor had gone on a certain journey, this abbot allowed anyone to depart home who would pay sufficient money and those who could not purchase their discharge, or were not allowed to return by their masters, he burdened with unending labors, as the Egyptians once afflicted the people of God. By such knavish tricks he gathered together a great mass of gold and silver and silken robes and exhibiting in his chamber only the least precious articles, he concealed in boxes and chests all the richest treasures. Well, one day there was brought to him on a sudden the news that his house was on fire. He ran, in great excitement, and pushed his way

---

[4] Adriatic or Agean seas.

through the bursting flames into the strong room where his boxes, stuffed with gold, were kept. He was not satisfied to take one away, but would only leave after he had loaded his servants with a box apiece. And as he was going out a huge beam, dislodged by the fire, fell on the top of him and then his body was burnt by temporal and his soul by eternal flames. Thus did the judgment of God keep watch for the most religious Emperor Charles, when his attention was withdrawn by the business of his kingdom.

There was another workman, the most skilled of all in the working of brass and glass. Now this man (his name was Tancho and he was at one time a monk of St. Gall) made a fine bell and the emperor was delighted with its tone. Then said that most distinguished, but most unfortunate worker in brass, "Lord emperor, give orders that a great weight of copper be brought to me that I may refine it and instead of tin give me as much silver as I shall need–a hundred pounds at least–and I will cast such a bell for you that this will seem dumb in comparison to it." Then Charles the most liberal of monarchs who "if riches abounded set not his heart upon them" readily gave the necessary orders, to the great delight of the knavish monk. He smelted and refined the brass but he used, not silver, but the purest sort of tin, and soon he made a bell, much better than the one that the emperor had formerly admired, and, when he had tested it, he took it to the emperor, who admired its exquisite shape and ordered the clapper to be inserted and the bell to be hung in the bell-tower. That was soon done and then the warden of the church, the attendants and even the boys of the place tried, one after the other, to make the bell sound. But all was in vain and so at last the knavish maker of the bell came up, seized the rope, and pulled at the bell. When, lo and behold! down from on high came the brazen mass; fell on the very head of the cheating brass founder and killed him on the spot and passed straight through his carcass and crashed to the ground carrying his bowels with it. When the aforementioned weight of silver was found, the most righteous Charles ordered it to be distributed among the poorest servants of the palace.

꒜꒜

Now it was a rule at that time that if the imperial mandate had gone out that any task was to be accomplished, whether it was the making of bridges, or ships or causeways, or the cleansing or paving or filling up of muddy roads, the counts might execute the less important work by the agency of their deputies or servants; but for the greater enterprises, and especially such as were of an original kind, no duke or count, no bishop or abbot could possibly get himself excused. The arches of the great bridge at Mainz bear witness to this for all Europe, so to speak, labored at this work in orderly co-operation, and then the knavery of a few rascals, who wanted to steal merchandise from the ships that passed underneath, destroyed it.

If any churches, with the royal domain, wanted decorating with carved ceilings or wall paintings, the neighboring bishops and abbots had to take charge of the task; but if new churches had to be built then all bishops, dukes and counts, all abbots and heads of royal churches and all who were in occupation of any public office had to work at it with never-ceasing labor from its foundations to its roof. You may see the proof of the emperor's skill in the cathedral at Aix, which seems a work half human and half divine; you may see it in the mansions of the various dignitaries which, by Charles's device, were built round his own palace in such a way that from the windows of his chamber he could see all who went out or came in, and what they were doing, while they believed themselves free from observation; you may see it in all the houses of his nobles, which were lifted on high from the ground in such a fashion that beneath them the retainers of his nobles and the servants of those retainers and every class of man could be protected from rain or snow, from cold or heat, while at the same time they were not concealed from the eyes of the most vigilant Charles. But I am a prisoner within my monastery walls and your ministers are free and I will therefore leave to them the task of describing the cathedral, while I return to speak of how the judgment of God was made manifest in the building of it.

The most careful Charles ordered certain nobles of the neighborhood to support with all their power the workmen whom he had set to their task, and to supply everything that they required for it. Those workmen who came from a distance he gave in charge to a certain Liutfrid, the steward of his palace, telling him to feed and clothe them and also most carefully to provide anything that was wanting for the building. The steward obeyed these commands for the short time that Charles remained in that place but after his departure neglected them altogether, and by cruel tortures collected such a mass of money from the poor workmen that Dis and Pluto would require a camel to carry his ill-gotten gains to hell. Now this was found out in the following way.

The most glorious Charles used to go to lauds[5] at night in a long and flowing cloak, which is now neither used nor known: then when the morning was over he would go back to his chamber and dress himself in his imperial robes. All the clerks used to come ready dressed to the nightly office, and then they would wait for the emperor's arrival, and for the celebration of mass either in the church or in the porch which then was called the outer court. Sometimes they would remain awake, or if anyone had need of sleep he would lean his head on his companion's breast. Now one poor clerk, who used often to go to Liutfrid's house to get his clothes (rags I ought to call them) washed and mended, was sleeping with his head on a friend's knees, when he saw in a vision a giant, taller than the adversary of Saint Anthony, come from the king's court and hurry over the bridge, that spanned a little stream, to the house of the steward. He led with him an enormous camel, burdened with baggage of inestimable value. He was, in his dream, struck with amazement and he asked the giant who he was and whither he wished to go. And the giant made answer, "I come from the house of the king and I go to the house of Liutfrid and I shall place Liutfrid on these packages and I shall take him and them down with me to hell."

Thereupon the clerk woke up, in a fright lest Charles should find him sleeping. He lifted up his head and urged the others to wakefulness and cried, "Hear, I pray you, my dream. I seemed to see another Polyphemus, who walked on the earth and yet touched the stars, and passed through the Ionian Sea without wetting his sides. I saw him hasten from the royal court to the house of Liutfrid with a laden camel. And when I asked the cause of his

---

[5] Lauds is an early morning Mass or divine office celebrated in the Catholic church.

journey, he said, 'I am going to put Liutfrid on the top of the load, and then take him to hell.'"

The story was hardly finished when there came from that house, which they all knew so well, a girl who fell at their feet and asked them to remember her friend Liutfrid in their prayers. And, when they asked the reason for her words, she said, "My lord, he went out but now in good health, and, as he stayed a long time, we went in search of him, and found him dead." When the emperor heard of his sudden death, and was informed by the workmen and his servants of his grasping avarice, he ordered his treasures to be examined. They were found to be of priceless worth, and when the emperor, after God the greatest of judges, found by what wickedness they had been collected he gave this public judgment, "Nothing of that which was gained by fraud must go to the liberation of his soul from purgatory. Let his wealth be divided among the workmen of this our building, and the poorer servants of our palace."

ঔৎড়

In the preface to this little work I said I would follow three authorities only. But as the chief of these, Werinbert, died seven days ago and today (the thirteenth of May) we, his bereaved sons and disciples, are going to pay solemn honor to his memory, here I will bring this book to an end, concerning the piety of Lord Charles and his care of the Church, which has been taken from the lips of this same clerk, Werinbert.

The next book which deals with the wars of the most fierce Charles is founded on the narrative of Werinbert's father, Adalbert. He followed his master Kerold in the Hunnish, Saxon and Slavic wars, and when I was quite a child, and he a very old man, I lived in his house and he used often to tell me the story of these events. I was most unwilling to listen and would often run away but in the end by sheer force he made me hear.

BOOK II:
Concerning the wars and military exploits of Charles

As I am going to found this narrative on the story told by a man of the world, who had little skill in letters, I think it will be well that I should first recount something of earlier history on the credit of written books. When Julian,[6] whom God hated, was slain in the Persian war by a blow from heaven, not only did the transmarine provinces fall away from the Roman Empire, but also the neighboring provinces of Pannonia, Noricum, Rhætia, or in other words the Germans and the Franks or Gauls. Then too the kings of the Franks (or Gauls) began to decay in power because they had slain Saint Didier, Bishop of Vienna, and had expelled those most holy visitors, Columban and Gall. Whereupon the race of the Huns, who had already often ravaged Francia and Aquitania (that is to say the Gauls and the Spains), now poured out with all their forces, devastated the whole land like a wide-sweeping conflagration, and then carried off all their spoils to a very safe hiding place. Now Adalbert, whom I have already mentioned, used to explain the nature of this hiding place as follows, "The land of the Huns," he would say, "was surrounded by nine rings." I could not think of any rings except our ordinary wicker rings for sheepfolds and so I asked, "What, in the name of wonder, do you mean, sire?" "Well," he said, "it was fortified by nine hedges." I could not think of any hedges except those that protect our cornfields, so again I asked and he answered, "One ring was as wide, that is, it contained as much within it, as all the country between Tours and Constance. It was fashioned with logs of oak and ash and yew and was twenty feet wide and the same in height. All the space within was filled with hard stones and binding clay; and the surface of these great ramparts was covered with sods and grass. Within the limits of the ring shrubs were planted of such a kind that, when lopped and bent down, they still threw out twigs and leaves. Then between these ramparts hamlets and houses were so arranged that a man's voice could be made to reach from one to the other. And opposite to the houses, at intervals in those unconquerable walls, were constructed doors of no great size; and through these doors the inhabitants from far and near would pour out on marauding expeditions. The second ring was like the first and was distant twenty Teutonic miles (or forty Italian) from the third ring; and so on to the ninth: though of course the successive rings were each much narrower than the preceding one. But in all

_____

[6] Roman Emperor who ruled from 361 to 363.

the circles the estates and houses were everywhere so arranged that the peal of the trumpet would carry the news of any event from one to the other."

For two hundred years and more the Huns had swept the wealth of the western states within these fortifications, and as the Goths and Vandals were disturbing the repose of the world at the same time the western world was almost turned into a desert. But the most unconquerable Charles so subdued them in eight years that he allowed scarcely any traces of them to remain. He withdrew his hand from the Bulgarians, because after the destruction of the Huns they did not seem likely to do any harm to the kingdom of the Franks. All the booty of the Huns, which he found in Pannonia, he divided most liberally among the bishoprics and the monasteries.

About the same time also envoys of the Persians were sent to him. They knew not where Frankland lay but because of the fame of Rome, over which they knew that Charles had rule, they thought it a great thing when they were able to reach the coast of Italy. They explained the reason of their journey to the bishops of Campania and Tuscany, of Emilia and Liguria, of Burgundy and Gaul and to the abbots and counts of those regions; but by all they were either deceitfully handled or else actually driven off so that a whole year had gone round before, weary and footsore with their long journey, they reached Aix at last and saw Charles, the most renowned of kings by reason of his virtues. They arrived in the last week of Lent, and, on their arrival being made known to the Emperor, he postponed their presentation until Easter Eve. Then when that incomparable monarch was dressed with incomparable magnificence for the chief of festivals, he ordered the introduction of the envoys of that race that had once held the whole world in awe. But they were so terrified at the sight of the most magnificent Charles that one might think they had never seen king or emperor before. He received them however most kingly, and granted them this privilege–that they might go wherever they had a mind to, even as one of his own children, and examine everything and ask what questions and make what inquiries they chose. They jumped with joy at this favor, and valued the privilege of clinging close to Charles, of gazing upon him, of admiring him, more than all the wealth of the east.

They went up into the ambulatory that runs round the nave of the cathedral and looked down upon the clergy and the nobles. Then they returned to the emperor, and, by reason of the greatness of their joy, they could not refrain from laughing aloud and they clapped their hands and said, "We have seen only men of clay before: here are men of gold." Then they went to the nobles, one by one, and gazed with wonder upon arms and clothes that were strange to them and then came back to the emperor, whom they regarded with wonder still greater. They passed that night and the next Sunday continuously in church; and, upon the most holy day itself, they were invited by the most munificent Charles to a splendid banquet, along with the nobles of Frankland and Europe. There they were so struck with amazement at the strangeness of everything that they had hardly eaten anything at the end of the banquet.

"But when the Morn, leaving Tithonus' bed,
Illumined all the land with Phoebus' torch"
then Charles, who could never endure idleness and sloth, went out to the woods to hunt the bison and the urochs;[7] and made preparations to take the Persian envoys with him. But when they saw the immense animals they were stricken with a mighty fear and turned and fled. But the undaunted hero Charles, riding on a high-mettled charger, drew near to one of these animals and drawing his sword tried to cut through its neck. But he missed his aim, and the monstrous beast ripped the boot and leg-thongs of the emperor and, slightly wounding his calf with the tip of its horn, made him limp slightly: after that, furious at the failure of its stroke, it fled to the shelter of a valley, which was thickly covered with stones and trees. Nearly all his servants wanted to take off their own hose to give to Charles, but he forbade it saying, "I mean to go in this fashion to Hildigard." Then Isambard, the son of Warin (the same Warin that persecuted your patron Saint Othmar), ran after the beast and not daring to approach him more closely, threw his lance and pierced him to the heart between the shoulder and the wind-pipe, and brought the beast yet warm to the emperor. He seemed to pay no attention to the incident but gave the carcass

---

[7] Uroch: A large, extinct European wild ox

to his companions and went home. But then he called the queen and showed her how his leg-coverings were torn, and said, "What does the man deserve who freed me from the enemy that did this to me?" She made answer, "He deserves the highest boon." Then the emperor told the whole story and produced the enormous horns of the beast in witness of his truth so that the empress sighed and wept and beat her breast. But when she heard that it was Isambard, who had saved him from this terrible enemy, Isambard, who was in ill favor with the emperor and who had been deprived of all his offices–she threw herself at his feet and induced him to restore all that had been taken from him and a largess was given to him besides.

These same Persian envoys brought the emperor an elephant, monkeys, balsam, nard, unguents of various kinds, spices, scents and many kinds of drugs, in such profusion that it seemed as if the east had been left bare that the west might be filled. They came by-and-by to stand on very familiar terms with the emperor and one day, when they were in a specially merry mood and a little heated with strong beer, they spoke in jest as follows, "Sir emperor, your power is indeed great but much less than the report of it which is spread through all the kingdoms of the east." When he heard this he concealed his deep displeasure and asked jestingly of them, "Why do you say that, my children? How did that idea get into your head?" Then they went back to the beginning and told him everything that had happened to them in the lands beyond the sea and they said, "We Persians and the Medes, Armenians, Indians, Parthians, Elamites, and all the inhabitants of the east fear you much more than our own ruler Haroun. And the Macedonians and all the Greeks (how shall we express it?) they are beginning to fear your overwhelming greatness more than the waves of the Ionian Sea. And the inhabitants of all the islands through which we passed were as ready to obey you, and as much devoted to your service, as if they had been reared in your palace and loaded with your favors. But the nobles of your own kingdom, it seems to us, care very little about you except in your presence: for when we came as strangers to them, and begged them to show us some kindness for the love of you, to whom we desired to make our way, they gave no heed to us and sent us away empty-handed." Then the emperor deposed all counts and abbots, through whose territories those envoys had come, from all the offices that they held and fined the bishops a huge sum of money. Then he ordered the envoys to be taken back to their own country with all care and honor.

Soon after the unwearied emperor sent to the emperor of the Persians horse and mules from Spain, Frisian robes, white, grey, red and blue, which in Persia, he was told, were rarely seen and highly prized. Dogs too he sent him of remarkable swiftness and fierceness, such as the King of Persia had desired, for the hunting and catching of lions and tigers. The King of Persia cast a careless eye over the other presents, but asked the envoys what wild beasts or animals these dogs were accustomed to fight with. He was told that they would pull down quickly anything they were set on to. "Well," he said, "experience will test that." Next day the shepherds were heard crying loudly as they fled from a lion. When the noise came to the palace of the king, he said to the envoys, "Now my friends of Frankland, mount your horses and follow me." Then they eagerly followed after the king as though they had never known toil of weariness. When they came in sight of the lion, though he was yet at a distance, the satrap of the satraps said to them, "Now set your dogs on to the lion." They obeyed and eagerly galloped forward. The German dogs caught the Persian lion, and the envoys slew him with swords of northern metal, which had already been tempered in the blood of the Saxons.

At this sight Haroun, the bravest inheritor of that name, understood the superior might of Charles from very small indications, and thus broke out in his praise, "Now I know that what I heard of my brother Charles is true: how that by the frequent practice of hunting, and by the unwearied training of his body and mind, he has acquired the habit of subduing all that is beneath the heavens. How can I make worthy recompense for the honors which he has bestowed upon me? If I give him the land which was promised to Abraham and shown to Joshua, it is so far away that he could not defend it from the barbarians: or if, like the high-souled king that he is, he tried to defend it I fear that the provinces which lie upon the frontiers of the Frankish kingdom would revolt from his empire. But in this way I will try to show my gratitude for his generosity. I will give that land into his power and I will rule over it as his representative. Whenever he likes or whenever there is a good opportunity he shall send me envoys; and he will find me a faithful manager of the revenue of that province."

Thus was brought to pass what the poet spoke of as an impossibility:

"The Parthian's eyes the Arar's stream shall greet
And Tigris' waves shall lave the German's feet";

for through the energy of the most vigourous Charles it was found not merely possible but quite easy for his envoys to go and return and the messengers of Haroun, whether young or old, passed easily from Parthia into Germany and returned from Germany to Parthia. (And the poet's words are true, whatever interpretation the grammarians put on "the river Arar," whether they think it an affluent of the Rhone or the Rhine for they have fallen into confusion on this point through their ignorance of the locality). I could call on Germany to bear witness to my words, for in the time of your glorious father Lewis, the land was compelled to pay a penny for every acre of land held under the law towards the redemption of Christian captives in the Holy Land and they made their wretched appeal in the name of the dominion anciently held over that land by your great-grandfather Charles and your grandfather Lewis.

But, after conquering the external foe, Charles was attacked at the hands of his own people in a remarkable but unavailing plot. For on his return from the Slavs into his own kingdom he was nearly captured and put to death by his son, whom a concubine had borne to him and who had been called by his mother by the ill-omened name of the most glorious Pippin. The plot was found out in the following manner. This son of Charles had been plotting the death of the emperor with a gathering of nobles, in the church of Saint Peter and when their debate was over, fearful of every shadow, he ordered search to be made, to see whether anyone was hidden in the corners or under the altar. And behold they found, as they feared, a clerk hidden under the altar. They seized him and made him swear that he would not reveal their conspiracy. To save his life, he dared not refuse to take the oath which they dictated but, when they were gone, he held his wicked oath of small account and at once hurried to the palace. With the greatest difficulty he passed through the seven bolted gates, and coming at length to the emperor's chamber knocked upon the door. The most vigilant Charles fell into a great astonishment as to who it was that dared to disturb him at that time of night. He however ordered the women (who followed in his train to wait upon the queen and the princesses) to go out and see who was at the door and what he wanted. When they went out and found the wretched creature, they bolted the door in his face and then, bursting with laughter and stuffing their dresses into their mouths, they tried to hide themselves in the corners of the apartments. But that most wise emperor, whose notice nothing under heaven could escape, asked straitly of the women who it was and what he wanted. When he was told that it was a smooth-faced, silly, half-mad knave, dressed only in shirt and drawers, who demanded an audience without delay, Charles ordered him to be admitted. Then he fell at the emperor's feet and showed all that had happened. So all the conspirators, entirely unsuspicious of danger, were seized before the third hour of the day and most deservedly condemned to exile or some other form of punishment. Pippin himself, a dwarf and a hunchback, was cruelly scourged, tonsured, and sent for some time as a punishment to the monastery of Saint Gall, the poorest, it was judged, and the straitest in all the emperor's broad dominions.

இ~ை

A short time afterwards some of the Frankish nobles sought to do violence to their king. Charles was well aware of their intentions, and yet did not wish to destroy them because, if only they were loyal, they might be a great protection to all Christian men. So he sent messengers to this Pippin and asked him his advice in the matter.

They found him in the monastery garden, in the company of the elder brothers, for the younger ones were detained by their work. He was digging up nettles and other weeds with a hoe, that the useful herbs might grow more vigorously. When they had explained to him the reason of their coming he sighed deeply, from the very bottom of his heart, and said in reply, "If Charles thought my advice worth having he would not have treated me so harshly. I give him no advice. Go, tell him what you found me doing." They were afraid to go back to the dreaded emperor without a definite answer, and again and again asked him what message they should convey to their lord. Then at last he said in anger, "I will send him no message except what I am doing! I am digging up the useless growths in order that the valuable herbs may be able to develop more freely."

So they went away sorrowfully thinking that they were bringing back a foolish answer. When the emperor asked them upon their arrival what answer they were bringing, they answered sorrowfully that after all their labor and long journeying they could get no definite information at all. Then that most wise king asked them carefully where they had found Pippin, and what he was doing, and what answer he had given them and they said, "We found him sitting on a rustic seat turning over the vegetable garden with a hoe. When we told him the cause of our journey we could extract no other reply than this, even by the greatest entreaties: 'I give no message except what I am doing! I am digging up the useless growths in order that the valuable herbs may be able to develop more freely.'" When he heard this the emperor, not lacking in cunning and mighty in wisdom, rubbed his ears and blew out his nostrils and said, "My good vassals, you have brought back a very reasonable answer." So while the messengers were fearing that they might be in peril of their lives, Charles was able to divine the real meaning of the words. He took all those plotters away from the land of the living which had previously been occupied by those unprofitable servants and so gave to his loyal subjects room to grow and spread. One of his enemies who had chosen as part of the spoil of the empire the highest hill in France and all that could be seen from it was, by Charles's orders, hanged upon a high gallows on that very hill. But he bade his bastard son Pippin choose the manner of life that most pleased him. Upon this permission being given him, he chose a post in a monastery then most noble but now destroyed.

৯৽৽৶

It happened too that on his wanderings Charles once came unexpectedly to a certain maritime city of Narbonensian, Gaul. When he was dining quietly in the harbor of this town it happened that some Norman scouts made a piratical raid. When the ships came in sight some thought them Jews, some African or British merchants, but the most wise Charles, by the build of the ships and their speed, knew them to be not merchants but enemies and said to his companions, "These ships are not filled with merchandise, but crowded with our fiercest enemies." When they heard this, in eager rivalry, they hurried in haste to the ships. But all was in vain

77

for when the Northmen heard that Charles, the Hammer, as they used to call him, was there, fearing lest their fleet should be beaten back or even smashed in pieces, they withdrew themselves, by a marvellously rapid flight, not only from the swords but even from the eyes of those who followed them. The most religious, just, and devout Charles had risen from the table and was standing at an eastern window. For a long time he poured down tears beyond price and none dared speak a word to him but at last he explained his actions and his tears to his nobles in these words, "Do you know why I weep so bitterly, my true servants? I have no fear of those worthless rascals doing any harm to me but I am sad at heart to think that even during my lifetime they have dared to touch this shore and I am torn by a great sorrow because I foresee what evil things they will do to my descendants and their subjects."

OLD ENGLISH LITERATURE

The ancient poem, *The Ruined City*, also known simply as *Ruin*, records the rise and fall of a city. Its language will remind you of *Beowulf.* This poem has been put together from fragments found by archaeologists and some parts of the poem are missing but even in its incomplete state, the poet paints a striking picture of the trials endured by those who lived during this turbulent time.

The Ruined City
Exeter Book (late 10th century)

Wondrously wrought and fair its wall of stone,
Shattered by Fate! The castles rend asunder,
The work of giants moldereth away,
Its roofs are breaking and falling; its towers crumble
In ruin. Plundered those walls with grated doors –
Their mortar white with frost. Its battered ramparts
Are shorn away and ruined, all undermined
By eating age. The mighty men that built it,
Departed hence, undone by death, are held
Fast in the earth's embrace. Tight is the clutch
Of the grave, while overhead for living men
A hundred generations pass away.
Long this red wall, now mossy gray, withstood,
While kingdom followed kingdom in the land,
Unshaken 'neath the storms of heaven–yet now
Its towering gate hath fallen . . .
Radiant the mead-halls in that city bright,
Yea, many were its baths. High rose its wealth
Of hornéd pinnacles, while loud within
Was heard the joyous revelry of men –
Till mighty Fate came with her sudden change!
Wide-wasting was the battle where they fell.
Plague-laden days upon the city came;
Death snatched away that mighty host of men . . .
There in the olden time fell many a thane,
Shining with gold, all gloriously adorned,

Haughty in heart, rejoiced when hot with wine;
Upon him gleamed his armor, and he gazed
On gold and silver and all precious gems;
On riches and on wealth and treasured jewels,
A radiant city in a kingdom wide.
There stood courts of stone. Hotly within,
The stream flowed with its mighty surge. The wall
Surrounded all with its bright bosom; there
The baths stood, hot within its heart. . . .

The Battle of Brunanburh, which took place in 937, was said to have been the "greatest single battle in Anglo-Saxon history before the Battle of Hastings." It marked the English defeat of the Norse kings and established England as a nation that could defend itself. You will recognize many of the terms from your reading of *Beowulf.*

The Battle of Brunanburh
Old English Chronicle, A.D. 937
Translation by Alfred Lord Tennyson, 1876

I

Athelstan King,
Lord among Earls,
Bracelet-bestower and
Baron of Barons,
He with his Brother,
Edmund Atheling,
Gaining a lifelong
Glory in battle,
Slew with the sword-edge
There by Brunanburh,
Brake the shield-wall,
Hew'd the linden-wood,
Hack'd the battle-shield,
Sons of Edward with hammer'd brands.

II

Theirs was a greatness
Got from their grand-sires –
Theirs that so often in
Strife with their enemies
Struck for their hoards and their hearths and their homes.

III

Bow'd the spoiler,
Bent the Scotsman,
Fell the ship-crews
Doom'd to the death.

All the field with blood of the fighters
 Flow'd, from when the first the great
 Sun-star of morning-tide
 Lamp of the Lord God
 Lord everlasting,
Glode over earth till the glorious creature
 Sank to his setting.

IV

 There lay many a man
 Marr'd by the javelin,
 Men of the Northland
 Shot over shield.
 There was the Scotsman
 Weary of war.

V

 We the West-Saxons,
 Long as the daylight
 Lasted, in companies
 Troubled the track of the host that we hated;
Grimly with swords that were sharp from the grindstone,
Fiercely we hack'd at the flyers before us.

VI

 Mighty the Mercian,
 Hard was his hand-play,
 Sparing not any of
 Those that with Anlaf,
 Warriors over the
 Weltering waters
 Borne in the bark's-bosom
 Drew to this island –
 Doom'd to the death.

VII

Five young kings put asleep by the sword-stroke,
Seven strong earls of the army of Anlaf

Fell on the war-field, numberless numbers,
Shipmen and Scotsmen.

VIII

Then the Norse leader –
Dire was his need of it,
Few were his following –
Fled to his war-ship;
Fleeted his vessel to sea with the king in it,
Saving his life on the fallow flood.

IX

Also the crafty one,
Constantinus,
Crept to his North again,
Hoar-headed hero!

X

Slender warrant had
He to be proud of
The welcome of war-knives –
He that was reft of his
Folk and his friends that had
Fallen in conflict,
Leaving his son too
Lost in the carnage,
Mangled to morsels,
A youngster in war!

XI

Slender reason had
He to be glad of
The clash of the war-glaive –
Traitor and trickster
And spurner of treaties –
He nor had Anlaf
With armies so broken
A reason for bragging
That they had the better

83

In perils of battle
On places of slaughter –
The struggle of standards,
The rush of the javelins,
The crash of the charges,
The wielding of weapons –
The play that they play'd with
The children of Edward.

XII

Then with their nail'd prow
Parted the Norsemen, a
Blood-redden'd relic of
Javelins over
The jarring breaker, the deep-sea billow,
Shaping their way toward Dyflen again,
Shamed in their souls.

XIII

Also the brethren,
King and Atheling,
Each in his glory,
Went to his own in his own West-Saxonland,
Glad of the war.

XIV

Many a carcass they left to be carrion,
Many a livid one, many a sallow-skin –
Left for the white-tail'd eagle to tear it, and
Left for the horny-nibb'd raven to rend it, and
Gave to the garbaging war-hawk to gorge it, and
That gray beast, the wolf of the weald.

XV

Never had huger
Slaughter of heroes
Slain by the sword edge –
Such as old writers
Have writ of in histories –

Hapt in this isle, since
Up from the East hither
Saxon and Angle from
Over the broad billow
Broke into Britain with
Haughty war-workers who
Harried the Welshman, when
Earls that were lured by the
Hunger of glory gat
Hold of the land.

ROMANESQUE LITERATURE

The Story of My Calamities
by Peter Abelard (1079-1142)
translated by Henry Adams Bellows, 1922

CHAPTER 1:
Of the birthplace of Pierre Abelard and of his parents

Know, then, that I am come from a certain town which was built on the way into lesser Brittany, distant some eight miles, as I think, eastward from the city of Nantes, and in its own tongue called Palets. Such is the nature of that country, or, it may be, of them who dwell there–for in truth they are quick in fancy–that my mind bent itself easily to the study of letters. Yet more, I had a father who had won some smattering of letters before he had girded on the soldier's belt. And so it came about that long afterwards his love thereof was so strong to it that each son of his should be taught in letters even earlier than in the management of arms. Thus indeed did it come to pass. And because I was his first born, and for that reason the more dear to him, he sought with double diligence to have me wisely taught. For my part, the more I went forward in the study of letters, and ever more easily, the greater became the ardor of my devotion to them, until in truth I was so enthralled by my passion for learning that, gladly leaving to my brothers the pomp of glory in arms, the right of heritage and all the honors that should have been mine as the eldest born, I fled utterly from the court of Mars that I might win learning in the bosom of Minerva.[1] And since I found the armory of logical reasoning more to my liking than the other forms of philosophy, I exchanged all other weapons for these, and to the prizes of victory in war I preferred the battle of minds in disputation. Thenceforth, journeying through many provinces, and debating as I went, going whithersoever I heard that the study of my chosen art most flourished, I became such an one as the Peripatetics.[2]

---

[1] Mars is the god of war and Minerva is the Roman goddess of wisdom.

[2] The students at a school in ancient Rome who were known for listening to lectures led by a teacher who walked as he taught.

CHAPTER II:

Of the persecution he had from his master William of Champeaux.
Of his adventures at Melun, at Corbeil, and at Paris. Of his
withdrawal from the city of the Parisians to Melun, and his return
to Mont Saint Genevieve. Of his journey to his old home.

I came at length to Paris, where above all in those days the art of dialectics[3] was most flourishing, and there did I meet William of Champeaux, my teacher, a man most distinguished in his science both by his renown and by his true merit. With him I remained for some time, at first indeed well liked of him, but later I brought him great grief, because I undertook to refute certain of his opinions, not infrequently attacking him in disputation, and now and then in these debates I was adjudged victor. Now this, to those among my fellow students who were ranked foremost, seemed all the more insufferable because of my youth and the brief duration of my studies.

Out of this sprang the beginning of my misfortunes, which have followed me even to the present day. The more widely my fame was spread abroad, the more bitter was the envy that was kindled against me. It was given out that I, presuming on my gifts far beyond the warranty of my youth, was aspiring despite my tender years to the leadership of a school; nay, more, that I was making ready the very place in which I would undertake this task, the place being none other than the castle of Melun, at that time a royal seat. My teacher himself had some foreknowledge of this, and tried to remove my school as far as possible from his own. Working in secret, he sought in every way he could before I left his following to bring to naught the school I had planned and the place I had chosen for it. Since, however, in that very place he had many rivals, and some of them men of influence among the great ones of the land, relying on their aid I won to the fulfillment of my wish; the support of many was secured for me by reason of his own unconcealed envy. From this small inception of my school, my fame in the art of dialectics began to spread abroad, so that little by

---

[3] The dialectical method is discourse between two or more people holding different points of view about a subject, who wish to establish the truth of the matter guided by reasoned arguments

little the renown, not alone of those who had been my fellow students, but of our very teacher himself, grew dim and was like to die out altogether. Thus it came about that, still more confident in myself, I moved my school as soon as I well might to the castle of Corbeil, which is hard by the city of Paris, for I knew there would be given more frequent chance for my assaults in our battle of disputation.

No long time thereafter I was smitten with a grievous illness, brought upon me by my immoderate zeal for study. This illness forced me to turn homeward to my native province, and thus for some years I was as if cut off from France. And yet, for that very reason, I was sought out all the more eagerly by those whose hearts were troubled by the lore of dialectics. But after a few years had passed, and I was whole again from my sickness, I learned that my teacher, that same William Archdeacon of Paris, had changed his former garb and joined an order of the regular clergy. This he had done, or so men said, in order that he might be deemed more deeply religious, and so might be elevated to a loftier rank in the prelacy,[4] a thing which, in truth, very soon came to pass, for he was made bishop of Chalons. Nevertheless, the garb he had donned by reason of his conversion did naught to keep him away either from the city of Paris or from his wonted study of philosophy; and in the very monastery wherein he had shut himself up for the sake of religion he straightway set to teaching again after the same fashion as before.

To him did I return for I was eager to learn more of rhetoric from his lips; and in the course of our many arguments on various matters, I compelled him by most potent reasoning first to alter his former opinion on the subject of the universals, and finally to abandon it altogether. Now, the basis of this old concept of his regarding the reality of universal ideas was that the same quality formed the essence alike of the abstract whole and of the individuals which were its parts: in other words, that there could be no essential differences among these individuals, all being alike save for such variety as might grow out of the many accidents of existence. Thereafter, however, he corrected this opinion, no longer

---

[4] Prelacy: the government of the Christian Church by clerics of high social rank and power.

maintaining that the same quality was the essence of all things, but that, rather, it manifested itself in them through diverse ways. This problem of universals is ever the most vexed one among logicians, to such a degree, indeed, that even Porphyry, writing in his "Isagoge" regarding universals, dared not attempt a final pronouncement thereon, saying rather, "This is the deepest of all problems of its kind." Wherefore it followed that when William had first revised and then finally abandoned altogether his views on this one subject, his lecturing sank into such a state of negligent reasoning that it could scarce be called lecturing on the science of dialectics at all; it was as if all his science had been bound up in this one question of the nature of universals.

Thus it came about that my teaching won such strength and authority that even those who before had clung most vehemently to my former master, and most bitterly attacked my doctrines, now flocked to my school. The very man who had succeeded to my master's chair in the Paris school offered me his post, in order that he might put himself under my tutelage along with all the rest, and this in the very place where of old his master and mine had reigned. And when, in so short a time, my master saw me directing the study of dialectics there, it is not easy to find words to tell with what envy he was consumed or with what pain he was tormented. He could not long, in truth, bear the anguish of what he felt to be his wrongs, and shrewdly he attacked me that he might drive me forth. And because there was naught in my conduct whereby he could come at me openly, he tried to steal away the school by launching the vilest calumnies against him who had yielded his post to me, and by putting in his place a certain rival of mine. So then I returned to Melun, and set up my school there as before; and the more openly his envy pursued me, the greater was the authority it conferred upon me. Even so held the poet, "Jealousy aims at the peaks; the winds storm the loftiest summits."[5]

Not long thereafter, when William became aware of the fact that almost all his students were holding grave doubts as to his religion, and were whispering earnestly among themselves about his conversion, deeming that he had by no means abandoned this world, he withdrew himself and his brotherhood, together with his

---

[5] From Ovid's *Remedy for Love*

students, to a certain estate far distant from the city. Forthwith I returned from Melun to Paris, hoping for peace from him in the future. But since, as I have said, he had caused my place to be occupied by a rival of mine, I pitched the camp, as it were, of my school outside the city on Mont Ste. Genevieve. Thus I was as one laying siege to him who had taken possession of my post. No sooner had my master heard of this than he brazenly returned post haste to the city, bringing back with him such students as he could, and reinstating his brotherhood in their former monastery, much as if he would free his soldiery, whom he had deserted, from my blockade. In truth, though, if it was his purpose to bring them succor, he did naught but hurt them. Before that time my rival had indeed had a certain number of students, of one sort and another, chiefly by reason of his lectures on Priscian, in which he was considered of great authority. After our master had returned, however, he lost nearly all of these followers, and thus was compelled to give up the direction of the school. Not long thereafter, apparently despairing further of worldly fame, he was converted to the monastic life.

Following the return of our master to the city, the combats in disputation which my scholars waged both with him himself and with his pupils, and the successes which fortune gave to us, and above all to me, in these wars, you have long since learned of through your own experience. The boast of Ajax, though I speak it more temperately, I still am bold enough to make:

"if fain you would learn now
How victory crowned the battle, by him was
I never vanquished."[6]

But even were I to be silent, the fact proclaims itself, and its outcome reveals the truth regarding it.

While these things were happening, it became needful for me again to repair to my old home, by reason of my dear mother, Lucia, for after the conversion of my father, Berengarius, to the monastic life, she so ordered her affairs as to do likewise. When all this had been completed, I returned to France, above all in order that I might study theology, since now my oft-mentioned teacher, William, was active in the episcopate of Chalons. In this field of

---

[6] From Ovid's *Metamorphoses*

learning Anselm of Laon, who was his teacher therein, had for long years enjoyed the greatest renown.

CHAPTER III:
Of how he came to Loan to seek Anselm as teacher

I sought out, therefore, this same venerable man, whose fame, in truth, was more the result of long established custom than of the potency of his own talent or intellect. If any one came to him impelled by doubt on any subject, he went away more doubtful still. He was wonderful, indeed, in the eyes of these who only listened to him, but those who asked him questions perforce held him as naught. He had a miraculous flow of words, but they were contemptible in meaning and quite void of reason. When he kindled a fire, he filled his house with smoke and illumined it not at all. He was a tree which seemed noble to those who gazed upon its leaves from afar, but to those who came nearer and examined it more closely was revealed its barrenness. When, therefore, I had come to this tree that I might pluck the fruit thereof, I discovered that it was indeed the fig tree which Our Lord cursed,[7] or that ancient oak to which Lucan likened Pompey, saying:
"he stands, the shade of a name once mighty,
Like to the towering oak in the midst of the fruitful field."[8]
It was not long before I made this discovery, and stretched myself lazily in the shade of that same tree. I went to his lectures less and less often, a thing which some among his eminent followers took sorely to heart, because they interpreted it as a mark of contempt for so illustrious a teacher. Thenceforth they secretly sought to influence him against me, and by their vile insinuations made me hated of him. It chanced, moreover, that one day, after the exposition of certain texts, we scholars were jesting among ourselves, and one of them, seeking to draw me out, asked me what I thought of the lectures on the Books of Scripture. I, who had as yet studied only the sciences, replied that following such lectures seemed to me most useful in so far as the salvation of the soul was concerned, but that it appeared quite extraordinary to me

---

[7] Matthew 21:19, Mark 11:13
[8] From Lucan's *Pharsalia*

that educated persons should not be able to understand the sacred books simply by studying them themselves, together with the glosses[9] thereon, and without the aid of any teacher. Most of those who were present mocked at me, and asked whether I myself could do as I had said, or whether I would dare to undertake it. I answered that if they wished, I was ready to try it. Forthwith they cried out and jeered all the more. "Well and good," said they "we agree to the test. Pick out and give us an exposition of some doubtful passage in the Scriptures, so that we can put this boast of yours to the proof." And they all chose that most obscure prophecy of Ezekiel.

I accepted the challenge, and invited them to attend a lecture on the very next day. Whereupon they undertook to give me good advice, saying that I should by no means make undue haste in so important a matter, but that I ought to devote a much longer space to working out my exposition and offsetting my inexperience by diligent toil. To this I replied indignantly that it was my wont to win success, not by routine, but by ability. I added that I would abandon the test altogether unless they would agree not to put off their attendance at my lecture. In truth at this first lecture of mine only a few were present, for it seemed quite absurd to all of them that I, hitherto so inexperienced in discussing the Scriptures, should attempt the thing so hastily. However, this lecture gave such satisfaction to all those who heard it that they spread its praises abroad with notable enthusiasm, and thus compelled me to continue my interpretation of the sacred text. When word of this was bruited about, those who had stayed away from the first lecture came eagerly, some to the second and more to the third, and all of them were eager to write down the glosses which I had begun on the first day, so as to have them from the very beginning.

---

[9] A gloss is an explanation of a purely verbal difficulty in a Biblical text. It does not explain issues of doctrinal, ritual, historical, or other significance.

CHAPTER IV:
Of the persecution he had from his teacher Anselm

Now this venerable man of whom I have spoken was acutely smitten with envy, and straightway incited, as I have already mentioned, by the insinuations of sundry persons, began to persecute me for my lecturing on the Scriptures no less bitterly than my former master, William, had done for my work in philosophy. At that time there were in this old man's school two who were considered far to excel all the others: Alberic of Rheims and Lotulphe the Lombard. The better opinion these two held of themselves, the more they were incensed against me. Chiefly at their suggestion, as it afterwards transpired, yonder venerable coward had the impudence to forbid me to carry on any further in his school the work of preparing glosses which I had thus begun. The pretext he alleged was that if by chance in the course of this work I should write anything containing blunders–as was likely enough in view of my lack of training–the thing might be imputed to him. When this came to the ears of his scholars, they were filled with indignation at so undistinguised a manifestation of spite, the like of which had never been directed against any one before. The more obvious this rancor became, the more it redounded to my honor, and his persecution did naught save to make me more famous.

CHAPTER V:
Of how he returned to Paris and finished the glosses which he had begun at Laon. Of his growing pride and his downfall.

And so, after a few days, I returned to Paris, and there for several years I peacefully directed the school which formerly had been destined for me, nay, even offered to me, but from which I had been driven out. At the very outset of my work there, I set about completing the glosses on Ezekiel which I had begun at Laon. These proved so satisfactory to all who read them that they came to believe me no less adept in lecturing on theology than I had proved myself to be in the field of philosophy. Thus my school was notably increased in size by reason of my lectures on subjects of both these kinds, and the amount of financial profit as well as glory which it brought me cannot be concealed from you, for the matter was talked of. But prosperity always puffs up the foolish and worldly comfort enervates the soul, rendering it an easy prey to carnal temptations. Thus I who by this time had come to regard myself as the only philosopher remaining in the whole world, and had ceased to fear any further disturbance of my peace, began to loosen the rein on my desires, although hitherto I had always lived in the utmost continence. And the greater progress I made in my lecturing on philosophy or theology, the more I departed alike from the practice of the philosophers and the spirit of the divines in the uncleanness of my life. For it is well known, methinks, that philosophers, and still more those who have devoted their lives to arousing the love of sacred study, have been strong above all else in the beauty of chastity.

Thus did it come to pass that while I was utterly absorbed in pride and sensuality, divine grace, the cure for both diseases, was forced upon me, even though I, forsooth would fain have shunned it. First was I punished for my sensuality, and then for my pride. For my sensuality I lost those things whereby I practiced it; for my pride, engendered in me by my knowledge of letters and it is even as the Apostle said "Knowledge puffeth itself up."[10] I knew the humiliation of seeing burned the very book in which I most gloried. And now it is my desire that you should know the stories of these two happenings, understanding them more truly from learning the very facts than from hearing what is spoken of them, and in the order in which they came about. Because I had ever held in abhorrence the foulness of prostitutes, because I had diligently kept myself from all excesses and from association with the women of noble birth who attended the school, because I knew so little of the common talk of ordinary people, perverse and subtly flattering chance gave birth to an occasion for casting me lightly down from the heights of my own exaltation. Nay, in such case not even divine goodness could redeem one who, having been so proud, was brought to such shame, were it not for the blessed gift of grace.

---

[10] I Corinthians 8:1

CHAPTER VI:

Of how, brought low by his love for Heloise, he was wounded in body and soul

Now there dwelt in that same city of Paris a certain young girl named Heloise, the niece of a canon who was called Fulbert. Her uncle's love for her was equalled only by his desire that she should have the best education which he could possibly procure for her. Of no mean beauty, she stood out above all by reason of her abundant knowledge of letters. Now this virtue is rare among women, and for that very reason it doubly graced the maiden, and made her the most worthy of renown in the entire kingdom. It was this young girl whom I, after carefully considering all those qualities which are wont to attract lovers, determined to unite with myself in the bonds of love, and indeed the thing seemed to me very easy to be done. So distinguished was my name, and I possessed such advantages of youth and comeliness, that no matter what woman I might favor with my love, I dreaded rejection of none. Then, too, I believed that I could win the maiden's consent all the more easily by reason of her knowledge of letters and her zeal therefor; so, even if we were parted, we might yet be together in thought with the aid of written messages. Perchance, too, we might be able to write more boldly than we could speak, and thus at all times could we live in joyous intimacy.

Thus, utterly aflame with my passion for this maiden, I sought to discover means whereby I might have daily and familiar speech with her, thereby the more easily to win her consent. For this purpose I persuaded the girl's uncle, with the aid of some of his friends to take me into his household–for he dwelt hard by my school–in return for the payment of a small sum. My pretext for this was that the care of my own household was a serious handicap to my studies, and likewise burdened me with an expense far greater than I could afford. Now he was a man keen in avarice and likewise he was most desirous for his niece that her study of letters should ever go forward, so, for these two reasons I easily won his consent to the fulfillment of my wish, for he was fairly agape for my money, and at the same time believed that his niece would vastly benefit by my teaching. More even than this, by his own earnest entreaties he fell in with my desires beyond anything I had dared to hope, opening the way for my love, for he entrusted her wholly to my guidance, begging me to give her instruction whensoever I might be free from the duties of my school, no matter whether by day or by night, and to punish her sternly if ever I should find her negligent of her tasks. In all this the man's simplicity was nothing short of astounding to me; I should not have been more smitten with wonder if he had entrusted a tender lamb to the care of a ravenous wolf. When he had thus given her into my charge, not alone to be taught but even to be disciplined, what had he done save to give free scope to my desires, and to offer me every opportunity, even if I had not sought it, to bend her to my will with threats and blows if I failed to do so with caresses? There were, however, two things which particularly served to allay any foul suspicion: his own love for his niece, and my former reputation for continence.

Why should I say more? We were united first in the dwelling that sheltered our love, and then in the hearts that burned with it. Under the pretext of study we spent our hours in the happiness of love, and learning held out to us the secret opportunities that our passion craved. Our speech was more of love than of the books which lay open before us; our kisses far outnumbered our reasoned words. Our hands sought less the book than each other's bosoms—love drew our eyes together far more than the lesson drew them to the pages of our text. In order that there might be no suspicion, there were, indeed, sometimes blows, but love gave them, not anger; they were the marks, not of wrath, but of a tenderness surpassing the most fragrant balm in sweetness. What followed? No degree in love's progress was left untried by our passion, and if love itself could imagine any wonder as yet unknown, we discovered it. And our inexperience of such delights made us all the more ardent in our pursuit of them, so that our thirst for one another was still unquenched.

In measure as this passionate rapture absorbed me more and more, I devoted ever less time to philosophy and to the work of the school. Indeed it became loathsome to me to go to the school or to linger there; the labor, moreover, was very burdensome, since my nights were vigils of love and my days of study. My lecturing became utterly careless and lukewarm; I did nothing because of inspiration, but everything merely as a matter of habit. I had become nothing more than a reciter of my former discoveries, and though I still wrote poems, they dealt with love, not with the secrets of philosophy. Of these songs you yourself well know how some have become widely known and have been sung in many lands, chiefly, methinks, by those who delighted in the things of this world. As for the sorrow, the groans, the lamentations of my students when they perceived the preoccupation, nay, rather the chaos, of my mind, it is hard even to imagine them.

A thing so manifest could deceive only a few, no one, methinks, save him whose shame it chiefly bespoke, the girl's uncle, Fulbert. The truth was often enough hinted to him, and by many persons, but he could not believe it, partly, as I have said, by reason of his boundless love for his niece, and partly because of the well-known continence of my previous life. Indeed we do not easily suspect shame in those whom we most cherish, nor can there be the blot of foul suspicion on devoted love. Of this St. Jerome in his epistle to Sabinianus says, "We are wont to be the last to know the evils of our own households, and to be ignorant of the sins of our children and our wives, though our neighbors sing them aloud." But no matter how slow a matter may be in disclosing itself, it is sure to come forth at last, nor is it easy to hide from one what is known to all. So, after the lapse of several months, did it happen with us. Oh, how great was the uncle's grief when he learned the truth, and how bitter was the sorrow of the lovers when we were forced to part! With what shame was I overwhelmed, with what contrition smitten because of the blow which had fallen on her I loved, and what a tempest of misery burst over her by reason of my disgrace! Each grieved most, not for himself, but for the other. Each sought to allay, not his own sufferings, but those of the one he loved. The very sundering of our bodies served but to link our souls closer together; the plentitude of the love which was denied to us inflamed us more than ever. Once the first wildness of shame had passed, it left us more shameless than before, and as shame died within us the cause of it seemed to us ever more desirable. And so it chanced with us as, in the stories that the poets tell, it once happened with Mars and Venus when they were caught together.

It was not long after this that Heloise found that she was pregnant, and of this she wrote to me in the utmost exultation, at the same time asking me to consider what had best be done. Accordingly, on a night when her uncle was absent, we carried out the plan we had determined on, and I stole her secretly away from her uncle's house, sending her without delay to my own country. She remained there with my sister until she gave birth to a son, whom she named Astrolabe. Meanwhile her uncle after his return, was almost mad with grief; only one who had then seen him could rightly guess the burning agony of his sorrow and the bitterness of his shame. What steps to take against me, or what snares to set for me, he did not know. If he should kill me or do me some bodily hurt, he feared greatly lest his dear-loved niece should be made to suffer for it among my kinsfolk. He had no power to seize me and imprison me somewhere against my will, though I make no doubt he would have done so quickly enough had he been able or dared, for I had taken measures to guard against any such attempt.

At length, however, in pity for his boundless grief, and bitterly blaming myself for the suffering which my love had brought upon him through the baseness of the deception I had practiced, I went to him to entreat his forgiveness, promising to make any amends that he himself might decree. I pointed out that what had happened could not seem incredible to any one who had ever felt the power of love, or who remembered how, from the very beginning of the human race, women had cast down even the noblest men to utter ruin. And in order to make amends even beyond his extremest hope, I offered to marry her whom I had seduced, provided only the thing could be kept secret, so that I might suffer no loss of reputation thereby. To this he gladly assented, pledging his own faith and that of his kindred, and sealing with kisses the pact which I had sought of him–and all this that he might the more easily betray me.

CHAPTER VII:
Of the arguments of Heloise against wedlock and of how none the less he made her his wife.

Forthwith I repaired to my own country, and brought back thence my mistress, that I might make her my wife. She, however, most violently disapproved of this, and for two chief reasons: the danger thereof, and the disgrace which it would bring upon me.

She swore that her uncle would never be appeased by such satisfaction as this, as, indeed, afterwards proved only too true. She asked how she could ever glory in me if she should make me thus inglorious, and should shame herself along with me. What penalties, she said, would the world rightly demand of her if she should rob it of so shining a light! What curses would follow such a loss to the Church, what tears among the philosophers would result from such a marriage! How unfitting, how lamentable it would be for me, whom nature had made for the whole world, to devote myself to one woman solely, and to subject myself to such humiliation! She vehemently rejected this marriage, which she felt would be in every way ignominious and burdensome to me.

Besides dwelling thus on the disgrace to me, she reminded me of the hardships of married life, to the avoidance of which the Apostle exhorts us, saying, "Art thou loosed from a wife? Seek not a wife. But and marry, thou hast not sinned; and if a virgin marry she hath not sinned. Nevertheless such shall have trouble in the flesh: but I spare you."[11] And again, "But I would have you to be free from cares."[12] But if I would heed neither the counsel of the Apostle nor the exhortations of the saints regarding this heavy yoke of matrimony, she bade me at least consider the advice of the philosophers, and weigh carefully what had been written on this subject either by them or concerning their lives. Even the saints themselves have often and earnestly spoken on this subject for the purpose of warning us. Thus St. Jerome, in his first book against Jovinianus, makes Theophrastus set forth in great detail the intolerable annoyances and the endless disturbances of married life, demonstrating with the most convincing arguments that no wise man should ever have a wife, and concluding his reasons for this philosophic exhortation with these words, "Who among Christians would not be overwhelmed by such arguments as these advanced by Theophrastus?"

Again, in the same work, St. Jerome tells how Cicero, asked by Hircius after his divorce of Terentia whether he would marry the sister of Hircius, replied that he would do no such thing, saying that he could not devote himself to a wife and to philosophy at the

---

[11] I Cor. 7:27
[12] I Cor. 7:32

same time. Cicero does not, indeed, precisely speak of "devoting himself," but he does add that he did not wish to undertake anything which might rival his study of philosophy in its demands upon him.

Then, turning from the consideration of such hindrances to the study of philosophy, Heloise bade me observe what were the conditions of honorable wedlock. What possible concord could there be between scholars and domestics, between authors and cradles, between books or tablets and distaffs, between the stylus or the pen and the spindle? What man, intent on his religious or philosophical meditations, can possibly endure the whining of children, the lullabies of the nurse seeking to quiet them, or the noisy confusion of family life? Who can endure the continual untidiness of children? The rich, you may reply, can do this, because they have palaces or houses containing many rooms, and because their wealth takes no thought of expense and protects them from daily worries. But to this the answer is that the condition of philosophers is by no means that of the wealthy, nor can those whose minds are occupied with riches and worldly cares find time for religious or philosophical study. For this reason the renowned philosophers of old utterly despised the world, fleeing from its perils rather than reluctantly giving them up, and denied themselves all its delights in order that they might repose in the embraces of philosophy alone. One of them, and the greatest of all, Seneca, in his advice to Lucilius, says philosophy is not a thing to be studied only in hours of leisure; we must give up everything else to devote ourselves to it, for no amount of time is really sufficient hereto".

It matters little, she pointed out, whether one abandons the study of philosophy completely or merely interrupts it, for it can never remain at the point where it was thus interrupted. All other occupations must be resisted; it is vain to seek to adjust life to include them, and they must simply be eliminated. This view is maintained, for example, in the love of God by those among us who are truly called monastics, and in the love of wisdom by all those who have stood out among men as sincere philosophers. For in every race, gentiles or Jews or Christians, there have always been a few who excelled their fellows in faith or in the purity of their lives, and who were set apart from the multitude by their continence or by their abstinence from worldly pleasures.

Among the Jews of old there were the Nazarites, who consecrated themselves to the Lord, some of them the sons of the prophet Elias and others the followers of Eliseus, the monks of whom, on the authority of St. Jerome, we read in the Old Testament. More recently there were the three philosophical sects which Josephus defines in his Book of Antiquities, calling them the Pharisees, the Sadducees and the Essenes. In our times, furthermore, there are the monks who imitate either the communal life of the Apostles or the earlier and solitary life of John. Among the gentiles there are, as has been said, the philosophers. Did they not apply the name of wisdom or philosophy as much to the religion of life as to the pursuit of learning, as we find from the origin of the word itself, and likewise from the testimony of the saints?

There is a passage on this subject in the eighth book of St. Augustine's *City of God*, wherein he distinguishes between the various schools of philosophy. "The Italian school," he says, "had as its founder Pythagoras of Samos, who, it is said, originated the very word 'philosophy'. Before his time those who were regarded as conspicuous for the praiseworthiness of their lives were called wise men, but he, on being asked of his profession, replied that he was a philosopher, that is to say a student or a lover of wisdom because it seemed to him unduly boastful to call himself a wise man." In this passage, therefore, when the phrase "conspicuous for the praiseworthiness of their lives" is used, it is evident that the wise, in other words the philosophers, were so called less because of their erudition than by reason of their virtuous lives. In what sobriety and continence these men lived it is not for me to prove by illustration, lest I should seem to instruct Minerva herself.

Now, she added, if laymen and gentiles, bound by no profession of religion, lived after this fashion, what ought you, a cleric and a canon, to do in order not to prefer base voluptuousness to your sacred duties, to prevent this Charybdis[13] from sucking you down headlong, and to save yourself from being plunged shamelessly and irrevocably into such filth as this? If you care nothing for your privileges as a cleric, at least uphold your dignity

---

[13] In Greek mythology a sea monster, later rationalized as a whirlpool.

as a philosopher. If you scorn the reverence due to God, let regard for your reputation temper your shamelessness. Remember that Socrates was chained to a wife, and by what a filthy accident he himself paid for this blot on philosophy, in order that others thereafter might be made more cautious by his example. Jerome thus mentions this affair, writing about Socrates in his first book against Jovinianus, "Once when he was withstanding a storm of reproaches which Xantippe was hurling at him from an upper story, he was suddenly drenched with foul slops; wiping his head, he said only, 'I knew there would be a shower after all that thunder.'"

Her final argument was that it would be dangerous for me to take her back to Paris, and that it would be far sweeter for her to be called my mistress than to be known as my wife; nay, too, that this would be more honorable for me as well. In such case, she said, love alone would hold me to her, and the strength of the marriage chain would not constrain us. Even if we should by chance be parted from time to time, the joy of our meetings would be all the sweeter by reason of its rarity. But when she found that she could not convince me or dissuade me from my folly by these and like arguments, and because she could not bear to offend me, with grievous sighs and tears she made an end of her resistance, saying, "Then there is no more left but this, that in our doom the sorrow yet to come shall be no less than the love we two have already known." Nor in this, as now the whole world knows, did she lack the spirit of prophecy.

So, after our little son was born, we left him in my sister's care, and secretly returned to Paris. A few days later, in the early morning, having kept our nocturnal vigil of prayer unknown to all in a certain church, we were united there in the benediction of wedlock her uncle and a few friends of his and mine being present. We departed forthwith stealthily and by separate ways, nor thereafter did we see each other save rarely and in private, thus striving our utmost to conceal what we had done. But her uncle and those of his household, seeking solace for their disgrace, began to divulge the story of our marriage, and thereby to violate the pledge they had given me on this point. Heloise, on the contrary, denounced her own kin and swore that they were speaking the most absolute lies. Her uncle, aroused to fury thereby, visited her repeatedly with punishments. No sooner had I learned this than I sent her to a convent of nuns at Argenteuil, not far from Paris, where she herself had been brought up and educated as a young girl. I had them make ready for her all the garments of a nun, suitable for the life of a convent, excepting only the veil, and these I bade her put on.

When her uncle and his kinsmen heard of this, they were convinced that now I had completely played them false and had rid myself forever of Heloise by forcing her to become a nun. Violently incensed, they laid a plot against me, and one night while I all unsuspecting was asleep in a secret room in my lodgings, they broke in with the help of one of my servants whom they had bribed. There they had vengeance on me with a most cruel and most shameful punishment, such as astounded the whole world; for they cut off those parts of my body with which I had done that which was the cause of their sorrow. This done, straightway they fled, but two of them were captured and suffered the loss of their eyes and their genital organs. One of these two was the aforesaid servant, who even while he was still in my service, had been led by his avarice to betray me.

CHAPTER VIII:
Of the suffering of his body, of how he became a monk in the monastery of St. Denis and Heloise a nun at Argenteuil.

When morning came the whole city was assembled before my dwelling. It is difficult, nay, impossible, for words of mine to describe the amazement which bewildered them, the lamentations they uttered, the uproar with which they harassed me, or the grief with which they increased my own suffering. Chiefly the clerics, and above all my scholars, tortured me with their intolerable lamentations and outcries, so that I suffered more intensely from their compassion than from the pain of my wound. In truth I felt the disgrace more than the hurt to my body, and was more afflicted with shame than with pain. My incessant thought was of the renown in which I had so much delighted, now brought low, nay, utterly blotted out, so swiftly by an evil chance. I saw, too, how justly God had punished me in that very part of my body whereby I had sinned. I perceived that there was indeed justice in my betrayal by him whom I had myself already betrayed; and then I thought how eagerly my rivals would seize upon this manifestation of justice, how this disgrace would bring bitter and enduring grief to my kindred and my friends, and how the tale of this amazing outrage would spread to the very ends of the earth.

What path lay open to me thereafter? How could I ever again hold up my head among men, when every finger should be pointed at me in scorn, every tongue speak my blistering shame, and when I should be a monstrous spectacle to all eyes? I was overwhelmed by the remembrance that, according to the dread letter of the law, God holds eunuchs in such abomination that men thus maimed are forbidden to enter a church, even as the unclean and filthy; nay, even beasts in such plight were not acceptable as sacrifices. Thus in Leviticus [22:24] is it said, "Ye shall not offer unto the Lord that which hath its stones bruised, or crushed, or broken, or cut." And in Deuteronomy [23:1], "He that is wounded in the stones, or hath his privy member cut off, shall not enter into the congregation of the Lord."

I must confess that in my misery it was the overwhelming sense of my disgrace rather than any ardor for conversion to the religious life that drove me to seek the seclusion of the monastic cloister. Heloise had already, at my bidding, taken the veil and entered a convent. Thus it was that we both put on the sacred garb, I in the abbey of St. Denis, and she in the convent of Argenteuil, of which I have already spoken. She, I remember well, when her fond friends sought vainly to deter her from submitting her fresh youth to the heavy and almost intolerable yoke of monastic life, sobbing and weeping replied in the words of Cornelia:

"O husband most noble
Who ne'er shouldst have shared my couch!
Has fortune such power
To smite so lofty a head?
Why then was I wedded
Only to bring thee to woe?
Receive now my sorrow,
The price I so gladly pay."[14]

With these words on her lips did she go forthwith to the altar, and

---

[14] From Lucan's "Pharsalia"

lifted therefrom the veil, which had been blessed by the bishop, and before them all she took the vows of the religious life. For my part, scarcely had I recovered from my wound when clerics sought me in great numbers, endlessly beseeching both my abbot and me myself that now, since I was done with learning for the sake of pain or renown, I should turn to it for the sole love of God. They bade me care diligently for the talent which God had committed to my keeping, [15] since surely He would demand it back from me with interest. It was their plea that, inasmuch as of old I had labored chiefly in behalf of the rich, I should now devote myself to the teaching of the poor. Therein above all should I perceive how it was the hand of God that had touched me, when I should devote my life to the study of letters in freedom from the snares of the flesh and withdrawn from the tumultuous life of this world. Thus, in truth, should I become a philosopher less of this world than of God.

The abbey, however, to which I had betaken myself was utterly worldly and in its life quite scandalous. The abbot himself was as far below his fellows in his way of living and in the foulness of his reputation as he was above them in priestly rank. This intolerable state of things I often and vehemently denounced, sometimes in private talk and sometimes publicly, but the only result was that I made myself detested of them all. They gladly laid hold of the daily eagerness of my students to hear me as an excuse whereby they might be rid of me; and finally, at the insistent urging of the students themselves, and with the hearty consent of the abbot and the rest of the brotherhood, I departed thence to a certain hut, there to teach in my wonted way. To this place such a throng of students flocked that the neighborhood could not afford shelter for them, nor the earth sufficient sustenance.

Here, as befitted my profession, I devoted myself chiefly to lectures on theology, but I did not wholly abandon the teaching of the secular arts, to which I was more accustomed, and which was particularly demanded of me. I used the latter, however, as a hook, luring my students by the bait of learning to the study of the true philosophy, even as the Ecclesiastical History tells of Origen, the greatest of all Christian philosophers. Since apparently the Lord

---

[15] Matthew 25:15

had gifted me with no less persuasiveness in expounding the Scriptures than in lecturing on secular subjects, the number of my students in these two courses began to increase greatly, and the attendance at all the other schools was correspondingly diminished. Thus I aroused the envy and hatred of the other teachers. Those who sought to belittle me in every possible advantage of my absence to bring two principal charges against me: first, that it was contrary to the monastic profession to be concerned with the study of secular books; and, second, that I had presumed to teach theology without ever having been taught therein myself. This they did in order that my teaching of every kind might be prohibited, and to this end they continually stirred up bishops, archbishops, abbots and whatever other dignitaries of the Church they could reach.

CHAPTER IX:
Of his book on theology and his persecution at the hands of his fellow students. Of the Council against him.

It so happened that at the outset I devoted myself to analyzing the basis of our faith through illustrations based on human understanding, and I wrote for my students a certain tract on the unity and trinity of God. This I did because they were always seeking for rational and philosophical explanations, asking rather for reasons they could understand than for mere words, saying that it was futile to utter words which the intellect could not possibly follow, that nothing could be believed unless it could first be understood, and that it was absurd for any one to preach to others a thing which neither he himself nor those whom he sought to teach could comprehend. Our Lord Himself maintained this same thing when He said, "They are blind leaders of the blind."[16]

Now, a great many people saw and read this tract, and it became exceedingly popular, its clearness appealing particularly to all who sought information on this subject. And since the questions involved are generally considered the most difficult of all, their complexity is taken as the measure of the subtlety of him who succeeds in answering them. As a result, my rivals became

---

[16] Matthew 15:14

furiously angry, and summoned a council to take action against me, the chief instigators therein being my two intriguing enemies of former days, Alberic and Lotulphe. These two, now that both William and Anselm, our erstwhile teachers, were dead, were greedy to reign in their stead, and, so to speak, to succeed them as heirs. While they were directing the school at Rheims, they managed by repeated hints to stir up their archbishop, Rodolphe, against me, for the purpose of holding a meeting, or rather an ecclesiastical council, at Soissons, provided they could secure the approval of Conon, Bishop of Praeneste, at that time papal legate in France. Their plan was to summon me to be present at this council, bringing with me the famous book I had written regarding the Trinity. In all this, indeed, they were successful, and the thing happened according to their wishes.

Before I reached Soissons, however, these two rivals of mine so foully slandered me with both the clergy and the public that on the day of my arrival the people came near to stoning me and the few students of mine who had accompanied me thither. The cause of their anger was that they had been led to believe that I had preached and written to prove the existence of three gods. No sooner had I reached the city, therefore, than I went forthwith to the legate; to him I submitted my book for examination and judgment, declaring that if I had written anything repugnant to the Catholic faith, I was quite ready to correct it or otherwise to make satisfactory amends. The legate directed me to refer my book to the archbishop and to those same two rivals of mine, to the end that my accusers might also be my judges. So in my case was fulfilled the saying, "Even our enemies are our judges."[17]

These three, then, took my book and pawed it over and examined it minutely, but could find nothing therein which they dared to use as the basis for a public accusation against me. Accordingly they put off the condemnation of the book until the close of the council, despite their eagerness to bring it about. For my part, every day before the council convened I publicly discussed the Catholic faith in the light of what I had written, and all who heard me were enthusiastic in their approval alike of the frankness and the logic of my words. When the public and the

---

[17] Deuteronomy 32: 31

clergy had thus learned something of the real character of my teaching, they began to say to one another, "Behold, now he speaks openly, and no one brings any charge against him. And this council, summoned, as we have heard, chiefly to take action upon his case is drawing toward its end. Did the judges realize that the error might be theirs rather than his?"

As a result of all this, my rivals grew more angry day by day. On one occasion Alberic, accompanied by some of his students, came to me for the purpose of intimidating me, and, after a few bland words, said that he was amazed at something he had found in my book, to the effect that, although God had begotten God, I denied that God had begotten Himself, since there was only one God. I answered unhesitatingly, "I can give you an explanation of this if you wish it." "Nay," he replied, "I care nothing for human explanation or reasoning in such matters, but only for the words of authority." "Very well, I said, "turn the pages of my book and you will find the authority likewise." The book was at hand, for he had brought it with him. I turned to the passage I had in mind, which he had either not discovered or else passed over as containing nothing injurious to me. And it was God's will that I quickly found what I sought. This was the following sentence, under the heading "Augustine, On the Trinity, Book I": "Whosoever believes that it is within the power of God to beget Himself is sorely in error; this power is not in God, neither is it in any created thing, spiritual or corporeal. For there is nothing that can give birth to itself."

When those of his followers who were present heard this, they were amazed and much embarrassed. He himself, in order to keep his countenance, said, "Certainly, I understand all that." Then I added, "What I have to say further on this subject is by no means new, but apparently it has nothing to do with the case at issue, since you have asked for the word of authority only, and not for explanations. If, however, you care to consider logical explanations, I am prepared to demonstrate that, according to Augustine's statement, you have yourself fallen into a heresy in believing that a father can possibly be his own son." When Alberic heard this he was almost beside himself with rage, and straightway resorted to threats, asserting that neither my explanations nor my citations of authority would avail me aught in this case. With this he left me.

On the last day of the council, before the session convened, the legate and the archbishop deliberated with my rivals and sundry others as to what should be done about me and my book, this being the chief reason for their having come together. And since they had discovered nothing either in my speech or in what I had hitherto written which would give them a case against me, they were all reduced to silence, or at the most to maligning me in whispers. Then Geoffroi, Bishop of Chartres, who excelled the other bishops alike in the sincerity of his religion and in the importance of his see, spoke thus:

"You know, my lords, all who are gathered here, the doctrine of this man, what it is, and his ability, which has brought him many followers in every field to which he has devoted himself. You know how greatly he has lessened the renown of other teachers, both his masters and our own, and how he has spread as it were the offshoots of his vine from sea to sea. Now, if you impose a lightly considered judgment on him, as I cannot believe you will, you well know that even if mayhap you are in the right there are many who will be angered thereby and that he will have no lack of defenders. Remember above all that we have found nothing in this book of his that lies before us whereon any open accusation can be based. Indeed it is true, as Jerome says, `Fortitude openly displayed always creates rivals, and the lightning strikes the highest peaks.' Have a care, then, lest by violent action you only increase his fame, and lest we do more hurt to ourselves through envy than to him through justice. A false report, as that same wise man reminds us, is easily crushed, and a man's later life gives testimony as to his earlier deeds. If, then, you are disposed to take canonical action against him, his doctrine or his writings must be brought forward as evidence, and he must have free opportunity to answer his questioners. In that case if he is found guilty or if he confesses his error, his lips can be wholly sealed. Consider the words of the blessed Nicodemus, who, desiring to free Our Lord Himself, said, 'Doth our law judge any man before it hear him and know what he doeth?'"[18]

When my rivals heard this they cried out in protest, saying, "This is wise counsel, forsooth, that we should strive against the

---

[18] John 7:51

wordiness of this man, whose arguments, or rather, sophistries, the whole world cannot resist!" And yet, methinks, it was far more difficult to strive against Christ Himself, for Whom, nevertheless, Nicodemus demanded a hearing in accordance with the dictates of the law. When the bishop could not win their assent to his proposals, he tried in another way to curb their hatred, saying that for the discussion of such an important case the few who were present were not enough, and that this matter required a more thorough examination. His further suggestion was that my abbot, who was there present, should take me back with him to our abbey, in other words to the monastery of St. Denis, and that there a large convocation of learned men should determine, on the basis of a careful investigation, what ought to be done. To this last proposal the legate consented, as did all the others.

Then the legate arose to celebrate mass before entering the council, and through the bishop sent me the permission which had been determined on, authorizing me to return to my monastery and there await such action as might be finally taken. But my rivals, perceiving that they would accomplish nothing if the trial were to be held outside of their own diocese, and in a place where they could have little influence on the verdict, and in truth having small wish that justice should be done, persuaded the archbishop that it would be a grave insult to him to transfer this case to another court, and that it would be dangerous for him if by chance I should thus be acquitted. They likewise went to the legate, and succeeded in so changing his opinion that finally they induced him to frame a new sentence, whereby he agreed to condemn my book without any further inquiry, to burn it forthwith in the sight of all, and to confine me for a year in another monastery. The argument they used was that it sufficed for the condemnation of my book that I had presumed to read it in public without the approval either of the Roman pontiff or of the church, and that, furthermore, I had given it to many to be transcribed. Methinks it would be a notable blessing to the Christian faith if there were more who displayed a like presumption. The legate, however, being less skilled in law than he should have been, relied chiefly on the advice of the archbishop, and he, in turn, on that of my rivals. When the Bishop of Chartres got wind of this, he reported the whole conspiracy to me, and strongly urged me to endure meekly the manifest violence of their enmity. He bade me not to doubt that this violence would in the end react upon them and prove a blessing to me, and counseled me to have no fear of the confinement in a monastery, knowing that within a few days the legate himself, who was now acting under compulsion, would after his departure set me free. And thus he consoled me as best he might, mingling his tears with mine.

CHAPTER X:
Of the burning of his book. Of the persecution he had at the hands of his abbot and the brethren.

Straightaway upon my summons I went to the council, and there, without further examination or debate, did they compel me with my own hand to cast that memorable book of mine into the flames. Although my enemies appeared to have nothing to say while the book was burning, one of them muttered something about having seen it written therein that God the Father was alone omnipotent. This reached the ears of the legate, who replied in astonishment that he could not believe that even a child would make so absurd a blunder. "Our common faith," he said, "holds and sets forth that the Three are alike omnipotent." A certain Tirric, a schoolmaster, hearing this, sarcastically added the Athanasian phrase, "And yet there are not three omnipotent Persons, but only One."

This man's bishop forthwith began to censure him, bidding him desist from such treasonable talk, but he boldly stood his ground, and said, as if quoting the words of Daniel, "Are ye such fools, ye sons of Israel, that without examination or knowledge of the truth ye have condemned a daughter of Israel?[19] Return again to the place of judgment," and there give judgment on the judge himself. You have set up this judge, forsooth, for the instruction of faith and the correction of error, and yet, when he ought to give judgment, he condemns himself out of his own mouth. Set free today, with the help of God's mercy, one who is manifestly innocent, even as Susanna was freed of old from her false accusers."

---

[19] Daniel 13: 48, The History of Susanna

Thereupon the archbishop arose and confirmed the legate's statement, but changed the wording thereof, as indeed was most fitting. "It is God's truth," he said, "that the Father is omnipotent, the Son is omnipotent, the Holy Spirit is omnipotent. And whosoever dissents from this is openly in error, and must not be listened to. Nevertheless, if it be your pleasure, it would be well that this our brother should publicly state before us all the faith that is in him, to the end that, according to its deserts, it may either be approved or else condemned and corrected."

When, however, I fain would have arisen to profess and set forth my faith, in order that I might express in my own words that which was in my heart, my enemies declared that it was not needful for me to do more than recite the Athanasian Symbol,[20] a thing which any boy might do as well as I. And lest I should allege ignorance, pretending that I did not know the words by heart, they had a copy of it set before me to read. And read it I did as best I could for my groans and sighs and tears. Thereupon, as if I had been a convicted criminal, I was handed over to the Abbot of St. Médard, who was there present, and led to his monastery as to a prison. And with this the council was immediately dissolved.

The abbot and the monks of the aforesaid monastery, thinking that I would remain long with them, received me with great exultation, and diligently sought to console me, but all in vain. O God, who dost judge justice itself, in what venom of the spirit, in what bitterness of mind, did I blame even Thee for my shame, accusing Thee in my madness! Full often did I repeat the lament of St. Anthony, "Kindly Jesus, where wert Thou?" The sorrow that tortured me, the shame that overwhelmed me, the desperation that wracked my mind, all these I could then feel, but even now I can find no words to express them. Comparing these new sufferings of my soul with those I had formerly endured in my body, it seemed that I was in very truth the most miserable among men. Indeed that earlier betrayal had become a little thing in comparison with this later evil, and I lamented the hurt to my fair name far more than the one to my body. The latter, indeed, I had brought upon myself through my own wrongdoing, but this other violence had come

---

[20] The Athanasian Symbol or Creed is a Christian statement of belief focused on Trinitarian doctrine and Christology.

upon me solely by reason of the honesty of my purpose and my love of our faith, which had compelled me to write that which I believed.

The very cruelty and heartlessness of my punishment, however, made every one who heard the story vehement in censuring it, so that those who had a hand therein were soon eager to disclaim all responsibility, shouldering the blame on others. Nay, matters came to such a pass that even my rivals denied that they had had anything to do with the matter, and as for the legate, he publicly denounced the malice with which the French had acted. Swayed by repentance for his injustice, and feeling that he had yielded enough to satisfy their rancor he shortly freed me from the monastery whither I had been taken, and sent me back to my own. Here, however, I found almost as many enemies as I had in the former days of which I have already spoken, for the vileness and shamelessness of their way of living made them realize that they would again have to endure my censure.

After a few months had passed, chance gave them an opportunity by which they sought to destroy me. It happened that one day, in the course of my reading, I came upon a certain passage of Bede, in his commentary on the Acts of the Apostles, wherein he asserts that Dionysius the Areopagite was the bishop, not of Athens, but of Corinth. Now, this was directly counter to the belief of the monks, who were wont to boast that their Dionysius, or Denis, was not only the Areopagite but was likewise proved by his acts to have been the Bishop of Athens. Having thus found this testimony of Bede's in contradiction of our own tradition, I showed it somewhat jestingly to sundry of the monks who chanced to be near. Wrathfully they declared that Bede was no better than a liar, and that they had a far more trustworthy authority in the person of Hilduin, a former abbot of theirs, who had travelled for a long time throughout Greece for the purpose of investigating this very question. He, they insisted, had by his writings removed all possible doubt on the subject, and had securely established the truth of the traditional belief.

One of the monks went so far as to ask me brazenly which of the two, Bede or Hilduin, I considered the better authority on this point. I replied that the authority of Bede, whose writings are held in high esteem by the whole Latin Church, appeared to me the better. Thereupon in a great rage they began to cry out that at last I had openly proved the hatred I had always felt for our monastery, and that I was seeking to disgrace it in the eyes of the whole kingdom, robbing it of the honor in which it had particularly gloried, by thus denying that the Areopagite was their patron saint. To this I answered that I had never denied the fact, and that I did not much care whether their patron was the Areopagite or some one else, provided only he had received his crown from God. Thereupon they ran to the abbot and told him of the misdemeanor with which they charged me.

The abbot listened to their story with delight, rejoicing at having found a chance to crush me, for the greater vileness of his life made him fear me more even than the rest did. Accordingly he summoned his council, and when the brethren had assembled he violently threatened me, declaring that he would straightway send me to the king, by him to be punished for having thus sullied his crown and the glory of his royalty. And until he should hand me over to the king, he ordered that I should be closely guarded. In vain did I offer to submit to the customary discipline if I had in any way been guilty. Then, horrified at their wickedness, which seemed to crown the ill fortune I had so long endured, and in utter despair at the apparent conspiracy of the whole world against me, I fled secretly from the monastery by night, helped thereto by some of the monks who took pity on me, and likewise aided by some of my scholars.

I made my way to a region where I had formerly dwelt, hard by the lands of Count Theobald (of Champagne). He himself had some slight acquaintance with me, and had compassion on me by reason of my persecutions, of which the story had reached him. I found a home there within the walls of Provins, in a priory of the monks of Troyes, the prior of which had in former days known me well and shown me much love. In his joy at my coming he cared for me with all diligence. It chanced, however, that one day my abbot came to Provins to see the count on certain matters of business. As soon as I had learned of this, I went to the count, the prior accompanying me, and besought him to intercede in my behalf with the abbot. I asked no more than that the abbot should absolve me of the charge against me, and give me permission to live the monastic life wheresoever I could find a suitable place.

The abbot, however, and those who were with him took the matter under advisement, saying that they would give the count an answer the day before they departed. It appeared from their words that they thought I wished to go to some other abbey, a thing which they regarded as an immense disgrace to their own. They had, indeed, taken particular pride in the fact that, upon my conversion, I had come to them, as if scorning all other abbeys, and accordingly they considered that it would bring great shame upon them if I should now desert their abbey and seek another. For this reason they refused to listen either to my own plea or to that of the count. Furthermore, they threatened me with excommunication unless I should instantly return; likewise they forbade the prior with whom I had taken refuge to keep me longer, under pain of sharing my excommunication. When we heard this both the prior and I were stricken with fear. The abbot went away still obdurate, but a few days thereafter he died.

As soon as his successor had been named, I went to him, accompanied by the Bishop of Meaux, to try if I might win from him the permission I had vainly sought of his predecessor. At first he would not give his assent, but finally, through the intervention of certain friends of mine, I secured the right to appeal to the king and his council, and in this way I at last obtained what I sought. The royal seneschal, Stephen, having summoned the abbot and his subordinates that they might state their case, asked them why they wanted to keep me against my will. He pointed out that this might easily bring them into evil repute, and certainly could do them no good, seeing that their way of living was utterly incompatible with mine. I knew it to be the opinion of the royal council that the irregularities in the conduct of this abbey would tend to bring it more and more under the control of the king, making it increasingly useful and likewise profitable to him, and for this reason I had good hope of easily winning the support of the king and those about him.

Thus, indeed, did it come to pass. But in order that the monastery might not be shorn of any of the glory which it had enjoyed by reason of my sojourn there, they granted me permission to betake myself to any solitary place I might choose, provided only I did not put myself under the rule of any other abbey. This was agreed upon and confirmed on both sides in the presence of the king and his counsellors. Forthwith I sought out a lonely spot known to me of old in the region of Troyes, and there, on a bit of land which had been given to me, and with the approval of the bishop of the district, I built with reeds and stalks my first oratory in the name of the Holy Trinity. And there concealed, with but one comrade, a certain cleric, I was able to sing over and over again to the Lord, "Lo, then would I wander far off, and remain in the wilderness."[21]

[21] Psalm 4:7

ARTHURIAN LITERATURE

The Song of Roland
author unkown (12th century)
translated by Isabel Butler, 1904

PART I:
Ganelon's treachery

Charles the King, our great Emperor, has been for seven long years in Spain; he has conquered all the high land down to the sea; not a castle holds out against him, not a wall or city is left unshattered, save Saragossa, which stands high on a mountain. King Marsila holds it, who loves not God, but serves Muhammad, and worships Allah; ill hap must in sooth befall him.

King Marsila abides in Saragossa. And on a day he passes into the shade of his orchard; there he sits on a terrace of blue marble, and around him his men are gathered to the number of twenty thousand. He speaks to his dukes and his counts, saying, "Hear, lords, what evil overwhelms us; Charles the Emperor of fair France has come into this land to confound us. I have no host to do battle against him, nor any folk to discomfort his. Counsel me, lords, as wise men and save me from death and shame." But not a man has any word in answer, save Blancandrin of the castle of Val-Fonde.

Balcandrin was among the wisest of the paynims,[1] a good knight of much prowess, discreet and valiant in the service of his lord. He saith to the King, "Be not out of all comfort. Send to Charles the proud, the terrible, proffer of faithful service and goodly friendship; give him bears and lions and dogs, seven hundred camels and a thousand falcons past the moulting time, four hundred mules laden with gold and silver, that he may send before him fifty full wains. And therewith shall he richly reward his followers. Long has he waged war in this land; it is meet he return again to Aix in France. And do thou pledge thy word to follow him at the feast of Saint Michael, to receive the faith of the

---

[1] Paynim: an archaic Middle English term meaning a pagan or non-Christian, especially a Muslim.

Christians, and to become his man in all honor and loyalty. If he would have hostages, send them to him, or ten or twenty, to make good the compact. We will send him the sons of our wives; yea, though it be to death, I will send mine own. Better it were that they lose their lives than that we be spoiled of lands and lordship, and be brought to beg our bread.

"By this my right hand," saith Blancandrin, "and by the beard that the winds blows about my breast, ye shall see the Frankish host straightway scatter abroad, and the Franks return again to their land of France. When each is in his own home and Charles is in his chapel at Aix, he will hold high festival on the day of Saint Michael. The day will come, and the term appointed will pass, but of us he will have no word or tidings. The King is proud and cruel of heart, he will let smite off the heads of our hostages, but better it is that they lose their lives than that we be spoiled of bright Spain, the fair, or suffer so great dole and sorrow." And the paynims cry, "Let it be as he saith."

So King Marsila hath ended his council; he then called Clarin de Balaguer, Estramarin, and Endropin, his fellow, and Priamon, and Garlan the Bearded, Machiner, and Maheu his uncle, Joïmer, and Malbien from oversea, and Blancandrin, ten of the fiercest he hath called, to make known his will unto them. "Lords, barons," he saith, "go ye to Charlemagne, who is at the siege of the city of Cordova, bearing olive branches in your hands in token of peace and submission. If by your wit ye can make me a covenant with Charles, I will give you great store of gold and silver, and lands and fiefs as much as ye may desire." "Nay," say the paynims, "of these things we have and to spare."

King Marsila has ended his council. And again he saith to his men, "Go ye forth, lords, and bear in your hands branches of olive; bid Charles the King that he have mercy on me for the love of his God; say before this first month ends, I will follow him with a thousand of my true liege people, to receive the Christian faith and become his man in all love and truth. If he would have hostages, they shall be given him." Then said Blancandrin, "We will make thee a fair covenant."

And King Marsila let bring the ten white mules which had been sent him by the King of Suatilie; their bridles are of gold and their saddles wrought of silver. They who are to do the king's message set forth, bearing in their hands branches of olive. Anon thereafter they come before Charles, who holds France as his domain; alack, he cannot but be beguiled by them.

The Emperor is joyous and glad at heart; he has taken Cordova and overthrown its walls; and with his mangonels he has beaten down its towers. Great was the plunder which fell to his knights in gold and silver and goodly armor. Not a heathen is left in the city; all are either slain or brought to Christianity. The Emperor is in a wide orchard, and with him are Roland, and Oliver, Samson the Duke, and Anseïs the Proud, Geoffrey of Anjou, the King's standard bearer, and hereto are Gerin, and Gerier, and with them is many another man of France to the number of fifteen thousand. Upon the grass are spread cloths of white silk whereon the knights may sit; and some of these play at tables for their delight, but the old and wise play at chess, and the young lords practice the swordplay. Under a pine, besides an eglantine, stands a throne made all of beaten gold; there sits the King who rules sweet France; white in his beard and his head is hoary, his body is well fashioned and his countenance noble; those who seek him have no need to ask which is the King. And the messengers lighted down from their mules and saluted him in all love and friendship.

Blancandrin was the first to speak, and said to the King, "Greetings in the name of God the Glorious whom ye adore. Thus saith to you King Marsila the valiant: much has he enquired into the faith which brings salvation; and now he would fain give you good store of his substance, bears and lions, and greyhounds in leash, seven hundred camels and a thousand falcons past the moulting time, four hundred mules laden with gold and silver, that ye may carry away fifty full wains of treasure; so many bezants of fine gold shall there be that well may ye reward your men of arms therewith. Long have you tarried in this land, it is meet that ye return again to Aix in France; there my lord will follow you, he gives you his word (and will receive the faith that you hold; with joined hands he will become your man, and will hold for you the kingdom of Spain)." At these words the Emperor stretches his two hands towards heaven, and then bows his head and begins to think.

The Emperor sat with bowed head, for he was in no wise hasty of his words, but was ever wont to speak at his leisure. When again he raised his head, proud was his face, and he said to the messengers, "Fairly have ye spoken. Yet King Marsila is much mine enemy. By what token may I set my trust in the words that ye have said?" "By hostages," the Saracen made answer, "of which you shall have ten or fifteen or twenty. Though it be to death I will send mine own son, and you shall have others, methinks, of yet gentler birth. When you are in your kingly palace at the high feast of Saint Michael of the Peril, my lord will come to you, he gives you his word, and there in the springs that God made flow for you, he would be baptized a Christian." "Yea, even yet he may be saved," Charles made answer.

Fair was the evening and bright the sun. Charles has let stable the ten mules, and in a wide orchard has let pitch a tent wherein the ten messengers are lodged. Ten sergeants make them right good cheer, and there they abide the night through till the clear dawn. The Emperor has risen early, and heard mass and matins and now he sits under a pine tree, and calls his barons into council, for he would act in all matters by the advice of those of France.

The Emperor sits under the pine tree and summons his barons to council. Thither came Ogier, and Archbishop Turpin, Richard the Old, with Henry his nephew, and the brave Count Acelin of Gascony, Tedbalt of Rheims and Milon his cousin, and thereto Gerin and Gerier, and with them came Count Roland, and Oliver the brave, the gentle; of the Franks of France there are more than a thousand, and with the rest came Ganelon who did the treason. And now begins the council that wrought so great woe.

"Lords, barons," then saith Charles the Emperor, "King Marsila has sent me messengers: he would give me great store of his havings, bears and lions and leashed greyhounds, seven hundred camels and a thousand moulted falcons, four hundred mules laden with gold of Arabia, more than enough to fill fifty wains; but thereto he charges me that I go back to France, giving his word to come to me at my abiding place at Aix, and there to receive our most holy faith, and to hold his marches of me; but I know not what may be in his heart." "We must bethink ourselves," say the Franks in answer.

Now when the Emperor had ceased from speaking, Count Roland, who is in no wise in accord with his words, stands forth and naysays him. He saith to the King, "It were ill done to set thy trust in Marsila. It is seven full years since we came into Spain and for you I have conquered Noples and Commibles, and I have taken Valtierra and the land of Pina, and Balaguer, and Tudela, and Sezilie. Now King Marsila was ever a traitor; aforetime he sent fifteen of his paynims, each bearing an olive branch, and they came unto you with a like tale. Then ye advised with your Franks, who counseled you folly: you sent two of your counts, Basan and Basil, into the paynims, and thereafter, below Haltilie, their heads were smitten off. Wherefore I counsel carry on the war even as ye have begun it. Lead your assembled host unto Saragossa, lay siege to it, even though it be for all the days of your life, and revenge us for those who the felons slew aforetime."

The Emperor sat with bent head; he stroked his beard and tugged at his moustache, nor answered he his nephew for either good or ill. The Franks are silent, all save Ganelon. He rises and comes before Charles and speaks right haughtily, saying to the King, "It were ill done to hearken to a braggart–either me or any other–save that his counsel be to thine own profit. When King Marsila lets tell thee he will do homage to thee as thy vassal and will hold all Spain in fief for thee, and thereafter will receive the faith that we hold, he who counsels thee that thou reject this proffer, reckons little, lord, of what death we die. The counsel of pride should not prevail. Let us leave folly and hold with the wise."

Thereafter Naymes stood forth–no better vassal was there in all the court–and thus bespoke the King, "Thou hast heard the answer of Ganelon the Count, and wise it is, an it be but heeded. King Marsila is spent with war, thou hast taken his castles, and with thy mangonels hast beaten down his walls, thou has burned his cities and vanquished his men; when now that he entreats thy mercy, it were sin to press him further, the more that he would give thee surety by hostages. This great war should have an end." "The Duke hath spoken wisely," cry the Franks.

"Lords, barons, what messenger shall we send to King Marsila at Saragossa?" And Duke Naymes made answer, "By thy leave I will go; give me now the glove and the staff." But the King answered him, "Nay, thou art a man of good counsel, and thou shalt not at this time go thus far from me. Sit thou again in thy place since none hath summoned thee."

"Lords, barons, what messenger shall we send to the Saracen that holds Saragossa?" And Roland made answer, "Right glad were

I to go." "Nay certes, not you," saith Count Oliver, "for you are fierce and haughty of temper and I fear lest you embroil yourself; I will myself go, if the King so wills it." "Peace," the King answered, "nor you nor he shall go thither; and by my beard which thou seest whiten, not one of the Twelve Peers shall be chosen." The Franks answer not, and lo, all were silent.

Turpin of Rheims then stood forth from the rest and bespoke the King saying, "Let be thy Franks. Seven years hast thou been in this land, and much travail and woe hath been theirs. Give me, lord, the staff and the glove, and I will go to the Saracen[2] of Spain, and learn what manner of man he is." But wrathfully the King made answer, "Sit thou again in thy place upon the white silk and speak not, save as I command thee.

"Ye knights of France," then said Charles the Emperor, "now choose me a baron of my marches who shall do my message to King Marsila." Then saith Roland, "Let it be Ganelon my stepfather." "Yea," say the Franks, "well will he do your errand; if ye pass him by ye will send none so wise."

Then said the King, "Ganelon, come thou hither, and receive the glove and the staff. Thou hast heard thou art chosen of the Franks." "Sir," Ganelon answered him, "it is Roland who has done this thing. Never again shall I hold him in my love all the days of my life, nor yet Oliver in that he is his comrade, nor the Twelve Peers in that they hold him dear, and here in my sight, lord, I defy them." "Thy wrath is over great," then saith the King, "and certes, go thou must in that I command thee." Ganelon answered, "Go I may, but without surety. None was there for Basil and Basan his brother. Well I know I needs must go until Saragossa, but for him who goes thither there is no return. And more than that, thy sister is my wife, and I have a son, never was there a fairer, and if he lives he will be a man of good prowess. To him I leave my lands and honors; guard him well, for never again shall I see him with these eyes." "Thou art too tender of heart," Charles answered him, "since I command thee, needs must thou go."

And Count Ganelon was in sore wrath thereat; he lets slip from about his neck his great cloak of sables, and stands forth in

---

[2] Saracen, a term for Muslims widely used in Europe during the later medieval period.

his tunic of silk. Gray blue are his eyes and proud his face, well fashioned is he of body and broad of chest. So comely he is all his peers turn to look upon him. And he speaks to Roland, saying, "Thou fool, why art thou in so great wrath? It is known of all that I am thy stepfather and thou hast named me to go unto Marsila. If God grants me to return again I shall bring woe upon thee so great it shall endure all the days of thy life." "Thou speakest pride and folly," Roland answered him, "and all men know I reckon naught of threats. Bu a man of counsel should bear this message, and if the King wills it, I am ready to go in thy stead."

"Nay," Ganelon made answer, "in my stead thou shalt not go. Thou art not my man, nor am I thy over-lord. Charles has commanded me that I do his errand, and I will go unto Marsila in Saragossa. But mayhap I shall do there some folly to ease me of my great wrath." At these words Roland falls a-laughing.

When Ganelon sees that Roland bemocks him, so great anger is his he is near to bursting with wrath, and he wellnigh goes out of his senses. He saith to the Count, "Little love have I for thee in that thou has brought false judgment upon me. O just King, lo, I stand before thee, ready to do thy commandment."

The Emperor holds out to him his right glove, but fain had Count Ganelon been elsewhere, and when he should have taken it, he lets it fall to earth. And the Franks cry, "God, what may this betide? Great woe shall come upon us from the embassage." "Lords," saith Ganelon, "ye shall have tidings thereof.

"And O King," he said again, "I pray thy leave; since go I must I would not delay." "Go in Jesus' name and in mine," the King made answer. With his right had he shrove and blessed him, and then he gave him the staff and the letter.

Now Ganelon the Count gets him to his lodging and begins to don his armor, the goodliest he can find; he has fastened spurs of gold upon his feet, and at his side he has girt Murglais his sword; and when he mounted Tachebrun his steed, Guinemer his uncle it was, held his stirrup. Many a knight ye may see weep, and they saith to him, "Woe worth the day, baron! Long hast thou been in the King's court and ever hast though been accounted a man of worship. He who judged thee to go will be nowise shielded or saved by Charles. Count Roland ought never to have had the thought, for ye twain are near of kin." But Ganelon answers, "No, so help me God! Better it were that I die alone than that so many good knights take their end. Ye will return again into sweet France, lords; greet ye my wife for me, and likewise Pinabel my friend and peer, and aid ye Baldwin my son, who ye know, and make him your over-lord." Therewith he set forth and rode on his way.

As Ganelon fares forth under the high olives he overtakes the Saracen messengers. Anon Blancandrin falls back to ride beside him. Cunningly thy speak one to another. "A marvel of a man is this Charles," saith Blancandrin. "He has conquered Apulia and all Calabria; he has crossed the salt sea into England and has won tribute therefrom for the profit of Saint Peter; but what would he of us in our marches?" Quoth Ganelon, "Such is his will; and no man avails to withstand him."

"The Franks are goodly men," then saith Blancandrin, "but your dukes and counts do much hurt to their liege lord in so advising him; they will bring loss and discomfiture to him and to others." But Ganelon answer him saying, "In sooth, I know no man save only Roland who shall be brought to shame thereby. On a day, as the Emperor was seated under the shade of the trees, his nephew came to him, clad in his hauberk–for he was come from the taking of spoils below Carcassone–and in his hand he held a scarlet apple, 'Take it, fair sir," saith Roland to his uncle, 'for even so I give over to thee the crowns of all the kings of the earth.' Of a surety, his great pride must undo him, for each day he runs in hazard of death; and if he be but slain we shall have quiet on the earth."

Then saith Blandandrin, "Fell and cruel is this Roland who would make all peoples yield them, and claim all lands for his. But by means of what folk does he think to win thus much?" "By the folk of France," Ganelon answers, "for he is so beloved by them that they will never fail him. Many a gift he gives them of gold and silver, mules and war horses, silk and armor. And the Emperor likewise has all his desire; for him Roland will conquer all the lands from here even unto the East."

So Ganelon and Blancandrin rode on till each had pledged the other to do what he might to compass the death of Roland. So they rode by highways and bypaths till they alighted under a yew tree in Saragossa. Hard by, under the shade of a pine tree, stood a throne covered over with silk of Alexandria; there sat the King who held all Spain, and around him were his Saracens to the number of twenty thousand; yet not one opened his lips or spoke a word, so eager were they for tidings; and now behold you, Blancandrin and Ganelon.

So Blancandrin came before Marsila; he held Count Ganelon by the hand, and he spoke to the King, saying, "Greeting in the name of Muhammad and Allah whose blessed law we hold. We gave thy message to Charles, who lifted up both his hands towards heaven, and praised his God, nor made he other answer. But here he sends thee one of his barons, who is of France, and a mighty man, and from he thou shalt hear if thou art to have peace or war." Saith Marsila, "Now speak, for we listen."

Count Ganelon had well bethought himself, and begins to speak with much cunning, as one who is skillful in words, saying to the King, "Greetings in the name of God the Glorious whom we should adore. Thus saith to thee Charles the mighty; if thou wilt receive Christianity he will give thee the half of Spain in fee; the second half he will give unto Roland, in whom thou shalt find a haughty compeer. If thou wilt not accept this covenant, he will lay siege to Saragossa, and thou shalt be taken and bound by force, and brought unto the King's seat at Aix, and thou shalt be adjudged to end thy days, and there thou shalt die a vile and shameful death."

At these words King Marsila was sore troubled; in his hand he held a javelin tipped with gold, and with it he would have struck Ganelon had his men not withheld him. King Marsila hath waxed red with wrath, and hath shaken the shaft of his javelin. When Ganelon saw this, he laid a hand on his sword, and drew it forth from the sheath the length of two fingers, and spoke to it, saying, "Most fair and bright you art; so long as I wear thee at this King's court, the Emperor of France will never say I should die here alone in a strange land, before the bravest have paid thee dear." But the paynims cry, "Let us stay this quarrel."

And the best of the Saracens so besought him, that Marsila again took his place on the throne. He breaks the seal and casts away the wax, he looks at the letter and sees the sum of it. "Charles who holds France in his power bids me bethink me of his sorrow and wrath; that is to say of Basan, and Basil, his brother, whose heads I did smite off in the hills below Haltilie. If I would ransom the life of my body I must send him the Caliph my uncle, otherwise he will not hold me in his love." Thereafter spoke

Marsila's son and said to the King, "Ganelon hath uttered folly. Such words hath he said to thee it is unmeet that he live; give him over to me, and I will do justice upon him." When Ganelon hears him he brandishes his sword, and sets his back against the trunk of a pine tree.

Now for council the King hath passed into his orchard, and gathered his chief men about him. Thither came Blancandrin the hoary-headed, and Jurfaleu, his son and heir, and the Caliph, Marsila's uncle and faithful liegeman. Then saith Blancandrin, "Call thither the Frank. He has pledged me his faith to our welfare." "Do thou bring him," saith the King. And Blancandrin took Ganelon by the right hand, and brought him into the orchard before the Kind. And there they plotted the foul treason.

"Fair Sir Ganelon," saith the King, "I was guilty of some folly toward thee when I would have struck thee in my wrath. I give thee as a pledge these skins of sable, the border whereof is worth more than five hundred pounds. Before tomorrow at evening a fair amend shall be thine." "I will not refuse it," Ganelon answered him, "and may it please God give thee good thanks."

Then quoth Marsila, "Ganelon, in good faith I have it in my heart to love thee well. Tell me now of Charlemagne. Methinks he is of great age and has outlived his time, for I deem him more than two hundred years old. Through many lands has he journeyed, and many a blow has he taken on his embossed shield, and many a mighty king has he brought low; when will he yield him in the strife?" "Nay not such is Charles," Ganelon answered him, "Whosoever looks on the Emperor, or knows him, must account him a man of much prowess. I know not how to praise or glorify him to the full sum of his honor and bounty. Who can reckon his worth? And God has gifted him with such valor that rather had he die than give up his lordship.

"That will never be," saith Ganelon, "so long as his nephew is a living man, he hath not his fellow for courage under the cope of heaven and Oliver his comrade is of good prowess, and likewise the Twelve Peers whom Charles holds right dear. They, together with twenty thousand knights, make up the vanguard and Charles is safe and unafraid."

"Fair Sir Ganelon," thus saith King Marsila, "a fairer folk than mine ye shall not see. I have upon four hundred thousand knights and with them I may well do battle against Charles and his Franks." "Nay, not at this time," Ganelon answer him, "or great will be the slaughter of thy paynims. Leave thou folly and seek after wisdom; give such store of thy substance into the Emperor that there will be no Frank that does not marvel thereat. Send him thereto twenty hostages and the King will return again into fair France. But his rearguard he will leave behind him, and in it, of a surety, will be Count Roland, his nephew, and Oliver the valiant, the courteous; and both counts shall be slain, if thou wilt put thy trust in me. And the great pride of Charles shall come to its fall, and thenceforth he will have no desire to wage more war upon thee."

"Fair Sir Ganelon," then saith King Marsila, "how may I slay this Roland?" Quoth Ganelon, "Even that will I tell thee. The King will be at the main pass of Cizre, and he will have set his rearguard behind him; in it will be the mighty Count Roland, his nephew, and Oliver, in whom he sets his trust, and in their company will be twenty thousand Franks. But do thou send against them one hundred thousand of thy paynims, and do them battle a first time, that the men of France may be smitten and sore hurt. Now mayhap, in this first stour, thine own may be slain with great slaughter, but do thou set upon the Franks a second time, with like array, that Roland may in no wise escape. And for thy part thou wilt have done a noble deed of arms, and thou shalt be untroubled by war all the days of thy life.

"Whosoever may compass the death of Roland in that place will thereby smite off the right arm of Charles: his great armies will have an end, never again shall he call together such hosts, and the Great Land shall have peace." When Marsila heard this saying he kissed Ganelon upon the neck and then he began to open his treasures.

Quoth Marsila, "What need of more words? No counsel is good in which a man may not set his trust. Now do thou therefore swear me straight the treason." "Let it be as thou wilt," said Ganelon and he swore the treason upon the relics in his sword Murglais, and therewith became a traitor.

Hard by was a throne wrought of ivory, and to it Marsila let bring a book wherein was writ the law of Muhammad and Trevagant, and upon it the Saracen of Spain swore that if he found

Roland in the rearguard, he would set upon him with all his folk, and if that he might, forthwith slay him. "Blessed be our covenant," quoth Ganelon.

Then the King calls Malduit, the treasurer, saying, "Hast thou made ready the gifts for Charles?" "Yea, lord," he answers, "all is ready—seven hundred camels laden with gold and silver, and twenty hostage, the noblest under heaven."

Marsila lays a hand on Ganelon's shoulder and speaks to him, saying, "A goodly baron and wise thou art, but by that faith thou deemest most holy, have a heed that thou turn not thy heart from us; and I will give the great store of my substance, ten mules laden with the finest gold of Arabia; and each year thou shalt have a like gift. Now take thou the keys of this great city and convey thou to Charles the rich gifts, but thereafter have a care the rearguard be adjudged to Roland. And so be it I may come upon him in pass or defile, I will do him battle to the death." "Methinks I tarry too long," saith Ganelon in answer and therewith he mounts his horse and rides on his way.

Meantime the Emperor has turned back towards his own land and has come to the city of Valtierra, which aforetime Count Roland had taken, and so destroyed that thenceforward for the space of a hundred years it was waste and desolate. There the King awaits tiding of Ganelon, and the tribute of the great land of Spain. And now on a morning, at dawn, with the first light, comes Ganelon into the camp.

The Emperor had risen early and heard mass and matins and now he is on the green grass before his tent, and with him is Roland, and Oliver the valiant, Naymes the Duke and many another. Thither comes Ganelon, the felon, the traitor, and with cunning and falsehood speaks to the King, saying, "Blessed be thou of God! I bring thee thereby the keys of Saragossa, and great store of gift, and twenty hostages—guard thou them well. But King Marsila bids thee blame him not that the Caliph be among them; with mine own eyes I saw him and four hundred men of arms, clad in hauberks, with helms on head, and girt with swords whose hilts were inlaid with gold, embark together upon the sea. They were fleeing from Christianity which they would not receive or hold. But before they had sailed four leagues, storm and tempest fell upon them, and even there they were drowned. Never shall ye see them more. Had the Caliph been alive I had brought him hither. As for the paynim King, in very truth, this month shall not pass but he will come to thee in thy kingdom of France, and will receive the faith that thou holdest, and will join his hands in thine and become thy man, and will hold of thee his kingdom of Spain." Then saith the King, "Thanks be to God therefor. Well hast thou done and great shall be thy reward." Thereafter he let sound a thousand trumpets throughout the host, and the Franks break up their camp, and load their sumpters, and set forth together towards fair France.

Charles the Great has laid waste all Spain, he has taken its castles and sacked its cities. But now the war is ended, so saith the King, and he rides on towards fair France. Count Roland has set the King's standard on the crest of a hill against the sky and the Franks pitched their tents in all the country round about. Meantime the paynims ride on through the valleys, clad in their hauberks and two-fold harness, helms on head, and girt with their swords, shields on shoulder, and lances in hand. They made stay in a wood, on the top of the mountains, and there four hundred thousand await the dawn. God, what sorrow the Franks know it not!

The day fades and night darkens and Charles, the great Emperor, sleeps. He dreamed that he was come to the great pass of Cizre, and it seemed to him that he held the oaken shaft of his lance in his hand, but Ganelon the Count snatched it from him, brandished and broke it, that its pieces flew to towards heaven. But still Charles sleeps and does not waken.

Thereafter he dreamed another dream; that he was before his chapel at Aix and a bear bit him in his arm right cruelly; and anon, from towards Ardennes, he saw come a leopard which fiercely assaulted him; but even then, from within the hall a greyhound sprang out, and ran leaping to Charles; first he snapped off the right ear of the bear, then wrathfully he set upon the leopard; and the Franks cried that it was a great battle. Yet none knew which of the twin should conquer. But Charles still sleeps and doth not waken.

Night passes and the clear dawn shines forth. Proudly the Emperor gets to horse, and lets sound trumpets aloud throughout the host. "Lords, barons," then saith Charles, "nigh at hand is the pass and the strait defiles, now choose ye who shall be in the rearguard." And Ganelon answered, "Let it be Roland, my stepson, thou hast no baron so brave as he." Now when the King hears him, he looks at him haughtily, saying, "Thou art a very devil and a mortal anger has entered into thee. And who shall go before me in the vanguard?" And Ganelon answered, "Let it be Ogier of Denmark, no baron hast thou more apt thereto."

When Count Roland hears that he is chosen, he speaks out in knightly wise, saying, "Sir kinsman, I should hold thee right dear in that thou hast adjudged the rearguard to me; and by my faith, Charles the King shall lose naught thereby, neither palfrey nor warhorse, nor any he-mule or she-mule whereon man may ride, nay, not so much as a pack-horse or sumpter, an it be not first well paid for by the sword." "Yea, thou speakest truly," saith Ganelon, "that I know well."

And Count Roland turns to Charles, saying, "Give me now the bow that you bear in your hand; verily, you shall have no need to chide me that I let it fall, as did Ganelon your right glove when you gave him the herald's staff." But still the Emperor sits with bent head; he plucks at his beard and strokes his moustache, and he may not help but weep.

Thereafter Naymes came before him, a better vassal was not in all the court, and he spoke to the King, saying, "Well hast thou heard, Count Roland is all in wrath but the rearguard is adjudged to him and thou has no baron who would dare supplant him therein. Give him therefore the bow that you hold and take heed that he hath good aid." The King holds out the bow and Roland receives it.

And the Emperor speaks to Roland, saying, "Fair sir nephew, know for sooth that I will give over unto thee the half of my army, keep them with thee that they may be thy safeguard." "Nay, not so will I," saith the Count, "May God confound me if I belie my house. I will keep with me twenty thousand Franks of good valor, and do thou cross the mountains in all surety, for so long as I live thou needst fear no man."

Count Roland has mounted his horse and Oliver his comrade came to stand over against him, and thither came Gerier, and Oton, and Berengier, and thereto came Samson, and Anseïs the Proud, Ivon and Ivory whom the King holds full dear, and after them came Gerard the Old of Rousillon, and thereto Engelier the Gascon. Then said the Archbishop, "By my head, I too will go." "And I with thee," quoth Count Gualter, "I am Roland's man and to follow him is my desire." Then among them they chose out twenty thousand knights.

Thereafter Count Roland calls Gualter del Hum, saying, "Take thou one thousand Franks of our land of France and hold the hills and defiles that the Emperor may lose none of his own." "It is my part to do this for thee," saith Gualter. And with a thousand Franks of France he ranges through the hills and passes, nor will he leave the heights for any ill tidings before seven hundred swords have been drawn. Now the same day King Almaris of the kingdom of Belferne shall do him and his men fierce battle.

High are the hills and dark the valleys, brown are the rocks and dread the defiles. That same day the main host of the Franks pass with toil and travail, and fifteen leagues away men might hear the noise of their march. But when that they draw near to the Great Land, and see Gascony, their lord's domain, they call to mind their own fiefs and havings, their young maidens and gentle wives, till there is not one that does not weep for pity. More than all the rest is Charles heavy of heart, in that he has left his nephew in the passes of Spain; pity takes him, and he cannot help but weep.

The Twelve Peers abide in Spain, and in their fellowship are twenty thousand Franks who know not fear or any dread of death. But the Emperor, as he draws near to France, hides his face in his mantle. Beside him rides Duke Naymes and he speaks to the King, saying, "Why makest thou such sorrow?" "Ye do ill to ask it," Charles answer him, "such grief is mine I cannot help but make lament. I fear lest through Ganelon France shall be destroyed. This past night, by means of an angel, a dream came to me, and it seemed to me that Ganelon shattered to bits the lance I held in my hand. And he it was who adjudged the rearguard to Roland. And now him I have left behind in a strange land. God, if I lose him never shall I find his equal."

Charles the Great cannot help but weep, and a hundred thousand Franks are full of pity for him, and a marvelous fear for Roland. Ganelon the felon has done this treason, and rich are the gifts he has received therefor from the paynim king, gold and silver, silks and ciclatons, mules and horses, and camels and lions.

Meantime King Marsila calls together the barons of Spain, counts and viscounts, dukes, and almaçurs, and emirs, and sons of counts; four hundred thousand has he gathered together in three days. He lets sound his tabours throughout Saragossa; and on the topmost tower the paynims raise an image of Muhammad, and there is not a man but offers prayers to it and worships it. Thereafter they ride through the land of Cerdagne, over hill and through dale, each seeking to outdo other, till they see the gonfanons of the men of France, the rearguard of the Twelve Peers. They will not fail to do them battle.

The paynims arm themselves with Saracen hauberks, of which the greater part are of threefold thickness. They lace on helms of right good Saracen work and gird on swords of Viennese steel. Fair are their shields, and their lances are of Valencia, tipped with gonfanons white and blue and scarlet. They leave behind them the mules and palfries, and mounting their war-horses, ride forth in close ranks. Fair was the day and bright the sun, and all their harness glistens in the light. And for the more joy they let sound a thousand trumpets; so great is the noise thereof that the Franks hear it. Then saith Oliver, "Sir comrade, methinks we shall have ado with the Saracens." "Now God grant it be as thou sayest," Roland answers him, "for to make stand here for our King is to do as good men ought to do. Verily for his liege a man well ought to suffer pain and woe, and endure both great heat and great cold, and should hold him ready to lose both hide and hair in his lord's service. Now let each have a care that he strikes good blows and great, that no man may mis-say us in his songs. These misbelieving men are in the wrong, and right is with the Christians, and for my part I will give ye no ill example."

PART II:
The Battle at Roncevals

Then Oliver goes up into a high mountain, and looks away to the right, all down a grassy valley, and sees the host of the heathen coming on, and he called to Roland, his comrade, saying, "From the side of Spain I see a great light coming, thousands of white hauberks and thousands of gleaming helms. They will fall upon our Franks with great wrath. Ganelon the felon has done this treason and he it was adjudged us to the rearguard, before the Emperor." "Peace Oliver," saith Count Roland, "he is my mother's husband, speak thou no ill of him."

132

Oliver has fared up the mountain and from the summit thereof he sees all the kingdom of Spain and the great host of the Saracens. Wondrous is the shine of helmets studded with gold, of shields and broidered hauberks, of lances and gonfanons. The soldiers are so without number, and no man may give count thereof, so great is the multitude. Oliver is all astonished at the sight, he got him down

the hill as best he might, and came to the Franks, and gave them his tidings.

"I have seen the paynims," said Oliver, "never was so great a multitude seen of living men. Those of the vanguard are upon a hundred thousand, all armed with shields and helmets, and clad in white hauberks. Right straight are the shafts of their lances and bright the points thereof. Such a battle we shall have as was never before seen of man. Ye lords of France, may God give you might! And stand ye firm that we be not overcome." "Foul fall him who flees!" then said the Franks, "For no peril of death will we fail thee."

"Great is the host of the heathen," saith Oliver, "and few is our fellowship. Roland, fair comrade, I pray thee sound thy horn of ivory that Charles may hear it and return again with all his host." "That were but folly," quoth Roland, "and thereby would I lose all fame in sweet France. Rather I will strike good blows and great with Durendal, that the blade thereof shall be blooded even unto the hilt. Woe worth the paynims that they come into the passes! I pledge thee my faith short life shall be theirs."

"Roland, comrade, blow now thy horn of ivory and Charles shall hear it and bring hither his army again, and the King and his barons shall succor us." But Roland answers him saying, "Now God forfend that through me my kinsman be brought to shame, or aught of dishonor befall fair France. But first I will lay on with Durendal, the good sword that is girded here at my side, and thou shalt see the blade thereof all reddened. Woe worth the paynims when they gathered their hosts! I pledge me they shall all be given over to death."

"Roland, comrade, blow thy horn of ivory, that Charles may hear it as he passes the mountains, and I pledge me the Franks will return hither again." But Roland saith, "Now God forfend it be said of any living man that I sounded my horn for dread of paynims.

Nay, that reproach shall never fall upon my kindred. But when I am in the stour I will smite seven hundred blows, or mayhap a thousand, and thou shalt see the blade of Durendal all crimson. The Franks are goodly men, and they will lay on right valiantly, nor shall those of Spain have any surety from death."

Saith Oliver, "I see no shame herein. I have seen the Saracens of Spain, they cover the hills and the valleys, the heaths and the plains. Great are the hosts of this hostile folk, and ours is but a little fellowship." And Roland makes answer, "My desire is the greater thereby. May God and His most holy angels forfend that France should lose aught of worship through me. Rather I die than bring dishonor upon me. The Emperor loves us for dealing stout blows."

Roland is brave and Oliver is wise and both are good men of their hands, once armed and a-horseback, rather would they die than flee the battle. Hardy are the Counts and high their speech. The felon paynims ride on in great wrath. Saith Oliver, "Roland, prithee look. They are close upon us, but Charles is afar off. Thou wouldst not deign to sound thy horn of ivory but were the King here we should suffer no hurt. Look up towards the passes of Aspre and thou shalt see the woeful rearguard; they who are of it will do no more service henceforth." But Roland answers him, "Speak not so cowardly. Cursed be the heart that turns coward in the breast! Hold we the field and ours be the buffets and the slaughter."

When Roland sees that the battle is close upon them he waxes fiercer than lion or leopard. He calls to the Franks, and he saith to Oliver, "Comrade, friend, say not so. When the Emperor left us his Franks he set apart such a twenty thousand of men that, certes, among them is no coward. For his liege lord a man ought to suffer all hardship and endure great heat and great cold and give both his blood and his body. Lay on with thy lance and I will smite with Durendal, my good sword that the King gave me. If I die here, may he to whom it shall fall, say, 'This was the sword of goodly vassal.'"

Nigh at hand is Archbishop Turpin; he now spurs his horse to the crest of a knoll and speaks to the Franks and this is his sermon: "Lords, barons, Charles left us here and it is a man's devoir to die for his King. Now help ye to uphold Christianity. Certes, ye shall have a battle, for here before you are the Saracens. Confess your sins and pray God's mercy and that your souls may be saved I will absolve you. If ye are slain, ye will be held martyrs and ye shall have seats in the higher Paradise." The Franks light off their horses and kneel down and the Archbishop blesses them and, for a penance, bids them that they lay on with their swords.

The Franks get upon their feet, freed and absolved from sin and the Archbishop blesses them in the name of God. Then they mounted their swift horses, and armed themselves after the manner of knights, and made them ready for battle. Cound Roland calls to Oliver, saying, "Sir comrade, rightly thou saidest Ganelon hath betrayed us all and hath received gold and silver and goods therefor; but the Emperor will well revenge us. King Marsila hath bought and sold us, but he shall pay for it with the sword."

Roland rides through the passes of Spain on Veillantif, his good horse and swift. He is clad in his harness right well it becomes him, and as he rides he brandishes his spear, turning its point towards heaven; and to its top is bound a gonfanon of pure white, whereof the golden fringes fall down even unto his hands. Well fashioned is his body, and his face fair and laughing. Close behind him rides his comrade; and all the Franks claim him as their champion. Full haughtily he looks on the Saracen, but gently and mildly on the Franks, and he speaks to them courteously, saying, "Lords, barons, ride on softly. The paynims come seeking destruction, and this day we shall have plunder so goodly and great that no King of France hath ever taken any of so great price." At these words the two hosts come together.

Saith Oliver, "I have no mind for more words. Thou wouldst not deign to sound thy horn of ivory, and no help shalt thou get from Charles. Naught he knows of our case, nor is the wrong his. They who are beyond the mountains are no wise to blame. Now ride on with what might ye may. Lords, barons, hold ye the field! And in God's name I pray you bethink you both how to deal good blows and how to take them. And let us not forget the device of our King." At these words all the Franks cried out together, and whosoever may have heard that cry of Montjoy[3] must call to mind valor and worth. Then they rode forward, God! how proudly,

---

[3] Montjoy was the war-cry of Charles the Great and it was a source of courage for the soldiers.

spurring their horses for the more speed, and fell-asmiting–how else should they do? But no whit adread were the Saracens. And lo you, Franks and paynims come together in battle.

The nephew of Marsila, who was called Aelroth, rides before all his host, and foul are his words to our Franks, "Ye Frankish felons, today ye shall do battle with us. He who should have been your surety has betrayed you; mad is the King who left you behind in the passes. Today shall fair France lose her fame, and the right arm of Charles shall be smitten off from his body." When Roland hears this, God! how great his wrath. He spurs as fast as his horse may run and with all the might he hath he smites Aelroth and breaks his shield, and rends apart his hauberk, that he cleaves his breast and breaks the bone, and severs the spine from the back; with his lance he drives out the soul from the body, for so fierce is the blow Aelroth wavers, and with all the force of his lance Roland hurls him from his horse dead, his neck broken in two parts. Yet Roland still chides him, saying, "Out coward! Charles is not mad, nor loves he treason. He did well and knightly to leave us in the passes. Today shall France lose naught of her fame. Franks, lay on! Ours is the first blow. Right is with us and these swine are in the wrong."

Among the paynims is a duke, Falsaron by name, who was brother to King Marsila, and held the land of Dathan and Abiram; there is no more shameless felon on all the earth. So wide is his forehead that the space between his eyes measures a full half foot. When he sees his nephew slain, he is full of dole, and he drives through the press as swift as he may, and cries aloud the paynim war-cry. Great is his hatred of the Franks. "Today shall fair France lose her fame!" Oliver hears him and is passing wroth; with his golden spurs he pricks on his horse and ride upon him like a true baron. He breaks the shield, tears asunder the hauberk, and drives his lance into the body up to the flaps of his pennon, and with the might of his blow hurls him dead from the saddle. He looks to earth where lies the felon, and speaks him haughtily, "Coward, naught care I for thy threats. Lay on Franks, certes, we shall overcome them." And he cries out Montjoy, the war-cry of Charles.

A king there is, Corsablis by name; he is of Barbary, a far-off land, and he spoke to the Saracens, saying, "We shall win a fair day on these Franks, for few is their fellowship. And such as be here shall prove themselves of small avail, nor shall one be saved alive for Charles. The day has come whereon they must die." Archbishop Turpin hears him right well, and to no man under heaven has he ever borne such hate. With his spurs of fine gold he pricks on his horse, and rides upon the king with great might, cleaves his shield and rends his hauberk, and thrusts his great lance into his body, and so drives home the blow that sorely the king wavers, and with all the force of his lance Turpin hurls him dead into the path. He looks on the ground where he sees the glutton lie, nor doth he withhold him from speech, but saith, "Coward and heathen, thou hast lied! Charles, my liege lord, is ever our surety, and our Franks have no mind to flee; we shall have a care that thy comrades go not far hence; yea, and a second death must ye suffer. Lay on ye Franks, let no man forget himself! This first blow is ours, thanks be to God." And he cries out Montjoy.

And Gerin smites Malprimis de Brigal, that his good shield no whit avails him, he shatters the bejeweled boss thereof, and half of it falls to earth; he pierces the hauberk to the flesh, and drives his good lance into the body. The paynim falls down in a heap, and his soul is carried away by Satan.

And Gerier, the comrade of Gerin, smites the Emir, and shatters his shield and unmails his hauberk, and thrusts his good lance into his heart; so great is the blow his lance drives through the body and with all the force of his shaft he throws him to the ground dead. "Ours is a goodly battle," quoth Oliver.

Samson the Duke rides upon the Almaçur, and breaks his shield all flowered and set with gold, nor doth his good hauberk give him any surety, but Samson pierces him through heart and liver and lungs, and fells him dead, whether anyone grieves for him or no. Saith the Archbiship, "That was knightly stricken."

And Anseïs urges on his horse and encounters with Turgis of Tortosa, cleaves his shield below the golden boss, rends asunder his twofold hauberk, and sets the point of his good lance in his body and thrusts so well that the iron passes sheer through him, that the might of the blow hurls him to the ground dead. "That was the buffet of a man of good prowess," saith Roland.

And Engelier, the Gascon of Bordeaux, spurs his horse, slackens his rein, and encounters with Escremis of Valtierra, breaks and carves the shield from his shoulder, rends apart the ventail of his hauberk, and smites him in the breast between his two collar bones, and with the might of the blow hurls him from the saddle, saying, "Ye are all given over to destruction."

And Oton smites the paynim Esturgant upon the leathern front of his shield, marring all the blue and white thereof, breaks through the sides of his hauberk, and drives his good spear and sharp into his body, and casts him from his swift horse, dead. "Naught may save thee," saith Oliver thereat.

And Berengier rides on Estramaris, shatters his shield, rends asunder his hauberk, and drives his stout lance into his body, and smites him dead amid a thousand Saracens. Of the Twelve [Saracen] Peers ten are now slain and but two are still living men, to wit, Chernuble and Count Margaris.

Margaris is a right valiant knight, strong and goodly, swift and keen; he spurs his horse and rides on Oliver, breaks his shield below the boss of pure gold, that the lance passed along his body, but by God's help, it did not pierce the body; the shaft grazes him but doth not overthrow him, and Margaris drives on, in that he has no hinderance, and sounds his horn to call his men about him.

Now the battle waxes passing great on both parties. Count Roland spares himself no whit, but smites with his lance as long as the shaft holds, but by fifteen blows it is broken and lost; thereupon he draws out Durendal his good sword, all naked, spurs his horse and rides on Chernuble, breaks his helm whereon the carbuncles blaze, cleaves his mail-coif and the hair of his head that the sword cuts through eyes and face, and the white hauberk of fine mail, and all the body to the fork of the legs, sheer into the saddle of beaten gold, nor did the sword stint till it had entered the horse and cleft the backbone, never staying for joint, that man and horse fell dead upon the thick grass. Thereupon Roland cried, "Coward, woe worth the day thou camest hither! No help shalt thou get from Muhammad; nor by such swine as thou shall today's battle be achieved."

Count Roland rides through the press; in his hand he hath Durendal, right good for hacking and hewing, and doth great damage upon the Saracens. Lo, how he hurls one dead upon another, and the bright blood flows out on the field. All reddened are his hauberk and his arms, and the neck and shoulders of his good horse. Nor doth Oliver hold back from the battle; the Twelve

Peers do not shame themselves, and all the Franks smite and slay, that the paynims perish or fall swooning. Then saith the Archbishop, "Our barons do passing well," and he cries out Montjoy, the war-cry of Charles.

Oliver drives through the stour; his lance is broken and naught is left him but the truncheon; yet he smites the paynim Malsaron that his shield patterned with gold and flowers is broken, and his two eyes fly out from his head, and his brains fall at his feet; among seven hundred of his fellows Oliver smites him dead. Then he slew Turgin and Esturgus, and thereby broke his lance that it splintered even unto the pommel. Therat Roland saith, "Comrade what doest thou? I have no mind for a staff in so great battle, rather a man hath need of iron and steel. Where is thy sword Halteclere?" "I may not draw it," Oliver answered him. "So keen am I to smite."

But now the lord Oliver hath drawn his good sword, even as his comrade had besought him, and hath shown it to him in knightly wise; and therewith he smites the paynim Justin de Val Ferrée that he severs his head in twin, cuts through his broidered hauberk and his body, through his good saddle set with gold, and severs the backbone of his steed, that man and horse fall dead on the field before him. Then said Roland, "Now I hold you as my brother, and 'tis for such buffets the Emperor loves us." And on all sides they cry out Montjoy.

Count Gerin rides his horse Sorel, and Gerier, his comrade, rides Passecerf; both slacken rein, and spurring mightily set upon the paynim Timosel; one smites him on the shield, and the other on the hauberk, that both their lances break in his body; and he falls dead in the field. I wot not, nor have I ever heard man say, which of the twin was more swift. Then Esperveris, son of Borel, died at the hand of Engelier of Bordeaux. And the Archbishop slew Siglorel, that enchanter who of old had passed down into Hell, led thither by the spells of Jupiter. "Of him we are well rid," quoth Turpin. And Roland answered him, "Yea, the coward is overthrown. Oliver, my brother such buffets please me right well."

Meantime the battle waxes passing hard, and both Franks and paynims deal such blows that it is wonder to see; here they smite, and there make what defence they may; and many a lance is broken and reddened, and there is great rending of pennons and ensigns. Many a good Frank loses his youth and will never again see wife or mother or the men of France who await him in the passes. Charles the Great weeps for them and makes great sorrow; but what avails it? No help shall they get therefrom. An ill turn Ganelon did them the day he sold his own kindred in Saragossa. Thereafter he lost both life and limb therefor; then in the council of Aix, he was condemned to hang, and with him upon thirty of his kindred to whom death left no hope.

Dread and sore is the battle. Roland and Oliver lay valiantly and the Archbishop deals more than a thousand buffets, nor are the Twelve Peers backward, and all the Franks smite as a man. The Paynims are slain by hundreds and thousands; whosoever does not flee has no surety from death, but will he, nill he, must take his end. But the Franks lose their goodliest arms; never again shall they see father or kindred, or Charles their liege lord who abides for them in the passes.

Meantime, in France, a wondrous tempest broke forth,[4] a mighty storm of wind and lightning, with rain and hail out of all measure, and bolts of thunder that fell ever and again; and verily therewith came a quaking of the earth that ran through all the land from Saint Michael of the Peril, even unto Xanten, and from the Besançon to the port of Guitsand; and there was not a dwelling whose walls were not rent asunder. And at noon fell a shadow of great darkness, nor was there any light save as the heavens opened. They that saw these things were sore afraid and many a one said, "This is the day of judgment and the end of the world is at hand." But they were deceived, and knew not whereof they spoke; it was the great morning of the death of Roland.

Meantime the Franks smote manfully and with good courage, and the paynims were slain by thousands and by multitudes; of a hundred thousand not two may survive. Then said the Archbishop, "Our Franks are of good prowess, no man under heaven hath better. It is written in the annals of France that valiant they are for our Emperor." And the Franks fare through the field seeing their fellows, and weeping from dole and pity for their kin, in all love and kindness. But even now King Marsila is upon them with his great host.

---

[4] In classical literature nature often reflects the state of man. Here a storm and earthquake signal the downfall of Charlemagne's army.

Marsila comes on down the valley with the mighty host that he has assembled; full twenty battles the King has arrayed. There is a great shining of helmets, set with gold and precious stones, and of shields and of broidered hauberks. Trumpets to the number of seven thousand sound the onset, and the din thereof runs far and wide. Then saith Roland, "Oliver, comrade and brother, Ganelon the felon has sworn our death. The treason is manifest, and great vengeance shall the Emperor take therefor. The battle will be sore and great, such a one as was never before fought of man. I will smite with Durendal my sword, and do thou, comrade, lay on with Halteclere. Through many lands have we carried them, and with them have we conquered many a battle, no ill song must be sung of them."

When the Franks see how great is the multitude of the paynims, that on all sides they cover the field, they call upon Roland and Oliver and the Twelve Peers, that they be their defence. Then the Archbishop tells them his mind, saying, "Lords, barons, put from you all cowardly thoughts and in God's name I pray you give not back. Better it were that we die in battle than that men of [false] worship should speak foully of us in their songs. Certain it is we shall straightway take our end, nor shall we from today be living men; yet there is a thing I can promise ye, blessed paradise shall be opened to you, and ye shall take your place among the innocent." At his words, the Franks take heart, and every man cries out Montjoy.

Among the paynims is a Saracen of Saragossa, lord he is of half the city, and never will he flee from any living man. He it was who swore fellowship with Count Ganelon, kissed him in all friendship upon the lips, and gave him his helm and his carbuncle. And he hath sworn to bring the Great Land to shame, and to strip the Emperor of his crown. He rides his horse whom he calls Barbamusche, that is swifter than falcon or swallow; and slackening his rein, he spurs mightily, and rides upon Engelier of Gascony that neither shield nor byrnie may save him, but he drives the head of his lance into his body, thrusting so manfully that the pain thereof passes through to the other side, and with all the might of his lance hurls him in the field dead. Thereafter he cries, "These folk are good to slay!" But the Franks say, "Alack, that so good a knight should take his end."

And Count Roland speaks to Oliver, saying, "Sir comrade, now is Engelier slain, now have we any knight of more valor." And the Count answers him, saying, "Now God grant me to avenge him." He pricks on his horse with spurs of pure gold, and he grasps Halteclere–already is the blade thereof reddened–and with all his strength he smites the paynim; he drives the blow home so that the Saracen falls and the devils carry away his soul. Then Oliver slew Duke Alphaïen, and cut off the head of Escababi, and unhorsed seven Arabs–never again shall they do battle. Then said Roland, "Wroth is my comrade, and now at my side he wins great worship. For such blows Charles holds us the more dear." And he cried aloud, "To battle, knights, to battle!"

Hard by is the paynim Valdabrun, that had stood godfather to King Marsila; on the sea he is lord of four hundred dromonds, and well honored of all shipmen. He it was who aforetime took Jerusalem by treason, violated the temple of Solomon, and slew the patriarch before the baptismal fonts. And he had sworn fellowship with Ganelon and had given him a sword and a thousand mangons. He rides a horse called Gramimond, swifter than any falcon; he spurs him well with his sharp spurs, and rides upon Samson the mighty Duke, breaks his shield, and rends his hauberk, and drives the flaps of his gonfanon into his body, and with all the force of his lance hurls him from the saddle dead. "Lay on, paynims, for hardily we shall overthrow them!" But the Franks cry, "God, woe worth the good baron!"

When Roland sees that Samson is dead, ye may guess he is sore stricken. He spurs his horse and lets him run as fast as he may, in his hand he holds Durendal, of greater worth than is pure gold, and with all the might he hath, he smites the paynim on the helm set with gold and gems, and cuts through head and hauberk and body, and through the good saddle set with gold and jewels, deep into the back of the horse, and slays both him and his rider, whosoever has dole or joy thereof. Cry the paynims, "That was a woeful blow for us." Then quoth Roland, "No love have I for any of ye, for yours is the pride and the iniquity."

Among the paynims is an African, Malquiant, son of King Malcud; his armor is all of beaten gold, and brighter than all the rest it shines to heaven. His horse, which he calls Salt-Perdut, is so swift that he has not his fellow in any four-footed beast. And now

Malquiant rode on Anseïs, and smote him full on the shield that its scarlet and blue were hewn away, and he rent the sides of his hauberk, and drove his lance into his body, both point and shaft. Dead is the Count and done are his life days. Thereat cry the Franks, "Alack for thee, good baron!"

Through the press rides Turpin the Archbishop–never did another priest say mass who did with his own strength so great deeds of arms–and he saith to the paynim, "Now may God bring all evil upon thee! For thou has slain one for whom my heart is sore stricken." Then he set his good horse at a gallop, and smote Malquiant on his shield of Toledo, that he fell dead upon the green grass.

Hard by is the paynim Grandonie, son of Capuel, King of Capadocia; he rides a horse called Marmorie, swifter than any bird that flies; he now slackens rein, and spurring well, thrusts mightily upon Gerin, breaks his crimson shield that it falls from his shoulder and rends all asunder his hauberk, and thereafter drives all his blue gonfanon into his body that he falls dead beside a great rock. Then he slays Gerier, Gerin's comrade, and Berengier, and Guyon of Saint-Antonie: and thereafter he smote Austor, the mighty Duke that held Valence and the land along the Rhône, and felled him dead that the paynims had great joy thereof. But the Franks cry, "How many of ours are stricken!"

Roland holds his ruddied sword in his hand. He has heard the Franks make lament and so great is his sorrow that his heart is nigh to bursting, and he saith to the paynims, "Now may God bring all evil upon thee! Methinks thou shalt pay me dear for him thou hast slain." And he spurs his horse, which springs forward eagerly and let whoso will pay the price, the two knights join battle.

Grandonie was a man of good prowess, of much valor and hardiness, and amid the way he encounters with Roland, and albeit before that time he had never set eyes upon him, he none the less knew him of a certainty by his look and countenance; and he could not but be sore adread at the sight, and fain would he have fled, but he could not. The Count smites him mightily so that he rends all his helm down to the nasal, cleaves through nose and mouth and teeth, through the hauberk of fine mail, and all the body, splits the silver sides from off the golden saddle, and cuts deep into the back of the horse, that both he and his rider are slain beyond help.

Thereat those of Spain make great lament, but the Franks cry, "That was well stricken of our captain!"

Wondrous and fierce is the battle; the Franks lay on in their wrath and their might, that hands and sides and bones fall to earth, and garments are rent off to the very flesh, and the blood runs down to the green grass. The paynims cry, "We may not longer endure. May the curse of Muhammad fall upon the Great Land, for its folk have not their fellow for hardiness." And there was not a man but cried out, "Marsila! Haste, O King, for we are in sore need of thy help."

Wondrous and great is the battle. And still the Franks smite with their burnished lances. There is great dolor of folk, and many a man is slain and maimed and bleeding, and one lies on another, or on his back, or face down. The Saracens may not longer endure, but howsoever unwillingly they must give back.[5] And eagerly the Franks pursue after them.

Marsila sees the slaughter of his people, and lets sound his horns and bussynes, and gets to horse with all his vassal host. In the foremost front rides the Saracen Abisme, the falsest knight of his fellowship, all compact of evil and villainy. He believes not in God the son of Mary; and he is black as melted pitch. Dearer than all the gold of Galicia he loves treachery and murder, nor did any man ever see him laugh or take disport. But he is a good man of arms, and bold to rashness, wherefor he is well beloved of the felon King Marsila, and to him it is given to bear the Dragon, around which the paynims gather. The Archbiship hath small love for Abisme, and so soon as he sees him he is all desirous to smite him, and quietly, within himself, he saith, "This Saracen seems a misbelieving felon, I had liefer die than not set upon him to slay him; never shall I love coward or cowardice."

Whereupon the Archbishop begins the battle. He rides the horse that he won from Grossaille, a king whom he slew in Denmark; the good steed is swift and keen, featly fashioned of foot, and flat of leg; short in the thigh and large of croupe, long of flank and high of back; his tail is white and yellow his mane, his head is the color of the fawn, and small are his ears; of all four-footed beasts none may outstrip him. The Archbishop spurs

---

[5] To turn or give back would signal a sort of retreat, temporary or permanent.

mightily and will not fail to meet with Abisme and smite him on his shield, a very marvel, set with gems–topaz and amethysts, and precious crystals, and blazing carbuncles; the gift it was of Galafré the Admiral, who had received it of a devil in Val-Metas. Now Turpin smites it and spares it not, that after his buffet it has not the worth of a doit. And he pierces Abisme through the body, and hurls him dead in the open field. And the Franks say, "That was a good deed of arms; and in the hands of our Archbishop safe is the crosier."

And Count Roland speaks to Oliver, saying, "Sir Comrade, what say ye, is not the Archbishop a right good knight, that there is no better under heaven? For well he knows how to smite with lance and spear." "Now let us aid him," the Count makes answer. And at these words the Franks go into battle again; great are the blows and grievous the slaughter, and great is the dolor of the Christians.

Would ye had seen Roland and Oliver hack and hew with their swords and the Archbishop smite with his lance. We can reckon those that fell by their hands for the number thereof is written in the charter and record; the Geste says more than four thousand. In four encounters all went well with the Franks, but the fifth was sore and grievous to them, for in this all their knights were slain save only sixty, spared by God's mercy. Before they die they will sell their lives dear.

When Count Roland is aware of the great slaughter of his men, he turns to Oliver, saying, "Sir comrade, as God may save thee, see how many a good man of arms lies on the ground; we may well have pity on sweet France, the fair, that must now be desolate of such barons. Ah, King and friend, would thou wert here! Oliver, my brother, what shall we do? How shall we send him tidings?" "Nay, I know not how to seek him," saith Oliver, "but liefer had I die than bring dishonor upon me."

Then saith Roland, "I will sound my horn of ivory, and Charles, as he passes the mountains, will hear it: and I pledge thee my faith the Franks will return again." Then saith Oliver, "Therein would be great shame for thee, and dishonor for all thy kindred, a reproach that would last all the days of their life. Thou wouldst not sound it when I bid thee, and now thou shalt not by my counsel. And if thou dost sound it, it will not be hardily, for now both thy arms are stained with blood." "Yea," the Count answers him, "I have dealt some goodly blows."

Then saith Roland, "Sore is our battle, I will blow a blast, and Charles the King will hear it." "That would not be knightly," saith Oliver, "When I bid thee, comrade, thou didst disdain it. Had the King been here, we had not suffered this damage; but they who are afar off are free from all reproach. By this my beard, and I see again my sister, Aude the Fair, never shalt thou lie in her arms."

Then saith Roland, "Wherefore art thou wroth with me?" And Oliver answers him, saying, "Comrade, thou thyself art to blame. Wise courage is not madness, and measure is better than rashness. Through thy folly these Franks have come to their death; nevermore shall Charles the King have service at our hands. Hadst thou taken my counsel, my liege lord had been here, and this battle had been ended, and King Marsila had been taken or slain. Woe worth thy prowess, Roland! Henceforth Charles shall get no help of thee; never till God's Judgment Day shall there be such another man; but thou must die, and France shall be shamed thereby. And this day our loyal fellowship will have an end; before this evening grievously shall we be parted."

The Archbishop, hearing them dispute together, spurs his horse with his spurs of pure gold, and comes unto them, and rebukes them, saying, "Sir Roland, and thou, Sir Oliver, in God's name I pray ye, let be this strife. Little help shall we now have of thy horn; and yet it were better to sound it; if the King come, he will revenge us, and the paynims shall not go hence rejoicing. Our Franks will light off their horses and find us dead and maimed and they will lay us on biers, and on the backs of sumpters, and will weep for us with dole and pity; and they will bury us in the courts of churches, that our bones may not be eaten by wolves and swine and dogs." "Sir, thou speakest well and truly," quoth Roland.

And therewith he sets his ivory horn to his lips, grasps it well and blows it with all the might he hath. High are the hills and the sound echoes far and for thirty full leagues they hear it resound. Charles and all his host hear it, and the King saith, "Our men are at battle." But Count Ganelon denies it, saying, "Had any other said so, we had deemed it great falsehood."

With dolor and pain and in sore torment, Count Roland blows his horn of ivory and the bright blood springs out of his mouth, and the temples of his brain are broken. Mighty is the blast of the horn and Charles, passing the mountians, hears it and Naymes hears it, and all the Franks listen and hear. Then saith the King, "I hear the horn of Roland; never would he sound it if he were not at battle."

But Ganelon answers him, saying, "Battle is there none; thou art old and white and hoary and thy words are those of a child. Well thou knowest the great pride of Roland–a marvel it is that God hath suffered it thus long. Aforetime he took Noples against thy commandment and when the Saracens came out of the city and set upon Roland, the good knight, he slew them with Durendal his sword; thereafter with water he washed away the blood which stained the meadow that none might know of what he had done. And for a single hare he will blow his horn all day long and now he but boasts among his fellows for there is no folk on earth would dare do him battle. I prithee ride on. Why tarry we? The Great Land still lies far before us."

Count Roland's mouth has burst out a-bleeding, and the temples of his brain are broken. In dolor and pain he sounds his horn of ivory but Charles hears it and the Franks hear it. Saith the King, "Long drawn is the blast of that horn." "Yea," Naymes answers, "for in sore need is the baron who blows it. Certes, our men are at battle and he who now dissembles hath betrayed Roland. Take your arms and cry your war-cry and succor the men of your house. Dost thou not hear Roland's call?"

The Emperor has commanded that his trumpets be sounded and now the Franks light down from their horses and arm themselves with hauberks and helms and swords adorned with gold; fair are their shields, and goodly and great their lances, and their gonfanons are scarlet and white and blue. Then all the barons of the host get them to horse and spur through the passes and each saith to other, "An we may but see Roland a living man, we will strike good blows at his side." But what avails it? For they have abode too long.

Clear is the evening as was the day and all their armor glistens in the sun and there is great shining of hauberks, and helms, and shields painted with flowers, and lances, and gilded gonfanons. The Emperor rides on in wrath and the Franks are full of care and foreboding and not a man but weeps full sore and hath great fear for Roland. Then the King let take Count Ganelon, and gave him over to the cooks of his household; and he called Besgon their chief, saying, "Guard him well, as beseems a felon who had betrayed my house." Besgon took him, and set a watch about him of a hundred of his fellows of the kitchen, both best and worst. They plucked out the hairs of Ganelon's beard and moustache, and each one dealt him four blows with his fist, and hardily they beat him with rods and staves; then they put about his neck a chain and bound him even as they would a bear, and in derision, they set him upon a sumpter. So they guard him til they return him unto Charles.

High are the hills and great and dark, deep the valleys, and swift the waters. To answer Roland's horn all the trumpets are sounded, both rear and van. The Emperor rides on in wrath, and the Franks are full of care and foreboding; there is not a man but weepeth and maketh sore lament, praying to God that he spare Roland until they come unto the field, that at his side they may deal good blows. But what avails it? They have tarried too long and may not come in time.

Charles the King rides on in great wrath and over his hauberk is spread his white beard. And all the barons of France spur mightily, no one but is full of wrath and grief that he is not with Roland the captain who is at battle with the Saracens of Spain. If he be wounded, what hope that one soul be left alive? God, what a sixty he still hath in his fellowship; no king or captain ever had better.

Roland looks abroad over hill and heath and sees the great multitude of the Frankish dead and he weeps for them as beseems a gentle knight, saying, "Lords and barons now may God have mercy upon you and grant Paradise to all your souls, that ye may rest among the blessed flowers. Man never saw better men of arms than ye were. Long and well, year in and year out, have ye served me, and many wide lands have ye won for the glory of Charles. Was it to such an end that he nourished you? O France, fair land, today art thou made desolate by rude slaughter. Ye Frankish barons, I see ye die through me, yet can I do naught to save or defend you. May God, who knows no lie, aid you! Oliver, brother, I must not fail thee; yet I shall die of grief, and I be not slain by the sword. Sir comrade, let us get us into battle."

So Count Roland falls a-smiting again. He holds Durendal in

his hand, and lays on right valiantly, that he cleaves in twain
Faldron de Pui, and slays four and twenty of the most worshipful
of the paynims. Never shall ye see man more desirous to revenge
himself. And even as the hart flies before the hounds, so flee the
heather from before Roland. "Thou dost rightly," then said the
Archbishop, "such valor well beseems a knight who bears arms
and sits a good horse; in battle such a one should be fell and
mighty, or he is not worth four deniers, and it behooves him to turn
monk and get him into a monastery to pray the livelong day for our
sins." And Roland answered him, saying, "Smite and spare not."
And at these words the Franks go into battle again but great is the
slaughter of the Christians,

That man who knows he shall get no mercy defends himself
savagely in battle. Wherefore the Franks are fierce as lions.
Marsila like a true baron sits his horse Gaignon; he spurs him well
and rides on Bevon—lord he was of Beaune and Dijon—and breaks
his shield, and rends his hauberk, that without other hurt he smites
him dead to the ground. And thereafter he slew Ivon and Ivory and
with them Gerard the Old of Roussillon. Now nigh at hand is
Count Roland and he saith to the paynim, "May the Lord God
bring me thee to mishap! And because thou hast wrongfully slain
my comrades thou shalt thyself get a buffet before we twain dispart
and this day thou shalt learn the name of my sword." And
therewith he rides upon him like a true baron and smites off his
right hand, and thereafter he takes off the head of Jurfaleu the Fair,
the son of King Marsila. Thereat the paynims cry, "Now help us,
Muhammad! Ye, our gods, revenge us upon Charles! He has sent
out against us into our marches men so fierce they will not give
back." And one saith to another, "Let us fly." At these words a
hundred thousand turn and flee, and let whosoever will call them,
they will not return again.

King Marsila has lost his right hand and now he throws his
shield to earth and pricks on his horse with his sharp spurs, and
with slackened rein, flees away towards Spain. Upon twenty
thousand Saracens follow after him, nor is there one among them
who is not maimed or hurt of body, and they say one to another,
"The nephew of Charles has won the field."

But alack, what avails it? For though Marsila be fled, his uncle
the Caliph yet abides, he who ruled Aferne, Carthage, Garmalie,

and Ethiopia, a cursed land; under his lordship he has the black folk. . .and they are with him to the number of fifty thousand. And now they come up in pride and wrath and cry aloud the war-cry of the paynims. Then saith Roland, "Now must we needs be slain, and well I know we have but a little space to live; but cursed be he who doth not sell himself right dear. Lay on, lords with your burnished swords, and debate both life and death; let not sweet France be brought to shame through us. When Charles, my liege lord, shall come upon this field, he will see such slaughter of the Saracens, that he shall find fifteen of them dead over each man of ours, and he will not fail to bless us."

When Roland sees the cursed fold whose skin is blacker than any ink, and who have naught of white about them save their teeth, he saith, "Now I know in very sooth that we shall die this day. Lay on, lords, and yet again I bid thee, smite." "Now foul fall him who lags behind," quoth Oliver. And at this word the Franks haste into the fray.

Now when the paynims see how few are the Franks they have great pride and joy thereof; and one saith to another, "Certes, the Emperor is in the wrong." The Caliph bestrides a sorrel horse, he pricks him on with his spurs of gold and smites Oliver from behind, and amid the back, that he drives the mails of his white hauberk into his body and his lance passes out through his breast, "Now hast thou got a good buffet," quoth the Caliph, "On an ill day Charles the Great left thee in the passes; much wrong hath he done us, yet he shall not boast thereof, for on thee alone have I well revenged us."

Oliver feels that he is wounded unto death; in his hand he holds Halteclere, bright was its blade, and with it he smites the Caliph on his golden pointed helmet, that its flowers and gems fall to earth, and he cleaves the head even unto the teeth, and with the force of the blow smote him dead to earth and said, "Foul fall thee, paynim! Say not that I am come to my death through Charles; and neither to thy wife, nor any other dame, shalt thou ever boast in the land from which thou art come, that thou has taken from me so much as one farthing's worth, or has done any hurt to me or to others." And thereafter he called to Roland for succor.

Oliver feels that he is wounded unto death; never will he have his fill of vengeance. In the thick of the press he smites valiantly, cleaving lances and embossed shields, and feet and hands and flanks and shoulders. Whosoever saw him thus dismember the Saracens and hurl one dead upon another must call to mind true valiance; nor did he forget the war-cry of Charles, but loud and clear he cries out Montjoy! And he calls to Roland, his friend and peer: "Sir comrade, come stand thou beside me. In great dolor shall we twain soon be disported."

Roland looks Oliver in the face, pale it is and livid and all discolored; the bright blood flows down from amid his body and falls in streams to the ground. "God," saith the Count, "now I know not what to do. Sir comrade, woe worth thy valor! Never shall the world see again a man of thy might. Alas, fair France, today art thou stripped of goodly vassals, and fallen and undone. The Emperor will suffer great loss thereby." And so speaking he swoons upon his horse.

Lo, Roland has swooned as he sits his horse, and Oliver is wounded unto death, so much has he bled that his sight is darkened, and he can no longer distinguish any living man whether far off or near at hand; and now, as he meets his comrade, he smites him upon the helm set with gold and gems, and cleaves it down to the nasal, but does not come unto the head. At the blow Roland looks up at him and asks him full softly and gently, "Comrade, dost thou this wittingly? I am Roland who so loves thee. Never yet has thou mistrusted me." Then saith Oliver, "Now I hear thee speak, but I cannot see thee, may the Lord God guard thee. I have struck thee, but I pray thy pardon." "Thou has done me no hurt," Roland answers him; 'I pardon thee before God, as here and now." So speaking each leans forward towards other, and lo, in such friendship they are disported.

Oliver feels the anguish of death come upon him; his two eyes turn in his head; and his hearing goes from him, and all sight. He lights down from his horse and lies upon the ground, and again and again he confesses his sins; he holds out his clasped hands toward heaven and prays God that He grant him Paradise, and he blesses Charles and sweet France, and Roland, his comrade, above all men. Then his heart fails him and his head sinks upon his breast and he lies stretched at all his length upon the ground. Dead is the Count and gone from hence. Roland weeps for him and is sore troubled; never on earth shall ye see a man so sorrowful.

When Count Roland sees his friend lie prone and dead, facing the East, gently he begins to lament him, "Sir comrade, woe worth thy hardiness! We twain have held together for years and days, never didst thou me wrong or I thee. Since thou art dead, alack that I yet live." So speaking, the Count swoons as he sits Veillantif his horse, but his golden spurs hold him firm, and let him go where he will, he cannot fall.

So soon as Roland comes to his senses and is restored from his swoon, he is ware of the great slaughter about him. Slain are the Franks, he has lost them all save only Gualter del Hum and the Archbishop. Gualter has come down from the mountains where he fought hardily with those of Spain; the paynims conquered, and his men are slain, and howsoever unwillingly, he must perforce flee down into the valley and call upon Roland for succor. "O gentle Count, brave captain, where art thou? For where thou art I have no fear. It is I, Gualter, who conquered Maëlgut, I the nephew of Droön the old, the hoary, I whom thou were wont to love for my hardihood. Now my shield is pierced, and the shaft of my lance is broken, and my hauberk rent and unmailed; I have the wounds of eight lances in my body, and I must die, but dear have I sold myself." So he saith, and Roland hears him, and spurs his horse and rides towards him.

Count Roland is a full noble warrior and a right good knight is Gualter del Hum, the Archbishop is of good valor and well tried; no one would leave aught to his fellows, and together, in the thick of the press, they smite the paynims. A thousand Saracens get them to foot and there are still forty thousand on horseback, yet in sooth they dare not come nigh unto the three, but they hurl upon them lances and spears, arrows and darts and sharp javelins. In the first storm they slew Gualter and sundered the shield of Turpin of Rheims, broke his helmet and wounded him in the head, and rent and tore his hauberk that he was pierced in the body by four spears and his horse was slain under him. The Archbishop falls; great is the pity thereof.

But so soon as Turpin of Rheims finds himself beaten down to earth with the wounds of four lances in his body, he right speedily gets him afoot again; he looks toward Roland, and hastes to him, and saith, "I am nowise vanquished; no good vassal yields him so long as he is a living man." And he draws Almace, his sword of brown steel, and in the thick of the press he deals well more than a thousand buffets. Afterwards Charles bore witness that Turpin spared himself no whit, for around him they found four hundred dead, some wounded, some cut in twain amid the body, and some whose heads had been smitten off; so saith the Geste and he who was on the field, the valiant Saint Gilles, for whom God wrought miracles; for it was he who wrote the annals of the monastery of Laon. And he who knows not this, knows naught of the matter.

Count Roland fights right nobly but all his body is a-sweat and burning hot, and in his head he hath great pain and torment, for when he sounded his horn he rent his temples. But he would fain know that Charles were coming, and he takes his horn of ivory, and feebly he sounds it. The emperor stops to listen, "Lords," he saith, "now has great woe come upon us, this day shall we lose Roland my nephew, I wot from the blast of his horn that he is nigh to death. Let him who would reach the field ride fast. Now sound ye all the trumpets of the host." Then they blew sixty thousand, so loud that the mountains resound and the valleys give answer. The paynims hear them and have no will to laugh, but one saith to another, "We shall have ado with Charles anon."

Say the paynims, "The Emperor is returning, we hear the trumpets of France; if Charles come hither, we shall suffer sore loss. Yet is Roland alive, our war will begin again, and we shall lose Spain our land." Then four hundred armed in their helmets, and of the best of those on the field, gather together, and on Roland they make onset fierce and sore. Now is the Count hard bestead.

When Count Roland sees them draw near he waxes hardy and fierce and terrible; never will he yield as long as he is a living man. He sits his horse Veillantif and spurs him well with his spurs of fine gold and rides into the stour upon them all; and at his side is Archbishop Turpin. And the Saracens say one to another, "Now save yourselves, friends. We have heard the trumpets of France; Charles the mighty King is returning."

Count Roland never loved the cowardly, or the proud, or the wicked, or any knight who was not a good vassal, and now he calls to Archbishop Turpin, saying, "Lord thou art on foot and I am a-horseback, for thy love I will make halt, and together we will take the good and the ill; I will not leave thee for any living man; the blows of Almace and of Durendal shall give back this assault to the paynims." Then saith the Archbishop, "A traitor is he who doth not smite; Charles is returning and he will revenge us."

"In an evil hour," say the paynims, "were we born; woeful is the day that has dawned for us! We have lost our lords and our peers. Charles the valiant cometh hither again with his great host, we hear the clear trumpets of those of France, and great is the noise of their cry of Montjoy. Count Roland is of such might he cannot be vanquished by any mortal man. Let us hurl our missiles upon him and then leave him." Even so they did and cast upon him many a dart and javelin, and spears and lances and feathered arrows. They broke and rent the shield of Roland, tore open and unmailed his hauberk, but did not pierce his body, but Viellantif was wounded in thirty places, and fell from under the Count, dead. Then the paynims flee and leave him. Count Roland is left alone and on foot.

The paynims flee in anger and wrath and in all haste they fare toward Spain. Count Roland did not pursue after them, for he has lost his horse Veillantif, and whether he will or no, is left on foot. He went to the help of Archbishop Turpin and unlaced his golden helm from his head, and took off his white hauberk of fine mail, and he tore his tunic into strips and with the pieces bound his great wounds. Then he gathers him in his arms, and lays him down full softly upon the green grass and gently he beseeches him, "O gracious baron, I pray thy leave. Our comrades whom we so loved are slain and it is not meet to leave them thus. I would go seek and find them and range them before thee." "Go and return again," quoth the Archbishop. "Thank God, this field is thine and mine."

Roland turns away and fares on along through the field; he searches the valleys and the hills, and there he found Ivon and Ivory, and Gerin, and Gerier his comrade, and he found Englier the Gascon, and Berengier, and Oton, and he found Anseïs and Samson, and Gerard the Old of Rousillon. One by one he hath taken up the barons and hath come with them unto the Archbishop, and places them in rank before him. The Archbishop cannot help but weep; he raises his hand and gives them benediction, and thereafter saith, "Alas for ye, Lords! May God the Glorious receive your souls, and bring them into Paradise among the blessed flowers. And now my own death torments me sore; never again shall I see the great Emperor."

Again Roland turned away to search the field and when he found Oliver his comrade, he gathered him close against his breast, and as best he might returned again unto the Archbishop and laid his comrade upon a shield beside the others and the Archbishop absolved and blessed him. Then their sorrow and pity broke forth again, and Roland saith, "Oliver, fair comrade, thou wert son of the great Duke Renier, who held the Marches of Rivier and Genoa. For the breaking of lances or the piercing of shields, for vanquishing and affrighting the proud, for upholding and counseling the good, never in any land was there a better knight."

When Roland sees the peers and Oliver whom he so loved, lying dead, pity takes him and he begins to weep. His face is all discolored, so great is his grief he cannot stand upright, but will he, nill he, falls to the ground in a swoon. Saith the Archbishop, "Alack for thee, good baron."

When the Archbishop sees Roland swoon, he is such dole as he has never known before. He stretches out his hand and takes the horn of ivory, for in Roncevals there is a swift streamlet and he would go to it to bring of its water to Roland. Slowly and falteringly he sets forth, but so weak he is he cannot walk, his strength has gone from him, too much blood has he lost, and before a man might cross an acre his heart faileth and he falls forward upon his face and the anguish of death comes upon him.

When Count Roland recovers from his swoon he gets upon his feet with great torment; he looks up and he looks down, and beyond his comrades, on the green grass, he sees that goodly baron, the Archbishop, appointed of God in His stead. Turpin saith his *mea culpa*, and looks up, and stretches out his two hands towards heaven, and prays God that he grant him Paradise. And so he dies, the warrior of Charles. Long had he waged strong war against the paynims, both by his mighty battling and his goodly sermons. May God grant him his holy benison.

Count Roland sees the Archbishop upon the ground; his bowels have fallen out of his body and his brains are oozing out of his forehead; Roland takes his fair, white hands and crosses them upon his breast between his two collar bones and lifting up his voice, he mourns for him, after the manner of his people, "Ah gentle man, knight of high parentage, now I commend thee to the heavenly Glory. Never will there be a man who shall serve Him

155

more willingly. Never since the days of the apostles hath there been such a prophet to uphold the law, and win the hearts of men. May thy soul suffer no dole or torment, but may the doors of Paradise be opened to thee."

Now Roland feels that death is near him and his brains flow out at his ears; he prays to the Lord God for his peers that He will receive them, and he prays to the Angel Gabriel for himself. That he may be free from all reproach, he takes his horn of ivory in the one hand, and Durendal, his sword, in the other, and further than a crossbow can cast an arrow through a cornfield he goeth on towards Spain. At the crest of a hill, beneath two fair trees, are four stairs of marble; there he falls down on the green grass in a swoon, for death is close upon him.

High are the hills and very tall are the trees; the four stones are of shining marble and there Count Roland swoons upon the green grass. Meantime a Saracen is watching him; he has stained his face and body with blood, and feigning death, he lies still among his fellows, but now he springs to his feet and hastens forward. Fair he was, and strong and of good courage; and in his pride he breaks out into mighty wrath, and seizes upon Roalnd, both him and his arms, and he cries, "Now is the nephew of Charles overthrown. This his sword will I carry into Arabia." But at his touch the Count recovered his senses.

Roland feels that his sword hath been taken from him, he opens his eyes, and saith, "Certes, thou art not one of our men." He holds his horn of ivory which he never lets out of his grasp and he smites the Saracen upon the helm which was studded with gold and gems, and he breaks steel and head and bones that his two eyes start out, and he falls down dead at his feet. Then saith Roland, "Coward, what made thee so bold to lay hands upon me, whether right or wrong? No man shall hear it but shall hold thee a fool. Now is my horn of ivory broken in the bell, and its gold and its crystals have fallen."

Now Roland feels that his sight is gone from him. With much striving he gets upon his feet; the color has gone from his face. Before him lies a brown stone and in his sorrow and wrath he smites ten blows upon it. The sword grates upon the rock, but neither breaks nor splinters and the Count saith, "Holy Mary, help me now! Ah Durendal, alas for your goodness! Now I am near to death and have no more need of you. Many a fight in the field have I won with you, many a wide land have I conquered with you, lands now ruled by Charles with the white beard. May the man who would flee before another, never possess you. For many a day have you been held by a right good lord, never will there be such another in France the free."

Roland smote his sword upon the block of hard stone, and the steel grates, but neither breaks nor splinters. And when he sees that he can in nowise break it, he laments, saying, "O Durendal, how fair and bright thou art, in the sunlight how thou flashest and shinest! Charles was once in the valley of Moriane, when God commanded him by one of his angels that he should give thee to a chieftain Count; then the great and noble King girded thee upon me and with thee I won for him Anjou and Bretagne, and I conquered Poitou and Maine for him, and for him I conquered Normandy the free, and Provence, and Aquitaine; and Lombardy, and all of Romagna; and I conquered for him Bavaria, and Flanders, and Bulgaria, and all of Poland; Constantinople which now pays him fealty, and Saxony, where he may work his will. And I conquered for him Wales, and Scotland, and Ireland, and England which he holds as his demesne. Many lands and countries have I won with thee, lands which Charles of the white beard rules. And now I am heavy of heart because of this my sword. Rather would I die than that it should fall into the hands of the paynims. Lord God our Father, let not this shame fall upon France."

And again Roland smote upon the brown stone and beyond all telling shattered it; the sword grates, but springs back again into the air and is neither dinted nor broken. And when the Count sees he may in no wise break it, he laments, saying, "O Durendal, how fair and holy a thing thou art! In thy golden hilt is many a relic–a tooth of Saint Peter, and some of the blood of Saint Basil, and hairs from the head of my lord, Saint Denis, and a bit of the raiment of the Virgin Mary. It is not meet that thou fall into the hands of the paynims, only Christians should wield thee. May no coward ever possess thee! Many wide lands have I conquered with thee, lands which Charles of the white beard rules and thereby is the Emperor great and mighty."

Now Roland feels that death has come upon him and that it creeps down from his head to his heart. In all haste he fares under a

157

pine tree, and hath cast himself down upon his face on the green grass. Under him he laid his sword and his horn of ivory and he turned his face towards the paynim folk, for he would that Charles and all his men should say that the gentle Count had died a conqueror. Speedily and full often he confesses his sins, and in atonement he offers his glove to God.

Roland lies on a high peak looking towards Spain; he feels that his time is spent, and with one hand he beats his breast, "O God, I have sinned; forgive me through thy might the wrongs, both great and small, which I have done from the day I was born even to this day on which I was smitten." With his right hand he holds out his glove to God and lo, the angels of heaven come down to him.

Count Roland lay under the pine tree; he has turned his face towards Spain. And begins to recall many things to remembrance– all the lands he had won by his valor, and sweet France, and the men of his lineage, and Charles, his liege lord, who had brought him up in his household, and he cannot help but weep. But he would not wholly forget himself, and again he confesses his sins and begs forgiveness of God, "Our Father, Who art Truth, Who raised up Lazarus from the dead, and Who defended Daniel from the lions, save Thou my soul from the perils to which it is brought through the sins I wrought in my life days." With his right hand he offers his glove to God and Saint Gabriel has taken it from his hand. Then his head sinks on his arm and with clasped hands he hath gone to his end. And God sent him His cherubim, and Saint Michael of the Seas, and with them went Saint Gabriel, and they carried the soul of the Count into Paradise.

ROMANCE LITERATURE

Crusader's Farewell
by Thibaud, King of Navarre (1201-1253)

Lady, the fates command, and I must go –
Leaving the pleasant land so dear to me;
Here my heart suffered many a heavy blow
But what is left to love, thus leaving thee?
Alas: that cruel land beyond the sea
Why thus dividing many a faithful heart,
Never again from pain and sorrow free
Never again to meet when thus they part?

I see not, when they presence bright I leave
How health, or joy, or peace can be my lot;
Ne'er yet my spirit found such cause to grieve
As now in leaving thee: and if thy thought
Of me in absence should be sorrow fraught
Oft will my heart repentant turn to thee
Dwelling, in fruitless wishes, on this spot,
And all the gracious words here said to me.

O gracious God: to thee I bend my knee
For thy sake yielding all I love and prize;
And O how might must that influence be,
That steals me thus from all my cherished joys!
Here, ready, then, myself surrendering,
Prepared to serve thee; I submit; and ne'er
To one so faithful could I service bring,
So kind a master, so beloved and dear.

And strong my ties – my grief unspeakable!
Grief, all my choicest treasures to resign;
Yet stronger still the affections that impel
My heart toward him the God whose love is mine
That holy love, how beautiful! How strong!
Even wisdom's favorite sons take refuge there;

'Tis the redeeming gem that shines among
Man's darkest thoughts – forever bright and fair.

The Travels of Marco Polo
by Marco Polo (1254-1324) and Rusticien de Pise
translated by Sir Henry Yule, 1875

Marco Polo's epic travelogue introduced medieval Europeans to the wonders of central China and the Tartar empire. During his 24 years of travel, taking place between 1271 and 1295, Polo had ample opportunity to observe the cultural practices of the Tartars. The following excerpt from *The Travels of Marco Polo* begins with a story of Genghis Khan, the founder of the great Yuan Dynasty, and continues to relate Polo's personal observations of life under Kublai Khan, Genghis's descendant. The Yuan Dynasty achieved great power and ruled over and area equal to one fifth of the world's inhabited land mass! The stories related by Polo ignited the European imagination and came about during a time of rapidly expanding horizons as travelers and adventurers pressed beyond the boundaries of the known world.

PART I:
Genghis Khan

Originally the Tartars dwelt in the north on the borders of Chorcha. Their country was one of great plains and there were no towns or villages in it but excellent pasturelands, with great rivers and many sheets of water. In fact it was a very fine and extensive region. But there was no sovereign in the land. They did, however, pay tax and tribute to a great prince who was called in their tongue Unc Can, the same that we call Prester John, him in fact about whose great dominion all the world talks. The tribute he had of them was one beast out of every ten and also a tithe of all their other gear.

Now it came to pass that the Tartars multiplied exceedingly. And when Prester John saw how great a people they had become, he began to fear that he should have trouble with them. So he made a scheme to distribute them over sundry countries and sent one of his barons to carry this out. When the Tartars became aware of this they took it much amiss, and with one consent they left their country and went off across a desert to a distant region towards the north, where Prester John could not get at them to annoy them. And so things continued for a time.

Now it came to pass in the year of Christ's incarnation 1187 that the Tartars made themselves a king whose name was Genghis Khan. He was a man of great worth and of great ability, eloquence, and valor. And as soon as the news that he had been chosen King was spread abroad through those countries, all the Tartars in the world came to him and owned him for their Lord. And right well did he maintain the sovereignty they had given him. What shall I say? The Tartars gathered to him in astonishing multitude and when he saw such numbers he made a great furniture of spears and arrows and such other arms as they used, and set about the conquest of all those regions till he had conquered eight provinces.

When he conquered a province he did no harm to the people or their property, but merely established some of his own men in the country along with a proportion of theirs, whilst he led the remainder to the conquest of other provinces. And when those whom he had conquered became aware how well and safely he protected them against all others, and how they suffered no ill at his hands, and saw what a noble prince he was, then they joined him heart and soul and became his devoted followers. And when he had thus gathered such a multitude that they seemed to cover the earth, he began to think of conquering a great part of the world.

Now in the year of Christ 1200 he sent an embassy to Prester John, and desired to have his daughter to wife. But when Prester John heard that Genghis Khan demanded his daughter in marriage he waxed very wroth, and said to the envoys, "What impudence is this, to ask my daughter to wife! Wist he not well that he was my liegeman and serf? Get ye back to him and tell him that I had liever set my daughter in the fire than give her in marriage to him, and that he deserve death at my hand, rebel and traitor that he is!" So he bade the envoys begone at once, and never come into his presence again. The envoys, on receiving this reply, departed straightway, and made haste to their master, and related all that Prester John had ordered them to say, keeping nothing back.

When Genghis Khan heard the brutal message that Prester John had sent him such a rage seized him that his heart came nigh to bursting within him, for he was a man of a very lofty spirit. At last he spoke, and so loud that all who were present could hear him, "Never more might he be prince if he took not revenge for the brutal message of Prester John, and such revenge that insult never in this world so dearly paid for. And before long, Prester John should know whether he were his serf or no!"

So then he mustered all his forces and levied such a host as never before was seen or heard of, sending word to Prester John to be on his defense. And when Prester John had sure tidings that Genghis was really coming against him with such a multitude, he still professed to treat it as a jest and a trifle, for, quoth he, "These be no soldiers." Nevertheless he marshaled his forces and mustered his people and made great preparations, in order that if Genghis did come, he might take him and put him to death. In fact he marshaled such an host of many different nations that it was a world's wonder.

And so both sides gat them ready to battle. And why should I make a long story of it? Genghis Khan with all his host arrived at a vast and beautiful plain which was called Tanduc, belonging to Prester John, and there he pitched his camp. So great was the multitude of his people that it was impossible to number them. And when he got tidings that Prester John was coming, he rejoiced greatly, for the place afforded a fine and ample battle-ground, so he was right glad to tarry for him there, and greatly longed for his arrival.

Now the story goes that when Prester John became aware that Genghis with his host was marching against him, he went forth to meet him with all his forces, and advanced until he reached the same plain of Tanduc, and pitched his camp over against that of Genghis Khan at a distance of twenty miles. And then both armies remained at rest for two days that they might be fresher and heartier for battle.

So when the two great hosts were pitched on the plains of Tanduc as you have heard, Genghis Khan one day summoned before him his astrologers, both Christians and Saracens, and desired them to let him know which of the two hosts would gain the battle, his own or Prester John's. The Saracens tried to ascertain, but were unable to give a true answer; the Christians however did give a true answer, and showed manifestly beforehand how the event should be. For they got a cane and split it lengthwise, and laid one half on this side and one half on that, allowing no one to touch the pieces. And one piece of cane they called Genghis Khan, and the other piece they called Prester John.

And they said to Genghis, "Now mark! and you will see the event of the battle, and who shall have the best of it; for whose can soever shall get above the other, to him shall victory be." He replied that he would fain see it and bade them begin. Then the Christian astrologers read a Psalm out of the Psalter and went through other incantations. And lo! whilst all were beholding, the cane that bore the name of Genghis Khan, without being touched by anybody, advanced to the other that bore the name of Prester John, and got on the top of it. When the Prince saw that, he was greatly delighted, and seeing how in this matter he found the Christians to tell the truth, he always treated them with great respect, and held them for men of truth for ever after.

And after both sides had rested well those two days, they armed for the fight and engaged in desperate combat; and it was such a battle that ever was seen. The numbers that were slain on both sides were very great, but in the end Genghis Khan obtained the victory. And in the battle Prester John was slain. And from that time forward, day by day, his kingdom passed into the hands of Genghis Khan till the whole was conquered.

I may tell you that Genghis Khan reigned six years after this battle and engaged continually in conquest, taking many a province and city and stronghold. But at the end of those six years he went against a certain castle that was called Caaju, and there he was shot with an arrow in the knee, so that he died of his wound. A great pity it was, for he was a valiant man and a wise.

PART II:
Kublai Khan

Now am I come to that part of our Book in which I shall tell you of the great and wonderful magnificence of the Great Khan now reigning, by name Kublai Khan. Khan being a title which signifyeth "The Great Lord of Lords" or Emperor. And of a surety he had good right to such a title, for all men know for a certain truth that he is the most potent man, as regards forces and lands and treasure, that existeth in the world, or ever hath existed from the time of our first father Adam until this day. All this I make clear to you for truth, in this book of ours, so that everyone will be fain to acknowledge that his is the greatest lord now in the world, or ever hath been. And now ye shall hear how and wherefore.

Now this Kublai Khan is of the right imperial lineage, being descended from Genghis Khan, the first sovereign of all the Tartars. And he is the sixth Lord in that succession, as I have already told you in this book. He came to the throne in the year of Christ 1256, and the Empire fell to him because of his ability and valor and great worth, as was right and reason. His brothers, indeed, and other kinsmen disputed his claim, but his it remained, both because maintained by his great valor, and because it was in law and right his, as being directly sprung of the imperial line.

Up to the year of Christ now running, to wit 1298, he had reigned two and forty years, and his age is about eighty-five, so that he must have been about forty-three years of age when he first came to the throne. Before that time he had often been to the wars, and had shown himself a gallant soldier and an excellent captain. But after coming to the throne he never went to the wars in person save once.

The personal appearance of the Great Khan, Lord of Lords, whose name is Kublai, is such as I shall now tell you. He is of a good stature, neither tall nor short, but of a middle height. He has a becoming amount of flesh and is very shapely in all his limbs. His complexion is white and red, the eyes black and fine, the nose well formed and well set on. He has four wives, whom he retains permanently as his legitimate consorts, and the eldest of his sons by those four wives ought by rights to be emperor–I mean when his father dies. Those four ladies are called empresses, but each is distinguished also by her proper name. And each of them has a special court of her own, very grand and ample, no one of them having fewer than 300 fair and charming damsels. They have also many pages and eunuchs, and a number of attendants of both sexes, so that each of these ladies has not less than 10,000 persons attached to her court.

When the Emperor desires the society of one of these four consorts, he will sometimes send for the lady to his apartment and sometimes visit her at his own. He has also a great number of concubines.

❧❧

The Emperor hath, by those four wives of his, twenty-two male children; the eldest of whom was called Zhenjin for the love

165

of the good Genghis Khan, the first Lord of the Tartars. And this Zhenjin, as the Eldest Son of the Khan, was to have reigned after his father's death; but as it came to pass, he died. He left a son behind him, however, whose name is Temür, and he is to be the Great Khan and Emperor after the death of his grandfather, as is but right; he bring the child of the Great Khan's eldest son. And this Temür is an able and brave man, as he hath already proven on many occasions.

The Great Khan hath also twenty-five other sons by his concubines and these are good and valiant soldiers, and each of them is a great chief. I tell you moreover that of his children by his four lawful wives there are seven who are kings of vast realms or provinces, and govern them well, being all able and gallant men, as might be expected. For the Great Khan their sire is, I tell you, the wisest and most accomplished man, the greatest captain, the best to govern men and rule an empire, as well as the most valiant, that ever has existed among all the tribes of Tartars.

You must know that for three months of the year, to wit December, January, and February, the Great Khan resides in the capital city of Cathay, which is called Cambaluc and which is at the north-eastern extremity of the country. In that city stands his great palace, and now I will tell you what it is like.

It is enclosed all round by a great wall forming a square, each side of which is a mile in length; that is to say, the whole compass thereof is four miles. This you may depend on; it is also very thick, and a good ten paces in height, whitewashed and loop-holed all around. At each angle of the wall there is a very fine and rich palace in which the war-harness of the Emperor is kept, such as bows and quivers, saddles and bridles, and bowstrings, and everything needful for an army. Also midway between every two of these corner palaces there is another of the like so that taking the whole compass of the enclosure you will find eight vast palaces stored with the Great Lord's harness of war. And you must understand that each palace is assigned to only one kind of article; thus one is stored with bows, a second with saddles, a third with bridles, and so on in succession right round.

The great wall has five gates on its southern face, the middle one being the great gate which is never opened on any occasion except when the Great Khan himself goes forth or enters. Close on either side of this great gate is a smaller one by which all other people pass and then towards each angle is another great gate, also open to people in general; so that on that side there are five gates in all.

Inside of this wall there is a second, enclosing a space that is somewhat greater in length than in breadth. This enclosure also has eight palaces corresponding to those of the outer wall, and stored like them with the Lord's harness of war. This wall also hath five gates on the southern face, corresponding to those in the outer wall, and hath one gate on each of the other faces as the outer wall hath also. In the middle of the second enclosure is the Lord's Great Palace, and I will tell you what it is like.

You must know that it is the greatest palace that ever was. Towards the north it is in contact with the outer wall, whilst towards the south there is a vacant space which the barons and the soldiers are constantly traversing. The palace itself hath no upper story, but is all on the ground floor, only the basement is raised some ten palms above the surrounding soil and this elevation is retained by a wall of marble raised to the level of the pavement, two paces in width and projecting beyond the base of the palace so as to form a kind of terrace walk, by which people can pass round the building, and which is exposed to view, whilst on the outer edge of the wall there is a very fine pillared balustrade and up to this the people are allowed to come. The roof is very lofty and the walls of the palace are all covered with gold and silver. They are also adorned with representations of dragons sculptured and gilt, beasts and birds, knights and idols, and sundry other subjects. And on the ceiling too you see nothing but gold and silver and painting. On each of the four sides there is a great marble staircase leading to the top of the marble wall and forming the approach to the palace.

The hall of the palace is so large that it could easily dine 6000 people and it is quite a marvel to see how many rooms there are besides. The building is altogether so vast, so rich, and so beautiful, that no man on earth could design anything superior to it. The outside of the roof is also all colored with vermilion and yellow and green and blue and other hues, which are fixed with a varnish so fine and exquisite that they shine like crystal and lend a resplendent luster to the palace as seen for a great way round. This roof is made, too, with such strength and solidity that it is fit to last for ever.

On the interior side of the palace are large buildings with halls and chambers, where the Emperor's private property is placed, such as his treasures of gold, silver, gems, pearls, and gold plate, and in which reside the ladies and concubines. There he occupies himself at his own convenience, and no one else has access.

Between the two walls of the enclosure which I have described, there are fine parks and beautiful trees bearing a variety of fruits. There are beasts also of sundry kinds, such as white stags and fallow deer, gazelles and roebucks, and fine squirrels of various sorts, with numbers also of the animal that gives the musk and all manner of other beautiful creatures, insomuch that the whole place is full of them, and no spot remains void except where there is traffic of people going and coming. The parks are covered with abundant grass and the roads through them being all paved and raised two cubits above the surface, they never become muddy, nor does the rain lodge on them, but flows off into the meadows, quickening the soil and producing that abundance of herbage.

From that corner of the enclosure which is towards the north-west there extends a fine lake, containing foison of fish of different kinds which the Emperor hath caused to be put in there, so that whenever he desires any he can have them at his pleasure. A river enters this lake and issues from it, but there is a grating of iron or brass put up so that the fish cannot escape in that way.

Moreover on the north side of the palace, about a bow-shot off, there is a hill which has been made by art from the earth dug out of the lake; it is a good hundred paces in height and a mile in compass. This hill is entirely covered with trees that never lose their leaves but remain green. And I assure you that wherever a beautiful tree may exist, and the Emperor gets news of it, he sends for it and has it transported bodily with all its roots and the earth attached to them, and planted on that hill of his. No matter how big the tree may be, he gets it carried by his elephants, and in this way he had got together the most beautiful collection of trees in all the world. And he has also caused the whole hill to be covered with the ore of azure, which is very green. And thus not only are the trees all green, but the hill itself is all green likewise, and there is nothing to be seen on it that is not green and hence it is called the

Green Mount, and in good sooth 'tis named well.

On the top of the hill again there is a fine big palace which is all green inside and out and thus the hill and the trees and the palace form together a charming spectacle; and it is marvelous to see their uniformity of color! Everybody who sees them is delighted. And the Great Khan has caused this beautiful prospect to be formed for the comfort and solace and delectation of his heart.

You must know that beside the palace that we have been describing, i.e. the Great Palace, the Emperor has caused another to be built just like his own in every respect, and this he hath done for his son when he shall reign and be emperor after him. Hence it is made just in the same fashion and of the same size so that everything can be carried on in the same manner after his own death. It stands on the other side of the lake from the Great Khan's palace and there is a bridge crossing the water from one to the other. The Prince in question holds now a Seal of the Empire, but not with such complete authority as the Great Khan, who remains supreme as long as he lives.

Now I am going to tell you of the Chief City of Cathay, in which these palaces stand and why it was built and how. Now there was on that spot in old times a great and noble city called Cambaluc, which is as much as to say in our tongue "The City of the Emperor." But the Great Khan was informed by his astrologers that this city would prove rebellious and raise great disorders against his imperial authority. So he caused the present city to be built close beside the old one, with only a river between them. And he caused the people of the old city to be removed to the new town that he had founded; and this is called Taidu. However, he allowed a portion of the people which he did not suspect to remain in the old city, because the new one could not hold the whole of them, big as it is.

As regards the size of this new city you must know that it has a compass of twenty-four miles, for each side of it hath a length of six miles, and it is four-square. And it is all walled round with walls of earth which have a thickness as they rise, so that at top they are only about three paces thick. And they are provided throughout with loop-holed battlements, which are all whitewashed.

There are twelve gates, and over each gate there is a great and handsome palace, so that there are on each side of the square three gates and five palaces; for, I ought to mention, there is at each angle also a great and handsome palace. In those palaces are vast halls, in which are kept the arms of the city garrison.

The streets are so straight and wide that you can see right along them from end to end and from one gate to the other. And up and down the city there are beautiful palaces, and many great and fine hostelries and fine houses in great numbers. All the plots of ground on which the houses of the city are built are four-square and laid out with straight lines–all the plots being occupied by great and spacious palaces, with courts and gardens of proportionate size. All these plots were assigned to different heads of families. Each square plot is encompassed by handsome streets for traffic and thus the whole city is arranged in square just like a chess-board and disposed in a manner so perfect and masterly that it is impossible to give a description that should do it justice.

Moreover, in the middle of the city there is a great clock–that is to say, a bell–which is struck at night. After it is struck three times no one must go out in the city, unless it be for the needs of a woman in labor, or of the sick. And those who go about on such errands are bound to carry lanterns with them. Moreover, the established guard at each gate of the city is one thousand armed men; not that you are to imagine this guard is kept up for fear of any attack, but only as a guard of honor for the sovereign, who resides there, and to prevent thieves from doing mischief in the town.

You must know that the Great Khan, to maintain his state, hath a guard of twelve thousand horsemen, who are styled Keshican, which is as much to say "Knights devoted to their Lord." Not that he keeps these for fear of any man whatever, but merely because of his own exalted dignity. These twelve thousand men have four captains, each of whom is in command of three thousand, and each body of three thousand takes a turn of three days and nights to guard the palace, where they also take their meals. After the expiration of three days and nights they are relieved by another three thousand, who mount guard for the same space of time, and then another body takes its turn, so that there are always three thousand on guard. Thus it goes until the whole twelve thousand who are styled, as I said, Keshican, have been on duty; and then the tour begins again, and so runs on from year's end to year's end. And when the Great Khan sits at table on any great court occasion, it is in this fashion. His table is elevated a good deal above the others and he sits at the north end of the hall, looking towards the south, with his chief wife beside him on the left. On his right sit his sons and his nephews and other kinsmen of the Blood Imperial, but lower, so that their heads are on a level with the Emperor's feet. And then the other barons sit at other tables lower still. So also with the women; for all the wives of the Lord's sons, and of his nephews and other kinsmen, sit at the lower table to his right, and below them again the ladies of the other barons and knights, each in the place assigned by the Lord's orders. The tables are so disposed that the Emperor can see the whole of them from end to end, many as they are. Further, you are not to suppose that everybody sits at table; on the contrary, the greater part of the soldiers and their officers sit at their meal in the hall on the carpets. Outside the hall will be found more than forty thousand people; for there is a great concourse of folk bringing presents to the Lord, or come from foreign countries with curiosities.

In a certain part of the hall near where the Great Khan holds his table, there is set a large and very beautiful piece of workmanship in the form of a square coffer, or buffet, about three paces each way, exquisitely wrought with figures of animals, finely carved and gilt. The middle is hollow and in it stands a great vessel of pure gold, holding as much as an ordinary butt; and at each corner of the great vessel is one of smaller size of the capacity of a firkin, and from the former the wine or beverage flavored with fine and costly spices is drawn off into the latter. And on the buffet aforesaid are set all the Lord's drinking vessels, among which are certain pitchers of the finest gold, which are called verniques and are big enough to hold drink for eight or ten persons. And one of these is put between every two persons, besides a couple of gold cups with handles, so that every man helps himself from the pitcher that stands between him and his neighbor. And the ladies are supplied in the same way. The value of these pitchers and cups is something immense; in fact, the Great Khan has such a quantity of this kind of plate, and of gold and silver in other shapes as no one ever before saw or heard tell of or could believe.

There are certain barons specially deputed to see that

foreigners, who do not know the customs of the court, are provided with places suited to their rank; and these barons are continually moving to and fro in the hall, looking to the wants of the guests at table, and causing the servants to supply them promptly with wine, milk, meat, or whatever they lack. At every door of the hall (or, indeed, wherever the Emperor may be) there stand a couple of big men like giants, one on each side, armed with staves. Their business is to see that no one steps upon the threshold in entering, and if this does happen, they strip the offender of his clothes, and he must pay a forfeit to have them back again; or in lieu of taking his clothes, they give him a certain number of blows. If they are foreigners ignorant of the order, then there are barons appointed to introduce them and explain it to them. They think, in fact, that it brings bad luck if any one touches the threshold. Howbeit, they are not expected to stick at this in going forth again, for at that time some are like to be worse for liquor and incapable of looking to their steps.

And you must know that those who wait upon the Great Khan with his dishes and drink are some of the great barons. They have the mouth and nose muffled with fine napkins of silk and gold, so the no breath nor odor from their persons should taint the dish or the goblet presented to the Lord. And when the Emperor is going to drink, all the musical instruments, of which he has vast store of every kind, begin to play. And when he takes the cup all the barons and the rest of the company drop on their knees and make the deepest obeisance before him, and then the Emperor doth drink. But each time that he does so the whole ceremony is repeated.

I will say naught about the dishes, as you may easily conceive that there is a great plenty of every possible kind. But you should know that in every case where a baron or knight dines at those tables, their wives also dine there with the other ladies. And when all have dined and the tables have been removed, then come in a great number of players and jugglers, adepts at all sorts of wonderful feats, and perform before the Emperor and the rest of the company, creating great diversion and mirth, so that everyone is full of laughter and enjoyment. And when the performance is over, the company breaks up and everyone goes to his quarters.

You must know that the Tartars keep high festival yearly on their birthdays. And the Great Khan was born on the 28th day of the

September moon, so that on that day is held the greatest feast of the year at the Khan's Court, always excepting that which he holds on New Year's day.

Now, on his birthday, the Great Khan, dresses in the best of his robes, all wrought with beaten gold, and full twelve thousand barons and knights on that day come forth dressed in robes of the same color, and precisely like those of the Great Khan, except that they are not so costly, but still they are all of the same color as his, and are also of silk and gold. Every man so clothed has also a girdle of gold, and this, as well as the dress, is given him by the sovereign. And I will aver that there are some of those suits decked with so many pearls and precious stones that a single suite shall be worth full ten thousand gold bezants.

And of such raiment there are several sets. For you must know that the Great Khan, thirteen times in the year, presents to his barons and knights such suits of raiment as I am speaking of. And on each occasion they wear the same color that he does, a different color being assigned to each festival. Hence you may see what a huge business it is, and that there is no prince in the world but he alone who could keep up such customs as these.

On his birthday also, all the Tartars in the world, and all the countries and governments that owe allegiance to the Khan, offer him great presents according to their several ability, and as prescription or orders have fixed the amount. And many other persons also come with great presents to the Khan, in order to beg for some employment from him. And the Great Khan has chosen twelve barons on whom is laid the charge of assigning to each of these suppliants a suitable answer.

On this day likewise all the Idolaters, all the Saracens, and all the Christians and other descriptions of people make great and solemn devotions, with much chanting and lighting of lamps and burning of incense, each to the God whom he doth worship, praying that He would save the Emperor, and grant him long life and health and happiness.

And thus, as I have related, is celebrated the joyous feast of the Khan's birthday.

The three months of December, January, and February, during which the Emperor resides at his capital city, are assigned for hunting and fowling, to the extent of some forty days' journey round the city and it is ordained that the larger game taken be sent to the Court. To be more particular: of all the larger beasts of the chase, such as boars, roebucks, bucks, stags, lions, bears, &c., the greater part of what is taken has to be sent, and feathered game likewise. The animals are gutted and despatched to the Court on carts. This is done by all the people within twenty or thirty days' journey, and the quantity so despatched is immense. Those at a greater distance cannot send the game, but they have to send the skins after tanning them, and these are employed in the making of equipments for the Emperor's army.

The Emperor hath numbers of leopards trained to the chase, and hath also a great many lynxes taught in like manner to catch game, and which afford excellent sport. He hath also several great lions, bigger than those of Babylonia, beasts whose skins are colored in the most beautiful way, being striped all along the sides with black, red, and white. These are trained to catch boars and wild cattle, bears, wild asses, stags, and other great or fierce beasts. And 'tis a rare sight, I can tell you, to see those lions giving chase to such beasts as I have mentioned! When they are to be so employed the lions are taken out in a covered cart, and every lion has a little doggie with him. They are obliged to approach the game against the wind, otherwise the animals would scent the approach of the lion and be off.

There are also a great number of eagles, all broken to catch wolves, foxes, deer, and wild goats, and they do catch them in great numbers. But those especially that are trained to wolf-catching are very large and powerful birds, and no wolf is able to get away from them.

After he has stopped at his capital city those three months that I mentioned, to wit, December, January, February, he starts off on the 1st day of March, and travels southward towards the Ocean Sea, a journey of two days. He takes with him full ten thousand falconers and some five hundred gerfalcons besides peregrines, sakers, and other hawks in great numbers, and goshawks also to fly at the water-fowl. But do not suppose that he keeps all these together by him; they are distributed about, hither and thither, one hundred together, or two hundred at the upmost, as he thinks proper. But they are always fowling as they advance and the most part of the quarry taken is carried to the Emperor. And let me tell you when he goes thus afowling with his gerfalcons and other hawks, he is attended by full ten thousand men who are disposed in couples and these are called Toscaol, which is as much as to say, "Watchers." And the name describes their business. They are posted from spot to spot, always in couples, and thus they cover a great deal of ground! Every man of them is provided with a whistle and hood, so as to be able to call in a hawk and hold it in hand. And when the Emperor makes a cast, there is no need that he follow it up, for those men I speak of keep so good a lookout that they never lose sight of the birds, and if these have need of help they are ready to render it.

All the Emperor's hawks, and those of the barons as well, have a little label attached to the leg to mark them, on which is written the names of the owner and the keeper of the bird. And in this way the hawk, when caught, is at once identified and handed over to its owner. But if not, the bird is carried to a certain baron who is styled the Bularguchi, which is as much as to say "The Keeper of Lost Property." And I tell you that whatever may be found without a known owner, whether it be a horse, or a sword, or a hawk, or what not, it is carried to that baron straightway and he takes charge of it. And if the finder neglects to carry his trover to the baron, the latter punishes him. Likewise the loser of any article goes to the baron, and if the thing be in his hands it is immediately given up to the owner. Moreover, the said baron, always pitches on the highest spot of the camp, with his banner displayed, in order that those who have lost or found anything may have no difficulty in finding their way to him. Thus nothing can be lost but it shall be incontinently found and restored.

And so the Emperor follows this road that I have mentioned, leading along in the vicinity of the Ocean Sea, which is within two days' journey of his capital city Cambaluc, and as he goes there is many a fine sight to be seen, and plenty of the very best entertainment in hawking; in fact, there is no sport in the world equal it!

The Emperor himself is carried upon four elephants in a fine chamber made of timber, lined inside with plates of beaten gold, and outside with lions' skins, for he always travels in this way on his fowling expeditions because he is troubled with gout. He always keeps beside him a dozen of his choicest gerfalcons and is attended by several of his barons who ride on horseback alongside. And sometimes, as they may be going along, and the Emperor from his chamber is holding discourse with the barons, one of the latter shall exclaim, "Sire! Look out for cranes!" Then the Emperor instantly has the top of his chamber thrown open, and having marked the cranes he casts one of his gerfalcons, whichever he pleases, and often the quarry is struck within his view, so that he has the most exquisite sport and the barons with him get the enjoyment of it likewise! So it is not without reason that I tell you that I do not believe there ever existed in the world or ever will exist, a man with such sport and enjoyment as he has, or with such rare opporunties.

And when he has travelled till he reaches a place called Cachar Modun, there he finds his tents pitched, with the tents of his sons, and his barons, and those of his ladies and theirs, so that there shall be full ten thousand tents in all, and all fine and rich ones. And I will tell you how his own quarters are disposed. The tent in which he holds his courts is large enough to give cover easily to a thousand souls. It is pitched with its door to the south, and the barons and knights remain in waiting in it, whilst the Lord abides in another close to it on the west side. When he wishes to speak with any one he causes the person to be summoned to that other tent. Immediately, behind the great tent there is a fine large chamber where the Lord sleeps; and there are also many other tents and chambers, but they are not in contact with the Great Tent as these are. The two audience-tents and the sleeping-chamber are constructed in this way. Each of the audience-tents has three poles, which are of spice-wood, and are most artfully covered with lions' skins, striped with black and white and red, so that they do not suffer from any weather. All three apartments are also covered outside with similar skins of striped lions, a substance that lasts for ever. And inside they are all lined with ermine and sable, these two being the finest and most costly furs in existence. For a robe of sable, large enough to line a mantle, is worth two thousand bezants of gold, or one thousand at least, and this kind of skin is called by the Tartars "the king of furs." The beast itself is about the size of a marten. These two furs of which I speak are applied and inlaid so exquisitely that it is really something worth seeing. All the tent-ropes are of silk. And in short I may say that those tents with the two audience-halls and the sleeping-chamber, are so costly that it is not every king could pay for them.

Round about these tents are others, also fine ones and beautifully pitched, in which are the Emperor's ladies and the ladies of the other princes and officers. And then there are the tents for the hawks and their keepers, so that altogether the number of tents there on the plain is something wonderful. To see the many people that are thronging to and fro on every side and every day there, you would take the camp for a good big city. For you much reckon the leeches, and the astrologers, and the falconers, and all the other attendants on so great a company, and add that everybody there has his whole family with him, for such is their custom.

The Lord remains encamped there until the spring, and all that time he does nothing but go hawking round about among the cranebrakes along the lakes and rivers that abound in that region and across fine plains on which are plenty of cranes and swans, and all sorts of other fowl. The other gentry of the camp also are never done with hunting and hawking, and every day they bring home great store of venison and feathered game of all sorts. Indeed, without having witnessed it, you would never believe what quantities of game are taken, and what marvelous sport and diversion they all have whilst they are in camp there.

There is another thing I should mention; to wit, that for twenty days' journey round the spot nobody is allowed, be he who he may, to keep hawks or hounds, though anywhere else whosoever list may keep them. And furthermore throughout all the Emperor's territories, nobody however audacious dares to hunt any of these four animals, to wit, hare, stag, buck, and roe, from the month of March to the month of October. Anybody who should do so would rue it bitterly. But those people are so obedient to their Lord's commands that even if a man where to find one of these animals asleep by the roadside he would not touch it for the world! And thus the game multiplies at such a rate that the whole country swarms with it and the Emperor gets as much as he would desire. Beyond the term I have mentioned, however, to wit that from March to October, everybody may take these animals as he list.

You must know that the City of Cambaluc hath such a multitude of houses and such a vast population inside the walls and outside that it seems quite past all possibility. There is a suburb outside each of the gates, which are twelve in number and these suburbs are so great that they contain more people than the city itself, for the suburb of one gate spreads in width till it meets the suburb of the next, whilst they extend in length some three or four miles. In those suburbs lodge the foreign merchants and travellers, of whom there are always great numbers who have come to bring presents to the Emperor or to sell articles at Court, or because the city affords so good a market to attract traders. There are in each of the suburbs, to a distance of a mile from the city, numerous fine hostelries for the lodgment of merchants from different parts of the world, and a special hostelry is assigned to each description of people, as if we should say there is one for the Lombards, another for the Germans, and a third for the Frenchmen. And thus there are as many good houses outside of the city as inside, without counting those that belong to the great lords and barons, which are very numerous.

You must know that it is forbidden to bury any dead body inside the city. If the body be that of an Idolater it is carried out beyond the city and suburbs to a remote place assigned for the purpose, to be burnt. And if it be of one belonging to a religion the custom of which is to bury, such as the Christian, the Saracen, or what not, it is also carried out beyond the suburbs to a distant place assigned for the purpose. And thus the city is preserved in a better and more healthy state.

Guards patrol the city every night in parties of thirty or forty, looking out for any persons who may be abroad at unseasonable hours, i.e. after the great bell hath stricken thrice. If they find any such person he is immediately taken to prison, and examined next morning by proper officers. If these find him guilty of any misdemeanor they order him a proportionate beating with the stick. Under this punishment people sometimes die, but they adopt it in order to eschew bloodshed, for their Bacsis[1] say that it is an evil thing to shed man's blood.

To this city also are brought articles of greater cost and rarity and in greater abundance of all kinds than to any other city in the

---

[1] The custom of the Tartars was said to have prohibited the spilling of blood. This was accomplished through different modes of death, including beating, boiling, and breaking the back.

world. For people of every description and from every region bring things (including all the costly wares of India, as well as the fine and precious goods of Cathay itself with its provinces), some for the sovereign, some for the court, some for the city which is so great, some for the crowds of barons and knights, some for the great hosts of the Emperor which are quartered round about, thus between court and city the quantity brought in is endless.

As a sample, I tell you, no day in the year passes that there do not enter the city a thousand cart-loads of silk alone, from which are made quantities of cloth of silk and gold, and of other goods. And this is not to be wondered at; for in all the countries round about there is no flax, so that everything is to be made of silk. It is true, indeed, that in some parts of the country there is cotton and hemp, but not sufficient for their wants. This, however, is not of much consequence, because silk is so abundant and cheap, and it is a more valuable substance than either flax or cotton.

Round abut this great city of Cambaluc there are some two hundred other cities at various distances, from which traders come to sell their goods and buy others for their lords, and all find means to make their sales and purchases, so that the traffic of the city is passing great.

Now that I have told you in detail of the splendor of this city of the Emperor's, I shall proceed to tell you of the Mint which he hath in the same city, in the which he hath his money coined and struck, as I shall relate to you. And in doing so I shall make manifest to you how it is that the Great Lord may well be able to accomplish even much more than I have told you, or am going to tell you, in this book. For, tell it how I might, you never would be satisfied that I was keeping within truth and reason!

The Emperor's Mint then is in this same City of Cambaluc, and the way it is wrought is such that you might say he hath the secret of alchemy in perfection, and you would be right! For he makes his money after this fashion.

He makes them take the bark of a certain tree, in fact of the mulberry tree, the leaves of which are the food of the silkworms—these trees being so numerous that whole districts are full of them. What they take is a certain fine white bast or skin which lies between the wood of the tree and the thick outer bark, and this they make into something resembling sheets of paper, but black. When these sheets have been prepared they are cut up into pieces of different sizes. The smallest of these sizes is worth a half tornesel, the next, a little larger, one tornesel, one, a little larger still is worth half a silver groat of Venice, another a whole groat, others yet two groats, five groats, or ten groats. There is also a kind worth one bezant of gold and others of three bezants, and so up to ten. All these pieces of paper are issued with as much solemnity and authority as if they were of pure gold or silver; and on every piece a variety of officials, whose duty it is, have to write their names and put their seals. And when all is prepared duly, the chief officer deputed by the Khan smears the Seal entrusted to him with vermilion and impresses it on the paper so that the form of the Seal remains printed upon it in red; the money is then authentic. Any one forging it would be punished with death. And the Khan causes every year to be made such a vast quantity of this money, which costs him nothing, that it must equal in amount all the treasure in the world.

With these pieces of paper, made as I have described, he causes all payments on his own account to be made. And he makes them to pass current universally over all his kingdoms and provinces and territories, and whithersoever his power and sovereignty extends. And nobody, however important he may think himself, dares to refuse them on pain of death. And indeed everybody takes them readily, for wheresoever a person may go throughout the Great Khan's dominions he shall find these pieces of paper current, and shall be able to transact all sales and purchases of goods by means of them just as well as if they were coins of pure gold. And all the while they are so light that ten bezants' worth does not weigh one gold bezant.

Furthermore all merchants arriving from India or other countries, and bringing with them gold or silver or gems or pearls, are prohibited from selling to anyone but the Emperor. He has twelve experts chosen for this business, men of shrewdness and experience in such affairs; these appraise the articles and the Emperor then pays a liberal price for them in those pieces of paper. The merchants accept his price readily, for in the first place they would not get so good an one from anybody else, and secondly they are paid without delay. And with this paper-money they can buy what they like anywhere over the Empire, whilst it is also vastly lighter to carry about on their journeys. And it is a truth that merchants will several times in the year bring wares to the amount of 400,000 bezants, and the Grand Sire pays for all in that paper. So he buys such a quantity of those precious things every year that his treasure is endless, whilst all the time the money he pays away costs him nothing at all. Moreover several times in the year proclamation is made through the city that anyone who may have gold or silver or gems or pearls, by taking them to the Mint shall get a handsome price for them. And the owners are glad to do this, because they would find no other purchaser to give so large a price. Thus the quantity they bring in is marvelous, though those who do not choose to do so may let it alone. Still, in this way, nearly all the valuables in the country come into the Khan's possession.

When any of those pieces of paper are spoilt–not that they are so very flimsy neither–the owner carries them to the Mint, and by paying three per cent on the value he gets new pieces in exchange. And if any baron, or any one else soever, hath need of gold or silver or gems or pearls in order to make plate or girdles or the like, he goes to the Mint and buys as much as he list, paying in this paper-money.

Now you must know that from this City of Cambaluc proceed many roads and highways leading to a variety of provinces, one to one province, another to another; and each road receives the name of the province to which it leads, and it is a very sensible plan. And the messengers of the Emperor in travelling from Cambaluc, be the road whichsoever they will, find at every twenty-five miles of the journey a station which they call Yamb, or, as we should say, the "Horse-Post-House." And at each of those stations used by the messengers there is a large and handsome building for them to put up at, in which they find all the rooms furnished with fine beds and all other necessary articles in rich silk, and where they are provided with everything they can want. If even a king were to arrive at one of these, he would find himself well lodged.

At some of these stations, moreover, there shall be posted some four hundred horses standing ready for the use of the messengers; at others there shall be two hundred, according to the requirements, and to what the Emperor has established in each case. At every twenty-five miles, as I said, or anyhow at every thirty miles, you find one of these stations, on all the principal highways leading to the different provincial governments; and the same is the case throughout all the chief provinces subject to the Great Khan. Even when the messengers have to pass through a roadless tract where neither house nor hostel exists, still there the station-houses have been established just the same, excepting that the intervals are somewhat greater and the day's journey is fixed at thirty-five to forty-five miles instead of twenty-five to thirty. But they are provided with horses and all the other necessaries just like those we have described, so that the Emperor's messengers, come they from what region they may, find everything ready for them.

And in sooth this is a thing done on the greatest scale of magnificence that ever was seen. Never had emperor, king, or lord, such wealth as this manifests! For it is a fact that on all these posts taken together there are more than 300,000 horses kept up, specially for the use of the messengers. And the great buildings that I have mentioned are more than 10,000 in number, all richly furnished as I told you. The thing is on a scale so wonderful and costly that it is hard to bring oneself to describe it.

But now I will tell you another thing that I had forgotten, but which ought to be told whilst I am on this subject. You must know that by the Great Khan's orders there has been established between those post-houses, at every interval of three miles, a little fort with some forty houses round about it, in which dwell the people who act as the Emperor's foot runners. Every one of those runners wears a great wide belt, set all over with bells, so that as they run the three miles from post to post their bells are heard jingling a long way off. And thus in reaching the post the runner finds another man similarly equipt, and all ready to take his place, who instantly takes over whatsoever he has in charge, and with it receives a slip of paper from the clerk who is always at hand for the purpose; and so the new man sets off and runs his three miles. At the next station he finds his relief ready in like manner; and so the post proceeds, with a change at every three miles. And in this way the Emperor, who has an immense number of these runners, receives dispatches with news from places ten days' journey off in one day and night; or if need be, news from a hundreds days off in ten days and nights; and that is no small matter! In fact in the fruit season many a time fruit shall be gathered one morning in Cabaluc, and the evening of the next day it shall reach the Great Khan at

Chandu, a distance of ten days' journey. The clerk at each of the posts notes the time of each courier's arrival and departure; and there are often other officers whose business it is to make monthly visitations of all the posts, and to punish those runners who have been slack in their work. The emperor exempts these men from all tribute, and pays them besides.

Moreover, there are also at the stations other men equipt similarly with girdles hung with bells, who are employed for expresses when there is a call for great haste in sending dispatches to any governor of a province, or to give news when any baron has revolted, or in other such emergencies, and these men travel a good two hundred or two hundred and fifty miles in the day, and as much in the night. I'll tell you how it stands. They take a horse from those at the station which are standing ready saddled, all fresh and in wind, and mount and go at full speed, as hard as they can ride in fact. And when those at the next post hear the bells they get another horse and a man equipt in the same way, and he takes over the letter or whatever it be, and is off full-speed to the third station, where again a fresh horse is found all ready, and so the dispatch speeds along from post to post, always at full gallop with regular change of horses. And the speed at which they go is marvelous. By night, however, they cannot go so fast as by day, because they have to be accompanied by footmen with torches, who could not keep up with them at full speed.

Those men are highly prized; and they could never do it did they not bind hard the stomach, chest, and head with strong bands. And each of them carries with him a gerfalcon tablet, in sight that he is on an urgent express; so that if perchance his horse break down, or he meet with other mishap, whomsoever he may fall in with on the road, he is empowered to make him dismount and give up his horse. Nobody dares refuse in such a case; so that the courier hath always a good fresh nag to carry him.

Now all these numbers of post-horses cost the Emperor nothing at all; and I will tell you the how and the why. Every city, or village, or hamlet that stands near one of those post-stations has a fixed demand made on it for as many horses as it can supply, and these it must furnish to the post. And in this way are provided all the posts of the cities, as well as the towns and villages round about them; only in uninhabited tracts the horses are furnished at the expense of the Emperor himself.

It is a fact that all over the country of Cathay there is a kind of black stones existing in beds in the mountains, which they dig out and burn like firewood. If you supply the fire with them at night, and see that they are well kindled, you will find them still alight in the morning; and they make such capital fuel that no other is used throughout the country. It is true that they have plenty of wood also, but they do not burn it because those stones burn better and cost less.

Moreover with that vast number of people, and the number of hot-baths that they maintain–for every one has such a bath at least three times a week, and in winter if possible every day, whilst every nobleman and man of wealth has a private bath for his own use–the wood would not suffice for the purpose.

You must also know that when the Emperor sees that corn is cheap and abundant, he buys up large quantities, and has it stored in all his provinces in great granaries, where it is so well looked after that it will keep for three or four years.

And this applies, let me tell you, to all kinds of corn, whether wheat, barley, millet, rice, or what not, and when there is any scarcity of a particular kind of corn he causes that to be issued. And if the price of corn is at one bezant the measure, he lets them have it at a bezant for four measures, or at whatever price will produce general cheapness, and every one can have food in this way. And by this providence of the Emperor's his people can never suffer from dearth. He does the same over his whole Empire causing these supplies to be stored everywhere according to the calculation of the wants and necessities of the people.

LATE LATIN LITERATURE

Vespers on Corpus Christi
by Saint Thomas Aquinas (1227-1274)
translated by Edward Caswell

Pange lingua gloriosi
Corporis mysterium
Sanguinisque pretiosi,
Quem in mundi pretium
Fructus ventris generosi
Rex Effudit gentium.

Sing, my tongue, the Savior's glory,
Of his Flesh the mystery sing;
Of the Blood, all price exceeding,
Shed by our immortal King,
Destined, for the world's redemption
From a noble womb to spring.

Of a pure and spotless Virgin
Born for us on earth below,
He, as Man, with man conversing,
Stayed, the seeds of truth to sow;
Then He closed in solemn order
Wondrously His life of woe.

On the night of that Last Supper
Seated with His chosen band,
He, the Paschal victim eating,
First fulfills the Law's command;
Then as Food to all His brethren
Gives Himself with his own hand.

Word made Flesh, the bread of nature
By His word to Flesh He turns;
Wine into His blood He changes;
What though sense no change discerns?

Only be the heart in earnest,
Faith her lesson quickly learns.

Down in adoration falling,
Lo! the sacred Host we hail;
Lo! o'er ancient forms departing,
Newer rites of grace prevail;
Faith for all defects supplying,
Where the feeble senses fail.

To the everlasting Father,
And the Son who reigns on high,
With the Holy Ghost proceeding
Forth from Each eternally,
Be salvation, honor, blessing,
Might, and endless majesty.

The Song of the Creatures
Saint Francis of Assisi (1182-1226)
translated by Matthew Arnold

Most high, all powerful, all good Lord!
All praise is Yours, all glory, all honor, and all blessing.
To You, alone, Most High, do they belong.
No mortal lips are worthy to pronounce Your name.
Be praised, my Lord, through all Your creatures,
especially through my lord Brother Sun,
who brings the day; and You give light through him.
And he is beautiful and radiant in all his splendor!
Of You, Most High, he bears the likeness.
Be praised, my Lord, through Sister Moon and the stars;
in the heavens You have made them bright, precious and beautiful.
Be praised, my Lord, through Brothers Wind and Air,
and clouds and storms, and all the weather,
through which You give Your creatures sustenance.
Be praised, my Lord, through Sister Water;
she is very useful, and humble, and precious, and pure.
Be praised, my Lord, through Brother Fire,
through whom You brighten the night.
He is beautiful and cheerful, and powerful and strong.
Be praised, my Lord, through our sister Mother Earth,
who feeds us and rules us,
and produces various fruits with colored flowers and herbs.
Be praised, my Lord, through those who forgive for love of You;
through those who endure sickness and trial.
Happy those who endure in peace,
for by You, Most High, they will be crowned.
Be praised, my Lord, through our sister Bodily Death,
from whose embrace no living person can escape.
Woe to those who die in mortal sin!
Happy those she finds doing Your most holy will.
The second death can do no harm to them.
Praise and bless my Lord, and give thanks,
and serve Him with great humility.

DANTE

The Divine Comedy, selections from "Hell"
by Dante Alighieri (1265-1321)
translated by Charles Eliot Norton

CANTO I:
Dante, astray in a wood, reaches the foot of a hill which he begins to ascend; he is hindered by three beasts, he turns back and is met by Virgil, who proposes to guide him into the eternal world.

Midway upon the journey of my life I found myself in a dark wood, where the right way was lost.[1] Ah! How hard a thing it is to tell what this wild and rough and difficult wood was, which in thought renews my fear! So bitter is it that death is little more. But in order to treat of the good that I found in it, I will tell of the other things that I saw there.

I cannot well report how I entered it, so full was I of slumber at the moment when I abandoned the true way. But after I had reached the foot of a hill, where that valley ended which had pierced my heart with fear, I looked upward, and saw its shoulders clothed already with the rays of the planet which leads man aright along every path. Then was the fear a little quieted which had lasted in the lake of my heart through the night that I had passed so piteously. And even as one, who with spent breath, issued forth from the sea upon the shore, turns to the perilous water and gazes, so did my mind, which still was flying, turn back to look again upon the pass which never left person alive.

After I had rested a little my weary body, I again took my way along the desert slope, so that the firm foot was always lower. And lo! almost at the beginning of the steep was a she-leopard,[2] light and very nimble, which was covered with a spotted coat. And she did not withdraw from before my face, nay, hindered so my road that I often turned to go back.

The time was beginning of the morning, and the Sun was

---

[1] The action begins on the night before Good Friday, 1300. Dante was thirty-five years old.

[2] Symbolizing sensual pleasure.

mounting up with those stars that were with him when Love Divine first set in motion those beautiful things[3] so that the hour of the time and the sweet season were occasion to me of good hope concerning that wild beast with the dappled skin. But not so that the sight which appeared to me of a lion[4] did not give me fear. He appeared to be coming against me, with his head high and with ravening hunger, so that it appeared that the air itself was affrighted at him. And a she-wolf,[5] which in her leanness seemed laden with all cravings, and ere now had made many folk to live forlorn. She brought on me so much heaviness, with the fear that came from the sight of her, that I lost hope of gaining the top of the mountain. And such as is he who gains willingly, and the time arrives which makes him lose, so that in all his thoughts he laments and is sad, such did the beast without peace make me, which, coming on against me, was pushing me back, little by little, thither where the Sun is silent.

While I was falling back to the low place, one who appeared faint-voiced through long silence presented himself before my eyes. When I saw him in the great desert, "Have pity on me!" I cried to him, "whatso thou be, whether shade or real man." He answered me, "Not man; man once I was, and my parents were Lombards, and both Mantuans by country. I was born *sub Julio*, though late,[6] and I lived at Rome under the good Augustus, at the time of the false and lying gods. I was a poet and sang of that just son of Anchises[7] who came from Troy after proud Ilion had been burned. But thou, why dost thou return to such great annoy? Why dost thou not ascend the delectable mountain which is the source and cause of all joy?"

"Art thou then that Virgil and that fount which pours fourth so

---

[3] It was a common belief that the spring was the season of the Creation and that on March 25, the vernal equinox, the Sun was created and placed in Aries, to begin his course.

[4] Symbolizing pride.

[5] Symbolizing avarice or greed. See Jeremiah 5:6. These three beasts correspond with the triple division of sins into those of incontinence, of violence, and of fraud which Virgil makes in the eleventh canto, according to which the sinners in Hell are divided into three main classes.

[6] Virgil was twenty-five years old at the time of Caesar's death, 44 BC.

[7] Anchises' son is Aeneas, the hero of Virgil's *Aeneid.*

broad a stream of speech?" replied I with bashful front to him, "O honor and light of the other poets! May the long study avail me and the great love, which has made me search thy volume! Thou art my master and my author. Thou alone art he from whom I took the fair style that has done me honor. Behold the beast because of which I turned; help me against her, famous sage, for she makes my veins and pulses tremble."

"It behoves thee to hold another course," he replied, when he saw me weeping, "if thou wouldst escape from this savage place, for this beast, because of which thou criest out, lets not any one pass along her way, but so hinders him that she kills him. She has a nature so malign and evil that she never sates her greedy will, and after food has more hunger than before. Many are the animals with which she wives, and there shall be more yet, until the hound shall come that will make her die of grief. He shall not feed on land or pelf, but wisdom and love and valor, and his birthplace shall be between Feltro and Feltor. Of that low Italy shall he be the salvation, for which the virgin Camilla died, and Euryalus, and Turnus and Nisus of their wounds. He shall hunt her through every town till he shall have put her back again in Hell, there whence envy first sent her forth. Wherefore I think and deem it for thy best that thou follow me, and I will be thy guide,[8] and will lead thee hence through the eternal place where thou shalt hear the despairing shrieks, shalt see the ancient spirits woeful who each proclaim the second death.[9] And then thou shalt see those who are contented in the fire, because they hope to come, whenever it may be, to the blessed folk; to whom if thou wouldst ascend, there shall be a soul more worthy than I for that. With her I will leave thee at my departure; for that Emperor who reigns there above wills not, because I was rebellious[10] to His law, that through me any one should come into His city and His lofty seat. O happy the man who hereto He elects!" And I said to him, "Poet, I beseech thee that by God whom thou didst not know, in order that I escape this ill and worse, that thou lead me thither where thou now hast said so that I

---

[8] Here Virgil explains that he will be guiding Dante through Hell and Purgatory until they meet with another guide who is worthy of taking Dante through Paradise.

[9] Virgil speaks of Hell here. See Revelation 20:10, 14.

[10] See *Hell*, Canto IV.

may see the gate of St. Peter and those who thou reportest so afflicted."

Then he moved on, and I held behind him.

CANTO II:

Dante, doubtful of his own powers, is discouraged at the outset.
Virgil cheers him by telling him he has been sent to his aid by a
blessed Spirit from Heaven, who revealed herself as Beatrice.
Dante casts off fear, and the poets proceed.

The day was going and the dusky air was taking the living things that are on earth from their fatigues and I alone was preparing to sustain the war alike of the journey and of the woe, which my memory that errs not shall retrace.

O Muses! O lofty genius! Assist me. Oh memory that didst inscribe that which I saw, here shall thy nobility appear!

I began, "Poet, who guidest me, consider my power, if it be sufficient, before thou trust me to the deep pass. Thou sayest[1] that the parent of Silvius while still corruptible went to the immortal world and was there in the body and truly if the Adversary of every ill was courteous to him it seems not unmeet to the man of understanding, thinking on the high effect that should proceed from him, and on the who and the what, for in the empyrean heaven he was chosen for father of revered Rome and of her empire, both which (would one say truth) were ordained for the holy place where the successor of the greater Peter has his seat. Through this going, whereof thou givest him vaunt, he learned things which were the cause of his victory and of the papal mantle. Afterward the Chosen Vessel[2] went thither to bring thence comfort to that faith which is the beginning of the way of salvation. But I, why go I thither? And who grants it? I am not Aeneas, I am not Paul, neither I nor others believe me worthy of this. Wherefore if I yield myself to go, I fear lest the going may be mad. Thou art wise, thou understandest better than I speak."

And as is he who unwills what he willed and by reason of new thoughts changes his purpose so that he withdraws wholly from what he has begun, such I became on that dark hillside because in my thought I abandoned the enterprise which had been so hasty from its beginning.

"If I have rightly understood thy speech," replied that shade of

---

[1] This story appears in Virgil's *Aeneid*, vi.
[2] Saint Paul (Acts 9:15 and Corinthians 12:1-4).

the magnanimous one, "thy soul is hurt by cowardice which often encumbers a man so that it turns him back from honorable enterprise, as false seeing does a beast when it shies. In order that I loose thee from this fear I will tell thee why I came and what I heard at the first moment that I grieved for thee. I was among those who are suspended[3] and a Lady blessed and beautiful called me, such that I besought her command. Her eyes were more shining than the star and she began to say to me sweet and clear, with angelic voice, in her speech, 'O courteous Manutan soul of whom fame yet lasts in the world, and shall last so long as motion continues, my friend is so hindered on his road upon the desert hillside that he has turned for fear and I am afraid, through that which I have heard of him in heaven, lest he be already so astray that I may have risen late to his succor. Now do thou move, and with thy ornate speech and with whatever is needful for his deliverance, assist him so that I may be consoled thereby. I am Beatrice who make thee go. I come from a place whither I desire to return. Love moved me, that makes me speak. When I shall be before my Lord, I will often praise thee to Him.' Then she was silent and thereon I began, 'O Lady of Virtue through whom alone the human race excels all contained within that heaven which has the smallest circles,[4] thy command so pleases me that to obey it, where it already done, were slow to me. There is no need for thee further to open to me thy will, but tell me this reason why thou dost not beware of descending down here into this center, from the ample place[5] whither thou burnest to return.' 'Since thou wishest to know so inwardly, I will tell thee briefly,' she replied to me, 'wherefore I fear not to come here within. One need be afraid only of those things that have power to do one harm, of others not, for they are not fearful. I am made by God, thanks be to Him, such that your misery touches me not, nor does the flame of this burning assail me. A gentle Lady[6] is in heaven who feels compassion for this hindrance whereto I send thee, so that she breaks stern

---

[3] The souls suspended are those held in Limbo, the first Circle of Hell.

[4] The heaven of the moon.

[5] From the Empyrean (highest circle of Heaven) to Limbo (the first circle of Hell).

[6] The Virgin Mary, never spoken of by name in Hell.

judgment there above. She summoned Lucia[7] in her request and said, "Thy faithful one now has need of thee, and I commend him to thee." Lucia, foe of every cruel one, moved and came to the place where I was seated with the ancient Rachel.[8] She said, "Beatrice, true praise of God, why dost thou not succor him who so loved thee that for thee he came forth from the vulgar throng? Dost thou not hear the pity of his plaint? Dost thou not see the death that combats him on the stream where the sea has no vaunt?" Never were persons in the world swift to do their good, or to fly their harm, as I, after these words were uttered, came down here from my blessed seat, putting my trust in thy upright speech, which honors thee and them who have heard it.' After she had said this to me, weeping she turned her lucent eyes, whereby she made me more quick to come. And I came to thee thus as she willed. I withdrew thee from before that wild beast which took from thee the short way on the beautiful mountain. What is it then? Why, why dost thou hold back? Why dost thou harbor such cowardice in thy heart? Why has thou not daring and assurance, since three such blessed Ladies care for thee in the court of Heaven, and my speech pledges thee such good?"

As the flowerets, bent and closed by the chill of night, when the sun brightens them erect themselves all open on their stem, so I became with my dropping courage, and such good daring ran to my heart that I began like a person enfreed. "Oh compassionate she who succored me, and courteous thou who didst speedily obey the true words that she addressed to thee! Thou by thy words hast so disposed my heart with desire of going, that I have returned to my first intent. Now go, for one single will is in us both: thou leader, thou lord, and thou master." Thus I said to him and when he moved on I entered along the deep and savage road.

---

[7] Symbolizing Illuminating Grace
[8] Symbolizing the Contemplative Life.

CANTO III:

*The gate of Hell. Virgil leads Dante in. The punishment of those
who had lived without infamy and without praise. Acheron, and the
sinners on the bank. Charon. Earthquake. Dante swoons.*

I AM THE WAY INTO THE WOEFUL CITY,[1]
I AM THE WAY INTO ETERNAL GRIEF,
I AM THE WAY TO A FORSAKEN RACE.

JUSTICE IT WAS THAT MOVED MY GREAT CREATOR;
DIVINE OMNIPOTENCE CREATED ME,
AND HIGHEST WISDOM JOINED WITH PRIMAL LOVE.

BEFORE ME NOTHING BUT ETERNAL THINGS
WERE MADE, AND I SHALL LAST ETERNALLY.
ABANDON EVERY HOPE, ALL YOU WHO ENTER.

These words of obscure color I saw written at the top of a gate
whereat I said, "Master their meaning is dire to me."

And he to me, like a person well advised, "Here it behoves to
leave every fear, it behoves that all cowardice should here be dead.
We have come to the place where I have told thee that thou shalt
see the woeful people, who have lost the good of the under-
standing."

And when he had put his hand on mine with a cheerful look,
wherefrom I took courage, he brought me within to the secret
things. Here sighs, laments, and deep wailings were resounding
through the starless air, wherefore at first I wept thereat. Strange
tongues, horrible utterances, words of woe, accents of anger,
voices high and faint, and sounds of hands with them, were making
a tumult which whirls always in that air forever dark, like the sand
when the whirlwind breathes.

And I, who had my head girt with horror, said, "Master, what
is that which I hear? And what folk is it that seems so overcome
with its woe?"

And he to me, "The wretched souls of those who lived without

---

[1] Within Hell you will notice a particular lack of grace. The souls inhabiting the
dreadful region are shown no mercy and they do not show mercy to anyone else.

195

infamy and without praise maintain this miserable mode. They are mingled with that caitiff choir of the angels, who were not rebels, nor were faithful to God, but were for themselves. The heavens chased them out in order to be not less beautiful, nor does the deep Hell receive them, for the damned would have some boast of them." And I, "Master, what is so grievous to them, that makes them lament so bitterly?" He answered, "I will tell thee very briefly. These have not hope of death, and their blind life is so debased that they are envious of every other lot. Fame of them the world permits not to be, mercy and justice disdain them. Let us not speak of them, but do thou look and pass on."

And I, who was gazing, saw a banner, which, whirling, ran so swiftly that it seemed to me disdainful of any pause, and behind it came so long a train of folk, that I should never have believed death had undone so many. After I had recognized some among them, I saw and knew the shade of him who made, through cowardice, the great refusal.[2] At once I understood and was certain that this was the sect of the caitiffs displeasing to God *and* to his enemies. These wretches, who never were alive, were naked and much stung by gad-flies and by wasps that were there; these streaked their faces with blood which mingled with tears and was gathered at their feet by loathsome worms.[3]

And when I gave myself to looking onward, I saw people on the bank of a great river wherefore I said, "Master, now grant to me that I may know who these are, and what rule makes them appear so ready to pass over, as I discern through the faint light." And he to me, "The things will be clear to thee when we shall stay our steps on the sad shore of Acheron." Then with eyes ashamed and downcast, fearing lest my speech may be troublesome to him,

---

[2] Dante purposely refrains from naming anyone in this group and thereby immortalizing him. This soul is often identified with Pontius Pilate or Pope Celestine V.

[3] Here we see an excellent example of contrapasso, a literary device used by Dante in which he condemns sinners to suffer punishments that are the opposite of their sins. In this circle the sinners lived entirely for themselves and took no thought for anyone else. Since they lived for comfort, they are eternally tortured by gadflies biting them. They spilled blood and shed tears for no cause or person during their living days and thus bleed and cry continually. You will see many more examples of contrapasso throughout *Hell*.

far as to the river I refrained from speaking.

And behold! Coming toward us in a boat, an old man, white with ancient hair, crying, "Woe to you, wicked souls! Hope not ever to see the Heavens! I come to carry you to the other bank, into the eternal darkness, into heat and into frost. And thou who art there, living soul, depart from these that are dead." But when he saw that I did not depart, he said, "By another way, by other ports thou shalt come to the shore, not here, for passage; a lighter bark must carry thee."[4]

And my Leader to him, "Charon, vex not thyself. It is thus willed there where is power for that which is willed. Ask no more." Thereon were quiet the fleecy jaws of the ferryman of the livid marsh, who round about his eyes had wheels of flame.

But those souls, who were weary and naked, changed color and gnashed their teeth soon as they heard his cruel words. They blasphemed God and their parents, the human race, the place, the time and the seed of their sowing and of their birth. Then, all of them bitterly weeping, drew together to the evil bank, which awaits every man who fears not God. Charon the demon, with eyes of glowing coal, beckoning to them, collects them all. He beats with his oar whoever lingers.

As in autumn the leaves depart one after the other until the bough sees all its spoils upon the earth, in likewise the evil seed of Adam throw themselves from that shore one by one, at signals, as the bird at his recall. Thus they go over the dusky wave and before they have landed on the farther side already on this a new throng is assembled.

"My son," said the courteous Master, "those who die in the wrath of God all come together here from every land, and they are eager to pass over the stream for divine justice spurs them so that fear is turned to desire. A good soul never passes this way and therefore if Charon fret thee, well mayest thou now know what his speech signifies."

This ended, the gloomy plain trembles so mightily that the

---

[4] I.e., the boat to Purgatory. Charon recognizes that Dante is not among the damned. Personages of heathen mythology were held by the church to have been demons who had a real existence; they were adopted into the Christian mythology and hence appear with entire propriety as characters in Hell.

memory of the terror even now bathes me with sweat. The tearful land gave forth a wind that flashed a crimson light which vanquished all sensation in me and I fell as a man whom slumber seizes.

CANTO IV:

The further side of Acheron. Virgil leads Dante into Limbo, the First Circle of Hell, containing the spirits of those who lived virtuously but without faith in Christ. Greeting of Virgil by his fellow poets. They enter a castle, were are the shades of ancient worthies. After seeing them Virgil and Dante depart.

A heavy thunder broke the deep sleep in my head, so that I started up like a person who is waked by force, and, risen erect, I moved my rested eye round about and looked fixedly to distinguish the place I was. True it is that I found myself on the brink of the woeful valley of the abyss which collects a thunder of infinite wailings. It was so dark, deep, and cloudy, that though I fixed my sight on the depth, I could not discern anything there.

"Now let us descend here below into the blind world," began the Poet all deadly pale, "I will be first and thou shalt be second."

And I, who had observed his color, said, "How shall I come, if thou fearest, who art wont to be the comfort to my doubting?" And he to me, "The anguish of the folk who are here below paints on my face that pity which thou takest for fear. Let us go on for the long way urges us."

Thus he placed himself¹ and thus he made me enter into the first circle that girds the abyss. Here, as one listened, there was no lamentation but that of sighs which made the eternal air tremble. This came from the woe without torments felt by the crowds, which were many and great, of infants and of women and of men.

The good Master said to me, "Thou dost not ask what spirits are these that thou seest. Now I would have thee know, before thou goest farther, that these did not sin, and though they have merits it suffices not, because they did not have baptism, which is part of the faith that thou believest. And if they were before Christianity they did not duly worship God, and of such as these am I myself. For such defects, and not for other guilt, are we lost, and only so far harmed that without hope we live in desire."

Great woe seized me at the heart when I heard him, because I know that people of much worth were suspended in that limbo. "Tell me, my Master, tell me, Lord," I began, with wish to be

---

¹ In the lead, in front of Dante.

assured of that faith which vanquishes every error, "did ever any one who afterwards was blessed go forth from here, either by his own or by another's merit?" And he, who understood my covert speech, answered, "I was new in this state[2] when I saw a Mighty One come hither crowned with sign of victory.[3] He drew out hence the shade of the first parent, of Abel his son, and that of Noah, of Moses the law-giver and obedient, Abraham the patriarch, and David the King, Israel with his father and with his offspring, and with Rachel, for whom he did so much, and many others. He made them blessed. And I would have thee know that before these, human spirits were not saved."

We ceased not going on because he spoke but all the while were passing through the wood, the wood, I mean of crowded spirits; nor yet had our way been long from the place of my slumber, when I saw a fire which overcame a hemisphere of darkness. We were still a little distant from it, yet not so far but that I could in part discern that honorable folk possessed that place. "O thou who honorest both science and art, who are these who have such honor that it separates them from the manner of the others?" And he to me, "The honorable renown of them which sounds above in thy life wins grace in heaven which thus advances them." At this a voice was heard by me, "Honor the loftiest Poet! His shade returns which had departed." When the voice had stopped and was quiet, I saw four great shades coming to us, they had a semblance neither sad nor glad. The good Master began to say, "Look at him with that sword in hand who comes before the three, even as lord, he is Homer, the sovereign poet. The next who comes is Horace, the satirist. Ovid is the third, and the last is Lucan. Since each shares with me the name which the single voice sounded, they do me honor, and in that do well."

Thus I saw assembled the fair school of that Lord of the loftiest song who soars above the others like an eagle. After they had discoursed somewhat together, they turned to me with sign of salutation and my Master smiled thereat. And far more honor yet they did me, for they made me of their band, so that I was the sixth amid so much wisdom. Thus we went on as far as the light,

---

[2] Virgil died in 19 BC.
[3] Christ's Harrowing of Hell.

speaking things concerning which silence is becoming, even as was speech there where I was.

We came to the foot of a noble castle,[4] seven times circled by high walls,[5] defended round about by a fair streamlet. This we passed as if hard ground, through seven gates[6] I entered with the sages. We came to a meadow of fresh verdure. People were there with slow and grave eyes, of great authority in their looks. They spoke seldom and with soft voices. Thereon we withdrew ourselves upon one side, into an open, luminous, and high place, so that they all could be seen. There before me upon the green enamel were shown to me the great spirits, whom for having seen I inwardly exalt.

I saw Electra with many companions, among whom I recognized Hector and Aeneas, Caesar in armor, with his gerfalcon eyes. I saw Camilla and Penthesilea, on the other side I saw the King Latinus, who was sitting with Lavinia his daughter. I saw that Brutus who drove out Tarquine; Lucretian, Julia, Marcia, and Cornelia, and alone, apart, I saw the Saladin. When I raised my brows a little more, I saw the Master[7] of those who know, seated amid the philosophic family, all regard him and do him honor. Here I saw Socrates and Plato, who in front of the others stand nearest to him. Democritus, who ascribes the world to chance; Diogenes, Anaxagoras, and Thales, Empedocles, Heraclitus, and Zeno; and I saw the good collector of the qualities Dioscorides, I mean, and I saw Orpheus, Tully, and Linus, and moral Seneca, Euclid the geometer, and Ptolemy, Hippocrates, Avicenna, and Galen, and Averrhoës, who made the great comment. I cannot report of all in full, because the long theme so drives me that many times the speech comes short of the fact.

The company of six is reduced to two. By another way the wise guide leads me out from the quiet into the air that trembles,

---

[4] The castle is commonly thought to represent Natural Philosophy.

[5] Representing the Seven Virtues: prudence, justice, fortitude, temperance, intellect, science, and knowledge.

[6] Representing the Seven Liberal Arts, consisting of the *quadrivium* (music, arithmetic, geometry, astronomy) and the *trivium* (grammar, logic, and rhetoric). The stream may signify eloquence.

[7] Aristotle

and I come into a region where is nothing that can give light.

CANTO V:

Virgil and Dante proceed to the Second Circle, that of Carnal Sinners.[1] For the first time Dante will see sinners being punished for their sins. Barring their way is the mytical and hideous creature Minos, judge of the underworld. Dante is shown shades renowned of old and speaks with Francesca da Rimini.

Thus I descended from the first circle down into the second, which girdles less space, and so much more woe that it goads to wailing. There stands Minos horribly and snarling. He examines the transgressions at the entrance, he judges, and he sends according as he entwines himself. I mean that when the ill born soul comes there before him, it confesses itself wholly, and that discerner of the sins sees what place of Hell is for it. He girds himself with his tail so many times as the grades he wills that it be sent down. Always many of them stand before him, they go in turn each to the judgment, they speak and hear, and then are whirled below.

"O thou that comest to the woeful inn," said Minos to me, when he saw me, leaving the act of so great an office, "beware how thou enterest, and to who thou trustest thyself. Let not the amplitude of the entrance deceive thee." And my Leader to him, "Wherefore dost thou too cry out? Hinder not his fated going, this it is willed there where is power for that which is willed, and ask no more."

Now the notes of woe begin to make themselves heard by me. Now I am come where much wailing smites me. I had come into a place mute of all light, that bellows as the sea does in a tempest, if it be combated by contrary winds. The infernal hurricane which never rests carries along the spirits with its rapine, whirling and smiting it molests them. When they arrive before its rush, here are the shrieks, the complaint, and the lamentation. Here they blaspheme the divine power. I understood that to such torment are

---

[1] The carnal sinners are those who committed sins of incontinence. This reflects the ancient Platonic idea that sins fell in three categories. The sins of incontinence were those of the natural appetites such as lust and gluttony. These sins are the least offensive. The next category are the sins of violence. Finally the sins of fraud are those that render the greatest punishments as they do the most harm.

condemned the carnal sinners who subject the reason to the appetite. And as their wings bear along the starlings in the cold season in a large and full troop, so did that blast the evil spirits, hither, thither, down, up it carries them. No hope ever comforts them, neither of repose, nor of less pain.

And as the cranes go singing their lays, making in air a long line of themselves, so I saw come, uttering wails, shades borne along by the aforesaid strife. Wherefore I said, "Master, who are these folk whom the black air so castigates?" "The first of those whom thou wishest to have knowledge," he said to me then, "was empress of many tongues. She was so abandoned to the vice of lust she made allowed in her law to take away the blame into which she had been brought. She is Semiramis, of whom it is read that she succeeded Ninus and had been his wife. She held the land which the Sultan rules. The other is she[2] who, for love, slew herself and broke faith to the ashes of Sichaeus. Next is Cleopatra, the luxurious. See Helen, for whom so long a time of ill revolved. And see the great Achilles, who fought to the end with love. See Paris, Tristan..." and more than a thousand shades whom love had parted from our life he showed me, and pointing to them, named to me.

After I heard my Teacher name the dames of old and the cavaliers, pity overcame me, and I was well nigh bewildered. I began, "Poet, willingly would I speak with those two that go together and seem to be so light upon the wind."[3] And he said to me, "Thou shalt see when they are nearer to us, and do thou then pray them by that love which leads them, and they will come." Soon as the wind sways them toward us, I lifted my voice, "O wearied souls, come to speak with us, if Another[4] deny it not."

As doves, called by desire, with wings open and steady come through the air borne by their will to their sweet nest, these issued from the troop where Dido is, coming to us through the malign air, so strong was the compassionate cry.

---

[2] Dido

[3] Francesca da Remini, daughter of Guido Vecchio de Polenta, lord of Ravenna, and her lover, Paolo, the brother of her husband. Their death, at the hands of her husband, took place about 1285.

[4] With one exception, the name of God is never spoken by the spirits in Hell, nor by Dante in addressing them.

"O living creature, gracious and benign, that goest through the black air visiting us who stained the world blood-red, if the King of the universe were a friend we would pray Him for thy peace, since thou hast pity on our perverse will. Of what it pleases thee to hear, and what to speak, we will hear and we will speak to you, while the wind, as now, is hushed for us. The city where I was born sits upon the seashore, where the Po,[5] with his followers, descends to have peace. Love, which quickly lays hold on gentle heart, seized this one for the fair person that was taken from me, and the mode still hurts me. Love, which absolves no loved one from loving, seized me for the pleasing of him so strongly that, as thou seest, it does not even now abandon me. Love brought us to one death. Caina[6] awaits him who quenched our life." These words were borne to us from them.

Soon as I had heard those injured souls I bowed my face and held it down so long until the Poet said to me, "What art thou thinking?" When I replied, I began, "Alas! How many sweet thoughts, how great desire, led these unto the woeful pass." Then I turned me again to them and spoke saying, "Francesca, thy torments make me sad and piteous to weeping. But tell me, at the time of the sweet sighs, by what and how did love concede to thee to know thy dubious desires?" And she to me, "There is no greater woe than the remembering in misery the happy time, and that thy Teacher knows.[7] But if thou hast so great desire to know the first root of our love, I will do like one who weeps and tells.

"We were reading one day, for delight, of Lancelot, how love constrained him. We were alone and without suspicion. Many times that reading urged our eyes and took the color from our faces, but only one point was it that overcame us. When we read of the longed-for smile being kissed by such a lover, this one, who never shall be divided from me, kissed my mouth all trembling.

---

[5] Po, a river in Italy.

[6] A section in the Ninth Cicle of Hell devoted to those who kill their brothers. Named after Cain.

[7] She here refers to Virgil, one of the souls suspended in Limbo with only memories of life to give him comfort.

Galahad was the book, and he who wrote it.[8] That day we read no farther in it."

While the one spirit said this, the other was so weeping that through pity I swooned as if I had been dying and fell as a dead body falls.

---

[8] In the romance it was Galahad that prevailed on Guinevere to give a kiss to Lancelot

CANTO VI:

When Dante wakes he finds that he is in the Third Circle, where the Gluttons are punished. They are stuck in filthy mud and battered with cold and dirty rain, hail and snow.

CANTO VII:

The Travelers enter the Fourth Circle where the Avaricious and Prodigal are punished. They encounter Pluto and Fortune on their journey. They cross over the River Styx and enter the Fifth Circle, that of the Wrathful.

CANTO VIII:

Continuing through the Fifth Circle they come to the City of Dis.

CANTO IX:

Dante and Virgil continue to the City of Dis. They meet the Three Furies as well as a Heavenly Messenger that helps them on their way. They proceed to the Sixth Circle where heretics are eternally punished.

CANTO X:

The travelers are now in the Sixth Circle where they are met by the heresiarchs. [1] They speak with Farinata degli Uberti, Cavalcante Cavalcanti, and Frederick II.

Now, along a solitary path between the wall of the city and the torments, my Master goes on, and I behind his shoulders.

"O virtue supreme," I began, "that through the impious circles dost turn me according to thy pleasure, speak to me and satisfy my desires. The folk that are lying in the sepulchers, might they be seen? All the lids are now lifted, and no one keeps guard." And he to me, "All will be locked in when they shall return here from Jehoshaphat with the bodies which they have left on earth.[2] Upon this side Epicurus with all his followers, who make the soul mortal with the body, have their burial place. Therefore as to the request that thou makest of me, thou shalt soon be satisfied here within, and also as to the desire of which thou art silent to me." And I, "Good Leader, I hold not my heart hidden from thee except in order to speak little, and not only now hast thou disposed me to this."

"O Tuscan, who goest thy way alive through the city of fire, speaking thus modestly, may it please thee to stop in this place. Thy mode of speech makes manifest that thou art native of that noble fatherland to which perchance I was too molestful." Suddenly this sound issued from one of the coffers, wherefore in fear I drew a little nearer to my Leader. And he said to me, "Turn thee, what art thou doing? See here Farinata who has risen erect, all from the girdle upwards wilt thou see him."[3]

I had already fixed my face on his and he was straightening himself up with the breast and front as though he held Hell in great scorn. And the bold and ready hands of my Leader pushed me among the sepulchers to him, saying, "Let thy words be clear."

When I was at the foot of his tomb, he looked at me a little,

---

[1] Heresiarchs are those who who spread false teaching and they are entombed within the Sixth Circle in flaming sepulchers or coffins.

[2] Joel 3:12.

[3] Farinata degli Uberti was the head of the Ghibelline party in Tuscany for many years. He died shortly after Dante was born.

and then, as though disdainful, asked me, "Who were thy ancestors?"[4] I, who was desirous to obey, concealed it not from him, but disclosed it all to him, whereon he raised up his brows a little, then said, "They were fiercely adverse to me and to my forefathers and to my party, so that at two times I scattered them."[5] "If they were driven out, they returned from every side," I replied to him, "both the one and the other time, but yours have not learned well that art."[6]

Then there arose to sigh alongside of this one, a shade[7] uncovered far as the chin, I think it had risen on its knees. It looked round about me, as if it had desire to see if another were with me, but when its expectancy was quite spent, weeping it said, "If through this blind prison thou goest by reason of loftiness of genius, where is my son? And why is he not with thee?" And I to him, "I come not of myself, he who waits yonder is leading me through here, whom perchance your Guido [8] held in disdain."

His words and the mode of punishment had already read to me the name of this one, wherefore my answer was so full.

Suddenly straightening up, he cried, "How didst thou say, 'he had'? Lives he not still? Does not the sweet light strike his eyes?" When he became aware of some delay that I made before answering, he fell again supine, and appeared no more outside.

But that other magnanimous one, at whose insistence I had stayed, changed not aspect, nor moved his neck, no bent his side. "And if," he said, continuing his first discourse, "they have ill learned that art,[9] it torments me more than this bed. But the face of

---

[4] The irony that this figure is still concerned with Dante's ancestry is part of the comedy of Hell.

[5] Dante's ancestors were Guelfs, opposed to the Ghibellines. Farinata dispersed the Guelphs in 1248 and 1260.

[6] The Guelfs returned to Florence in 1251 and 1266 and, regaining power, finally expelled the Ghibellines permanently.

[7] Cavalcanti, father of Guido, a friend of Dante.

[8] Guido Cavalcanti, Dante's first friend, and Farinata's son-in-law. Guido died a few months after Dante's vision. Guido thought little of Virgil's writing.

[9] Farinata continues his conversation as though he was never interrupted and decries the fact that the Ghibellines have not been able to rise again. This shows a sad obsession with the things of the world.

the Lady who rules here[10] will not be rekindled fifty times ere thou shalt know how much that art weighs.[11] And, so mayest thou return to the sweet world, tell me wherefore is that people so pitiless against my party in its every law?" Thereon I to him, "The rout and the great carnage which colored the Arbia[12] red cause such prayer to be made in our temple." After he had, sighing, shaken his head, "In that I was not alone there,[13] where it was agreed by every one to destroy Florence, he who defended her with open face." "Ah! So may your seed ever have repose," I prayed to him, "loose for me that knot, which has here entangled my judgment. It seems, if I hear rightly, that ye see in advance that which time is bringing with it, and as to the present have another way."[14] "We see," he said, "like him who has bad light, the things that are far from us, so much the supreme Ruler still shines on us. When they draw near, or are, our intelligence is wholly vain, and if another report not to us, we know nothing of your human state; wherefore thou canst comprehend that our knowledge will be utterly dead from that moment when the gate of the future shall be closed." Then, as compunctious for my fault, I said, "No, then, will you tell to that fallen one that his son is still conjoined with the living, and if just now I was dumb to answer, make him know that I was so because I was already thinking in the error which you have solved for me."

And now my Master was recalling me, wherefore more hastily I prayed the spirit that he would tell me who was with him. He said to me, "Here I lie with more than a thousand, here within is the Second Frederick[15] and the Cardinal,[16] and of the others I am silent."

---

[10] Proserppine, identified with the mystical Hecate, and hence with the Moon.

[11] Farinata predicts that Dante will know the pain of exile from Florence.

[12] A river in Tuscany

[13] At Empoli, in 1260, after the terrible rout of the Florentine Guelfs at Montaperti on the Arbia.

[14] That is, are ignorant of the present. Farinata foretells future events, but Cavalcante shows himself ignorant of present conditions. In Hell the dead can see future events on earth but are ignorant of the present.

[15] The famous Frederick II, emperor from 1212 to 1250.

[16] Ottaviano degli Ubaldinin, a fierce Ghibelline, who was reported to say, "If there be a soul I have lost it for the Ghibellines." He died in 1273.

CANTO XI:

They continue their way within the Sixth Circle, encounterimg
other heretics. Dante and Virgil are then accosted by a stench that
is so strong they must stop in order to accustom themselves to the
odor. They pause beside the tomb of Pope Anastasius where Dante
expresses a wish to pass the time learning more about the
punishments in Hell.

Upon the edge of a high bank which great rocks broken in a circle made, we came upon a more cruel pen. And here, because of the horrible stench which the deep abyss throws out, we drew aside behind the lid of a great tomb, whereon I saw an inscription which said, "I hold Pope Anastasius, whom Photinus drew from the right way."

"It behoves that our descent be slow so that the sense may first accustom itself a little to the dismal blast and then it will be of no concern." Thus said the Master and I to him, "Some compensation do thou find that the time pass not lost." And he, "Behold, I am thinking of that. My son, within these rocks," he began then to say, "are three lesser circles from grade to grade, like those which thou art leaving. All are full of accused spirits, but in order that hereafter the sight alone may suffice thee, hear how and wherefore they are in bonds.

"Of every wickedness that acquires hate in heaven injury is the end, and every such end afflicts other either by force or by fraud. But because fraud is an evil peculiar to man, it more displeases God, and therefore the fraudulent are the lower, and woe assails them more.

"The first circle below is wholly of the violent but because violence is done to three persons it is divided and constructed in three rounds. To God, to one's self, and to one's neighbor may violence be done. I say to them and to their belongings, as thou shalt hear with plain discourse. By violence, death and grievous wounds are inflicted on one's neighbor and on his substance ruins, burnings, and harmful extortions. Wherefore the first round torments homicides and every one who smites wrongfully, all despoilers and plunderers, in various troops.

"Man may lay violent hands upon himself and on his goods and therefore, in the second round it behoves that he repent without avail who deprives himself of your world, gambles away or dissipates his property, and laments there where he ought to be joyous.

"Violence may be done to the Deity, by denying and blaspheming Him in the heart, and by showing contempt for nature and His bounty, and therefore the smallest round seals with its signet both Sodom and Cahors[1] and him who, showing contempt for God, speaks from his heart.

"The fraud, by which every conscience is stung, man may practice on one who confides in him, or on one that has not stock of confidence. This latter mode seems to destroy only the body of love which nature makes, wherefore in the second circle nest hypocrisy, flatteries, and he who bewitches, falsity, robbery, and simony, panders, barrators, and such like filth.

"By the other mode that love is forgotten which nature makes and that which is thereafter added, whereby special confidence is created. Hence, in the smallest circle, where is the point of the universe, upon which Dis sits, whoso betrays is consumed forever."

And I, "Master, full clear thy discourse proceeds, and full well divides this pit and the people that possess it, but tell me, they of the fat marsh, and they whom the wind drives, and they whom the rain beats, and they who encounter such rough tongues, why are they not punished with the ruddy city[2] if God be wroth with them? And if He be not so, why are they in such a plight?"

And he said to me, "Why does thy wit so wander beyond its wont? Or thy mind, where else is it gazing? Dost thou not remember those words with which thy *Ethics* treats in full of the three dispositions that Heaven abides not: incontinence, wickedness, and mad bestiality, and how incontinence less offends God, and incurs less blame?[3] If thou consider well this doctrine and bring to mind who are those that up above suffer punishment outside, you wilt see clearly why they are divided from these felons, and why less wroth the divine vengeance hammers them."

---

[1] Cahors, a town in southern France, on the river Lot, noted in the Middle Ages for usury.

[2] In this lower Hell, within the walls of the city of Dis.

[3] This argument is made in Aristotle's *Ethics*.

"O Sun that healest every troubled vision, thou dost content me so, when thou solvest, that doubt, not less than knowledge, pleases me, yet turn thee a little back," said I, "to where thou sayest that usury offends the Divine Goodness, and loose the knot."

"Philosophy," he said to me, "points out to him who understands it, not only in one part alone, how Nature takes her course from the Divine Intellect and from Its art. And if thou note thy *Physics*[4] well thou wilt find, after not many pages, that your art follows her so far as it can, as the disciple does the master, so that your art is as it were grandchild of God. From these two, if thou bring to mind Genesis at its beginning,[5] it behoves mankind to gain their life and to advance. But because the usurer holds another way, he contemns Nature in herself, and in her follower, since upon other things he sets his hope. But follow me now, for to go on pleases me, for the Fishes are quivering on the horizon and the Wain lies quite over Caurus,[6] and far onwards is the descent of the steep."

---

[4] Aristotle's *Physics*

[5] "in the sweat of thy face shalt thou eat bread." Genesis 3:19.

[6] The sign of the Fishes precedes that of the Ram and as the Sun was in the latter sign the time indicated is about 4, or between 4 and 5AM.

213

CANTO XII:
The travelers make their way to the first round of the Seventh Circle where they encounter the souls of those who did violence to others.

CANTO XIII:
The second round of the Seventh Circle, where those who have done violence to themselves and to their goods are punished.

CANTO XIV:
This is where Dante and Virgil encounter those who have done violence to God in the third round of the Seventh Circle.

CANTOS XV-XVII:
Further in the third round of the Seventh Circle, the travellers meet those who have done violence to Nature and violence to Art. Descent into the Eighth Circle.

CANTOS XVIII-XXV:
The Eighth Circle of Hell is where the fraudulent are punished and is divided into eight sections or pouches. All forms of fraud are punished here: panderers, seducers, simonists, diviners, soothsayers, magicians, barrators, hypocrites, thieves and fraudulent thieves.

CANTO XXVI:
Dante and Virgil make their way through the last pouch of the Eighth Circle where they encounter fraudulent counselors.

Rejoice, Florence, since thou art so great that thou beatest thy wings over sea and land, and thy name is spread through Hell! Among the thieves I found five such, thy citizens, whereat shame comes to me, and thou dost not mount unto great honor thereby. But, if near the morning one dreams of the truth, thou shalt feel within short time what Prato, as well as others, craves for thee. And if already it were, it would not be too soon. So were it since surely it must be! For it will weigh the more on me as the more I agree.

We departed thence and up along the stairs which the bourns had before made for our descent my Leader remounted and drew me. And pursuing the solitary way among the fragments and the rocks of the craggy bridge, the foot sped not without thy hand. I sorrowed then, and now I sorrow again when I direct my mind to what I saw, and I curb my genius more than I am wont, that it may not run unless virtue guide it. So that if a good star, or better thing, have given me the good, I may not grudge it to myself.[1]

As many as the fireflies which, in the season when he that brightens the world keeps his face least hidden from us, the rustic, who is resting on the hillside what time the fly yields to the gnat, sees down in the valley, perhaps there where he makes his vintage and ploughs, with so many flames all the eighth pit was gleaming, as I perceived so soon as I was there where the bottom became apparent. And as he[2] who was avenged by the bears saw the chariot of Elijah at its departure, when the horses rose erect to heaven (for he could not so follow it with his eyes as to see aught save the flame alone) thus each of those flames was moving through the gulley of the ditch, for not one shows its theft, and every flame steals away a sinner.

---

[1] Dante is coming to men distinguished for their natural gifts but who misued them and brought eternal condemnation on themselves. It turns his thoughts to the risks attending the use of his own genius.

[2] Elisha in 2 Kings 2:9-24.

I was standing on the bridge, risen up to look, so that, if I had not taken hold of a rock, I should have fallen below without being pushed. And my Leader, who saw me thus intent, said, "Within these fires are the spirits, each swathed by that wherewith he is burnt."[3] "My master," I replied, "through hearing thee am I more certain, but already I deemed that it was so, and already I wished to say to thee, who is in that fire which becomes so divided at its top that it seems to rise from the pyre on which Eteocles was put with his brother?"[4] He answered me, "Therewithin Ulysses and Diomed are tormented, and thus they go together in their punishment, as in their wrath. And within their flame they groan for an ambush of the horse which made the gate whence the noble seed of the Romans issued forth. Within it they lament the artifice whereby the dead Deidamia[5] still mourns for Achilles, and there they bear the penalty for the Palladium."[6] "If they have power to speak within those sparks," said I, "Master, much I pray thee, and repray, that my prayer avail a thousand, that thou make not to me denial of waiting till the horned flame come hither. Thou seest that with desire I bend me toward it." And he to me, "Thy prayer is worthy of much praise, and therefore I accept it. Mind that thy tongue restrain itself. Leave speech to me, for I have conceived that which thou wishest, for because they were Greeks, they would perhaps be disdainful of thy words."

When the flame had come there where it seemed to my Leader time and place, I heard him speak to it in this form, "O ye, who are two within one fire, if I deserved of you while I lived, if I deserved of you much or little, when in the world I wrote my lofty verses, move not, but let one of you tell, whither, being lost, he went away

---

[3] Each soul is engulfed in a flame that consumes it but never extinguishes.

[4] So great was the mutual hate of the brothers Eteocles and Polynices that, when their bodies burned on the same funeral pile, the flames divided in two. From *Thebaid* by Statius.

[5] Thetis committed her son Achilles, disguised as a maiden, to Deidamia that he might not go to the siege of Troy. Deidamia, who became the mother of a son by Achilles, killed herself, when, by the craft of Ulysses, accompanied by Diomed, Achilles was discovered and persuaded to go to Troy.

[6] The Palladium was the image of Athena, on which the safety of Troy depended, and which was stolen by the two heroes. From *Aeneid*.

to die." The greater horn[7] of the ancient flame began to wag, murmuring, even as a flame that the wind wearies. Then waving its tip to and fro, as if it were the tongue that spoke, it cast forth a voice and said, "When I departed Circe, who had detained me more than a year there near to Gaeta, before Aeneas had so named it,[8] neither fondness for my son, nor piety for my old father, nor the due love which should have made Penelope glad, could overcome within me the ardor which I had to become experienced of the world, and of the vices of men, and of their virtue. But I put forth on the deep, open sea, with one vessel only, and with that little company by which I had not been deserted. I saw one shore and the other as far as Spain, as far as Morocco and the island of Sardinia, and the others which the sea bathes round about. I and my companions were old and slow when we came to that narrow strait where Hercules set up his bounds,[9] to the end that man should not put out beyond. On the right hand I left Seville, on the other I had already left Cueta. 'O brothers,' I said, 'who through a hundred thousand perils have reached the West, to this so brief vigil of your senses which remains wish not to deny the experience, following the sun, of the world that has no people. Consider your origin, ye were not made to live as brutes, but to pursue virtue and knowledge.' With this little speech I made my companions so keen for the voyage that hardly afterwards could I have held them back. And turning our stern to the morning, with our oars we made wings for the mad flight, always gaining on the left hand side. The night saw now all the stars of the other pole, and ours so low that it rose not forth from the ocean floor. The light beneath the moon had been five times rekindled and as many quenched since we had entered on the passage of the deep, when there appeared to us a mountain dark in the distance, and it seemed to me so high as I had never seen one.[10] We rejoiced and soon it turned to lamentation, for from the new land a whirlwind rose and struck the fore part of the vessel. Three times it made her whirl

---

[7] Ulysses

[8] *Aeneid*, vii, 1-4.

[9] The Pillars of Hercules were the ancient name for the promontories the flank the Strait of Gibraltar.

[10] The Mount of Purgatory.

with all the waters, the fourth it made her stern lift up and the prow go down, as pleased Another, until the sea had closed over us."

CANTO XXVII:
After hearing Odysseus's tale, Dante and Virgil move through the eighth pouch of the Eighth Circle and make their way to the ninth pouch.

CANTO XXVIII:
In the ninth pouch of the Eighth Circle, the travelers encounter the sowers of discord and schism including Muhammad and Ali as well as several well-known Italians.

CANTO XXIX:
Deeper in the ninth pouch Virgil and Dante meet falsifiers of all sorts including alchemists.

CANTO XXX:
Eighth Circle, the tenth pouch, which contains false personators and counterfeiters as well as liars.

CANTO XXXI:
Making their way out of the tenth pouch the travelers meet the Giants surrounding the Eighth Circle and encounter Nimrod. The giant Antaeus sets the Poets down in the Ninth Circle.

CANTO XXXII:

As the travelers enter the Ninth Circle they encounter the first and second ring where lie the traitors.

If I had rhymes both harsh and raucous, such as would befit the dismal hole on which all the other rocks thrust, I would press out more fully the juice of my conception, but since I have them not, not without fear I bring myself to speak. For to describe the bottom of the whole universe is no enterprise to take up in jest, nor of a tongue that cries mamma and papa. [1] But may those Dames aid my verse, who aided Amphion to enclose Thebes, [2] so that the speech may not be diverse from the fact.

O ye, beyond all others, miscreated rabble, that are in the place whereof to speak is hard, better had ye here[3] been sheep or goats!

When we were down in the dark pit beneath the feet of the giant, far lower, and I was still gazing at the high wall, I heard say to me, "Take heed how thou steppest, go so that thou trample not with thy soles the heads of thy wretched weary brothers." Whereat I turned and saw before me, and under my feet, a lake which by reason of frost resembled glass and not water.

The Danube in Austria never made in winter so thick a veil for its current, nor of the Don yonder under the cold sky, as there was here. If Tambernich[4] had fallen on it, or Pietrapana, [5] it would not have given a creak even at the edge. And as the frog lies to croak with muzzle out of the water, what time the peasant woman often dreams of gleaning, so, livid up to where shame appears, were the woeful shades within the ice, setting their teeth to the note of the stork. Every one held his face turned downward, from the mouth

---

[1] Dante here means the task of describing the lowest circle of Hell is not one to be taken lightly and it is not subject for common language.

[2] The Muses endowed the lyre of Amphion with such power that its sound charmed the rocks to move from Mount Cithaeron and build themselves up for the walls of Thebes.

[3] On earth.

[4] A mountain, the locality of which is unknown.

[5] One of the Tuscan Apennines.

the cold, and from the eyes the sad heart provides testimony of itself among them.[6]

When I had looked round awhile, I turned to my feet, and saw two so close that they had the hair of their heads mixed together. "Tell me, ye who thus press tight your breasts," said I, "who are ye?" And they bent their necks, and after they had raised their faces to me, their eyes, which before were moist only within, gushed up through the lids, and the frost bound the tears between them, and locked them up again. Clamp never girt board to board so strongly. And thereupon they, like two he-goats, butted one another, and anger overcame them.

And one who had lost both his ears by the cold, with his face still downward, said to me, "Why dost thou so mirror thyself on us? If thou wouldst know who are these two, the valley whence the Bizenzio descends belonged to their father Albert and to them.[7] They issued from one body, and thou mayst search all Caina and thou wilt not find shade more worthy to be fixed in ice; not he whose breast and shadow were broken by one self-same blow by the hand of Arthur;[8] not Focaccia;[9] not this one who so encumbers me with his head that I see no further, and who was named Sassol Mascheroni.[10] If thou art a Tuscan, thou now knowest well who he was. And that thou mayest not put me to more speech, know that I

---

[6] The souls in this circle are encased in a lake of ice up to their necks. Their heads are all downturned and tears fall from their eyes before freezing on their faces.

[7] Count Napoleone and Alessandro degli Alberti, one Ghibelline, the other Guelf. They quarreled over their inheritance, and each seeking treacherously to kill the other, they were both slain. The Bizenzio flows into the Arno some ten miles below Florence.

[8] Sir Mordred. Arthur smote Sir Mordred with such a thrust of his spear that, on the withdrawal of the lance, a ray of light passed through the wound.

[9] Focaccia de' Cancellieri of Pistoia, who, enraged by a trifling offense committed by his cousin, cut off the boy's hand, and then treacherously killed the boy's father. From this crime sprang the feud of the Black and White factions, which, from Pistoia, was introduced into Florence.

[10] He murdered his nephew for an inheritance.

was Camicion de' Pazzi, [11] and I await Carlino[12] to exculpate me."

Then I saw a thousand faces made currish by the cold, whence a shudder comes to me, and will always come at frozen pools. And while we were going toward the center to which all gravity collects, and I was trembling in the eternal chill, whether it was will or destiny or fortune I know not, but walking among the heads, I struck my foot hard in the face of one. Wailing he railed at me, "Why dost thou kick me? If thou dost not come to increase the vengeance of Mont' Aperti, why dost thou molest me?" And I, "My Master, now wait here for me, so that by means of this one I may free me from a doubt, then thou shalt make as much haste for me as thou wilt." The Leader stopped and I said to that shade who was still bitterly blaspheming, "Who art thou that thus chidest another?" "Now who art thou, that goest through the Antenora,"[13] he answered, "smiting the cheeks of others, so that if thou wert alive, it would be too much?" "I am alive, and it may be dear to thee," was my reply, "if thou demandest fame, that I set thy name among my other notes." And he to me, "For one contrary have I desire, take thyself hence and give me no more trouble, for ill thou knowest to flatter on this swamp." Then I took him by the hair of the nape and said, "It shall needs be that thou name thyself, or that not a hair remain upon thee here." Whereon he to me, "Though thou strip me of hair, I will not tell thee who I am, nor show it to thee, though you fall a thousand times upon my head."

I had already twisted his hair in my hand, and had pulled out more than one tuft, he barking, with his eyes kept close down, when another cried out, "What ails thee, Bocca?[14] Is it not enough for thee to make a noise with thy jaws, but thou must bark too?

---

[11] He betrayed and killed his kinsman Ubertino.

[12] In 1302 the castle of Piantravigne was held by a body of the recently exiled "Whites" of Florence. The castle was besieged by the "Blacks" and Carlino, for a bribe, opened its gates to them. Many of the chief exiles were slain, others were held for ransom.

[13] The second division of the ninth circle. According to tradition Antenor betrayed Troy.

[14] Bocca degli Abati, the most infamous of Florentine traitors, in the heat of the battle of Mont' Aperti, in 1260, cut off the hand of the standard-bearer of the cavalry, so that the standard fell, and the Guelfs of Florence, disheartened thereby, were put to rout with frightful slaughter.

What devil is at thee?" "Now," said I, "I do not want thee to speak, accursed traitor, for to thy shame will I carry true news of thee." "Begone," he answered, "and tell what thou wilt, but be not silent, if thou go forth from here within, and him who now had his tongue so ready. He is lamenting here the silver of the French. I saw, thou canst say, him of Duera,[15] there where the sinners stand cold. Shouldst thou be asked who else was there, thou hast at thy side him of the Beccheria[16] whose gorge Florence cut. Gianni de' Soldanier[17] I think is further on with Ganelon, and Tribealdello who opened Faenza when it was sleeping."

We now departed from him when I saw two frozen in one hole, so that the head of one was a hood for the other. And as bread is devoured for hunger, so the upper one set his teeth upon the other where the brain joins with the nape. Not otherwise Tydeus gnawed for despite the temples of Menalippus,[18] than this one was doing to the skull and the other parts. "O thou that by so bestial a sign showest hatred against him whom thou art eating, tell me the wherefore," said I, "with this compact, that if thou with reason complainest of him, I knowing who ye are, and his sin, may yet make thee pardon with him in the world above, if that with which I speak be not dried up."

---

[15] Buoso da Duera, of Cremona, in command of a part of the Ghibelline forces in Lombardy, assembled to oppose the troops of Charles of Anjou in 1265. Bribed, he let them pass unmolested.

[16] Tesauro de' Beccheria, Abbot of Allombrosa and Papal Legate, beheaded by the Florentines in 1258 because of his treacherous dealings with the exiled Ghibellines.

[17] A Ghibelline of Florence, who, after the defeat of Manfred in 1266, plotted against his own party.

[18] Tydeus, one of the Seven Kings against Thebes, mortally wounded by Menalippus, slew his adversary, and then gnawed his cut-off head.

CANTO XXXIII:
Dante speaks with the souls in the Ninth Circle.

From his savage repast that sinner raised his mouth, wiping it with the hair of the head that he had spoiled behind and then he began, "Thou wishest that I should renew a desperate grief which oppresses my heart already only in thinking, ere I speak of it. But, if my words are to be seed that may bear fruit of infamy for the traitor whom I gnaw, thou shalt see me speak and weep together. I know not who thou art, nor by what mode thou art come down here, but Florentine thou seemest to me truly when I hear thee. Thou hast to know that I was Count Ugolino and this one the Archbishop Ruggieri.[1] Now I will tell thee why I am such a neighbor. That, by the effect of his evil thoughts, I, trusting to him, was taken and then put to death, there is no need to tell, but what thou canst not have heard, that is, how cruel my death was, thou shalt hear, and shalt know if he has wronged me.

"A narrow slit in the mew, which from me has the title of Hunger, and in the which others must yet be shut up, had already shown me through its opening many moons, when I had the bad dream which rent for me the veil of the future.

"This one appeared to me master and lord, chasing the wolf and his welps upon the mountain[2] because of which the Pisans cannot see Lucca. With lean, eager, and trained hounds, he had put before him at the front Gualandi with Sismondi and with Lanfranchi.[3] After short course, the father and his sons seemed to

---

[1] Ugolino della Gherardesca, Count of Donoratico, many years the most powerful citizen of Pisa, in 1285 was elected Podestà of Pisa and permitted his ambitious grandson, Nino dei Visconti, the "noble Judge Nino" whom Dante greets in Purgatory, to share in the rule of the city. Discord soon broke out between the old and the young man. The Ghibellines' chief, the Archbishop Ruggieri degli Ubaldinin, pretending friendship with Count Ugolino, joined forces with him to expel his grandson with his followers. The strength of the Guelfs in the city thus being weakened, the Archbishop turned against the Count and defeated the Guelfs. The Count and two of his sons and two of his grandsons were taken prisoner and were shut up in the tower of the Gualandi alle Sette Vie in July 1288. In the succeeding March the keys of the tower were thrown into the Arno and the prisoners were starved to death.

[2] Mont San Giuliano; Lucca is about fourteen miles northeast of Pisa.

[3] Three of the chief Ghibelline families of Pisa.

me weary, and it seemed to me I saw their flanks ripped by the sharp fangs.

"I awoke before the morrow, I heard my sons, who were with me, wailing in their sleep and asking for bread. Truly thou art cruel if already thou dost not grieve, at the thought of that which my heart was foreboding. And if thou dost not weep, at what art thou wont to weep? They were not awake and the hour was drawing near at which food used to be brought to us, and because of his dream each was apprehensive. And I heard the door below of the horrible tower being nailed up, whereat I looked on the faces of my sons without saying a word. I did not weep, I was so turned to stone within. They were weeping and my poor little Anselm said, 'Thou lookest so, Father, what ails thee?' I shed no tear for that nor did I answer all that day, nor the night after, until the next sun came forth upon the world. When a little ray made its way into the woeful prison and I discerned by their four faces my own very aspect, I bit both my hands for woe, and they, thinking I did it through desire of eating, of a sudden raised themselves up and said, 'Father, it will be far less pain to us if thou eat of us. Thou didst clothe us with this wretched flesh and do thou strip it off.' I quieted me then, not to make them more sad. That day and the next we all stayed dumb. Ah, thou hard earth! Why didst thou not open? After we came to the fourth day, Gaddo thew himself stretched out at my feet, saying, 'My father, why dost thou not help me?' Here he died and even as thou seest me, I saw the three fall one by one between the fifth day and the sixth. Then I betook me, already blind, to groping over each, and for two days I called them after they were dead. Then fasting was more powerful than woe."

When he had said this, with his eyes twisted, he seized again the wretched skull with his teeth, that were strong as a dog's upon the bone.

Ah Pisa! Reproach of the people of the fair country where the *sì* doth sound,[4] since thy neighbors are slow to punish thee, let Caprara and Gorgona[5] move and make a hedge for Arno at its mouth so that it may drown every person in thee. For even if Count

---

[4] Italy, whose language Dante calls *il volgare di sì*, the common tongue in which *sì* is the word for yes.

[5] Two little islands not far from the mouth of the Arno, on whose banks Pisa lies.

Ugolino had report of having betrayed thee in thy strongholds, thou oughtest not to have set his sons on such a cross. Their young age, thou modern Thebes, made Uguccione and Il Brigata[6] innocent, and the other two that my song names above.

We passed onward to where the ice roughly enswathes another folk, not turned downward but all reversed.[7] The very weeping allows not weeping there, and the grief, which finds a barrier on the eyes, turns inward to increase the anguish, for the first tears for a block and like a visor of crystal fill all the cup beneath the eyebrow.

And although, as in a callus, ill feeling, because of the cold, had ceased to abide in my face, it now seemed to me I felt some wind, wherefore I asked, "My Master, who moves this? Is not every vapor[8] quenched here below?" Whereon he to me, "Speedily shalt thou be where thine eye, beholding the cause that rains down the blast, shall make answer to thee of this."

And one of the wretches of the cold crust cried out to us, "O souls so cruel that the last station has been given to you, lift from my eyes the hard veils, so that, before the weeping recongeal, I may vent a little the woe which swells my heart." Wherefore I to him, "If thou wishest that I succor thee, tell me who thou art, and if I relieve thee not, may I have to go to the bottom of the ice."[9] He replied then, "I am friar Alberigo;[10] I am he of the fruits of the bad garden, who here get back a date for a fig."[11] "Oh!" said I to him,

---

[6] Uguccione was a son, and Il Brigata a grandson of Count Ugolion; they were in fact grown men.

[7] With faces upturned, so that the tears freeze in their eyes.

[8] Medievals thought that wind was caused by the action of the sun on the vapors of the atmosphere.

[9] Misleading words, with their double meaning.

[10] Alberigo de' Manfredi, of Faenza, having received a blow from his younger brother Manfred, pretended to forgive it, and invited him and his son to a feast. Toward the end of the meal he gave a preconcerted signal by calling out, "Bring the fruit," upon which his emissaries rushed in and killed the two guests. The "bad fruit of Brother Alberigo" became a proverb.

[11] A fig is the cheapest of Tuscan fruits, the imported date is more costly.

"art thou then dead already?"[12] And he to me, "How my body may fare in the world above I have no knowledge. Such vantage hath this Ptolomea[13] that oftentimes the soul falls down here before Atropos has given motion to it.[14] And that thou mayst the more willingly scrape the glassy tears from my face, know that soon as the soul betrays, as I did, its body is taken from it by a demon, who thereafter governs it until its time be all revolved. It falls headlong into such cistern as this, and perhaps the body of the shade that is wintering here behind me still appears above. Thou shouldst know him if thou comest down but now, he is Ser Branca d' Oria,[15] and many years have passed since he was thus shut up." "I believe," I said to him, "that thou art deceiving me, for Branca d'Oria is not yet dead, and he eats and drinks, and sleeps, and puts on clothes." "In the ditch of the Malebranche above," he said, "there where the sticky pitch is boiling, Michel Zanche[16] had not yet arrived, when this one left a devil in his stead in his own body, and in that of one of his next kin, who committed the treachery together with him. But now stretch hither thy hand, open my eyes for me." And I did not open them for him, for to be churlish to him was courtesy.[17]

Ah Genoese! Men strange to all mortality and full of all corruption, why are ye not scattered from the world? For with the worst spirit of Romagna[18] I found one of you, such that for his

---

[12] In Medieval times it was believed that if a person committed a crime of fraud against a guest or someone in his care, this sin was so heinous that the sinner's soul was immediately sent to hell and his earthly body was inhabited by a demon until it died a natural death.

[13] The third ring of ice, named for Ptolemy, Captain of Jericho, who, having invited them to the banquet, treacherously slew his father-in-law, the high-priest Simon, and his two sons. 1 Maccabees 16:11-16.

[14] That is, before Atropos has cut the thread of its life on earth.

[15] Murderer, in or about 1290, of his father-in-law, Michel Zanche, Governor of Logodoro, in Sardinia. The date of the death of Branca d' Oria is not known.

[16] In the fifth *bolgia*. Canto XXII.

[17] "Courtesy and propriety of behavior are one and the same thing". Pity or compassion may be rightly felt, according to St. Thomas Aquinas, for sinners still on earth, for they may yet repent and turn from sin. But in the future life there is no repentance. The punishment of the sinner is the evidence of the justice of God. There can be no pity for him, charity cannot wish the damned to be less wretched, for this would be to call in question the Divine justice.

[18] That is, with Friar Alberigo.

deeds he is already in soul bathed in Cocytus, and in body he appears till alive on earth.

CANTO XXXIV:

*Continuing through the Ninth Circle, the Poets come to the very
lowest pit of Hell where they find the three greatest traitors of all
time as well as Lucifer. Here they have reached the center of the
universe and must make their passage from Hell. They emerge in
the Southern Hemisphere.*

"*Bexilla regis prodeunt inferni*[1] toward us, so look forward,"
said my Master, "see if thou discern him." As when a thick fog
breathes, or when our hemisphere darkens to night, a mill which
the wind is turning seems from afar, such a structure it seemed to
me that I then saw.

Then because of the wind I drew me behind my Leader, for no
other shelter was there. I was now (and with fear I put it into verse,
there[2] where the shades were wholly covered, and showed through
like a straw in glass. Some are lying down, some are upright, this
one with his head, and that with his soles uppermost, another, like
a bow, bends his face to his feet.

When we had gone so far forward that it pleased my Master to
show me the creature which had the fair semblance, he took
himself from before me and made me stop, saying, "Lo Dis! And
lo the place where it is needful that thou arm thyself with
fortitude!" How frozen and faint I then became, ask it not Reader,
for I do not write it, because all speech would be little. I did not
die, and did not remain alive. Think now for thyself, if thou has a
grain of wit, what I became, deprived of one and the other.

The emperor of the woeful realm issued forth from the ice
from the middle of his breast, and I compare better with a giant,
than the giants do with his arms. See now how great must be that
whole which is conformed to such a part. If he was as fair as he
now is foul, and lifted up his brows against his Maker, well should
all tribulation proceed from him. Oh how great a marvel it seemed
to me when I saw three faces on his head! One in front, and that
was crimson. The others were two, which were adjoined to this
above the very middle of each shoulder, and they were joined up to
the place of the crest. The right seemed between white and yellow,

---

[1] "The banners of the King of Hell advance."

[2] In the fourth, innermost ring of ice of the ninth circle, the Judecca.

the left was such in appearance as those who come from there whence the Nile descends.[3] Beneath each came forth two great wings, of size befitting so great a bird, sails of the sea I never saw such. They had no feathers, but their fashion was of a bat, and he was flapping them so that three winds were proceeding from him, whereby Cocytus was all congealed. With six eyes he was weeping, and over three chins were trickling the tears and bloody drivel. At each mouth he was crushing a sinner with his teeth, in manner of a heckle, so that he thus was making three of them woeful. To the one in front the biting was nothing to the clawing, whereby sometimes his back remained all stripped of the skin.

"That soul up there which has the greatest punishment," said the Master, "is Judas Iscariot, who has his head within, and plies his legs outside. Of the other two who have their heads downwards, he who hangs from the black muzzle is Brutus. See how he writhes and says not a word. And the other is Cassius, who seems so large-limbed.[4] But the night is rising again and now we must depart for we have seen the whole."

As was his pleasure, I clasped his neck, and he took advantage of the time and place and when the wings were wide opened he caught hold on the shaggy flanks. Down from shag to shag he then descended between the matted hair and the frozen crusts. When we were where the thigh turns just on the thick of the haunch, my Leader, with effort and stress of breath, turned his head to where he had had his shanks,[5] and grappled to the hair like one who mounts, so that I believed we were returning again to hell.

"Cling fast hold," said the Master, panting like one weary, "for by such stairs must we depart from so great evil." Then he came forth through the cleft of a rock and placed me upon its edge to sit and then stretched toward me with a cautious step.

I raised my eyes and thought to see Lucifer as I had left him

---

[3] The three faces exhibit the devilish counterparts of the attributes of the three persons of the Godhead, that is Impotence, Ignorance, and Hate as opposed to Power, Wisdom, and Love. Impotence is scarlet with rage, Ignorance black with its own darkness, Hate pale yellow with jealousy and envy.

[4] Christ, betrayed by Judas was the head of the Church, the supreme spiritual authority. Caesar, betrayed by Brutus and Cassius, was regarded by Dante as the founder of the Empire, the supreme authority in temporal affairs.

[5] Possible symbolizing a *Conversion,* in the literal sense.

and I saw him holding his legs upward, and if I then became perplexed, let the dull folk suppose it, who see not what that point is which I had passed.[6]

"Rise up on foot," said the Master, "the way is long and the road is difficult, and already the sun returns to mid-tierce."[7]

It was no hallway of a palace where we were but a natural dungeon which had a bad floor and lacked light. "Before I tear myself from the Abyss," I said when I had risen up, "my Master, talk a little with me to draw me out of error. Where is the ice? And this one, how is he fixed thus upside down? And how in such short while has the sun made transit from the evening to morning?" And he to me, " Thou imagines that thou still art on the other side of the center, where I laid hold on the hair of the wicked Worm that pierces the world. On that side thou wast so long as I descended, when I turned thou didst pass the point to which from every part all weighty things are drawn[8] and thou art now arrived beneath the hemisphere which is opposite to that which the great dry land covers and beneath whose zenith the Man was slain who was born and lived without sin. Thou hast thy feet upon a little circle which forms the other face of the Judecca. Here it is morning when it is evening there, and this one who made a ladder for us with his hair is still fixed even as he was before. On this side he fell down from heaven and the earth, which before was spread out on this side, through fear of him made of the sea a veil, and came to our hemisphere. And perhaps to fly from him that land which appears on this side left here this vacant space and ran back upward."

A place is there below, stretching as far from Beelzebub as his tomb extends, which is not known by sight, but by the sound of a rivulet which descends here along the hollow of a rock that it has gnawed with its winding and gently sloping course.[9] My Leader and I entered by that hidden road to return into the bright world and without any care to have any repose we mounted up, he first and I second, so far that through a round opening I saw some of the beautiful things which Heaven bears, and thence we issued forth

---

[6] The prime meridian.

[7] 7:30AM.

[8] The center of gravity.

[9] The streamlet of sin from Purgatory, which finds it way back to Satan.

again to see the stars.

CPSIA information can be obtained at www.ICGtesting.com
Printed in the USA
LVOW12s0207160913

352555LV00003B/6/P